Bloom's Modern Critical Interpretations

250 - 280
   intro

Bloom's Modern Critical Interpretations

Toni Morrison's
THE BLUEST EYE
Updated Edition

Edited and with an introduction by
Harold Bloom
Sterling Professor of the Humanities
Yale University

BLOOM'S
LITERARY CRITICISM
An imprint of Infobase Publishing

Editorial Consultant, Brian L. Johnson

Bloom's Modern Critical Interpretations:
Toni Morrison's The Bluest Eye—Updated Edition
Copyright ©2007 by Infobase Publishing

Introduction ©2007 by Harold Bloom

Bloom's Literary Criticism
An imprint of Infobase Publishing
132 West 31st Street
New York NY 10001

Library of Congress Cataloging-in-Publication Data

Toni Morrison's The Bluest Eye / edited with an introduction by Harold Bloom.
     p. cm. — (Bloom's modern criticial views)
  Includes bibliographical references and index.
  ISBN-13: 978-0-7910-96154 (hardcover : alk. paper)
  1. Toni Morrison's The Bluest Eye—Criticism and interpretation. I. Bloom, Harold.
PS3525.I5156Z5145 2007
812'.52—dc22   2006102701

Bloom's Literary Criticism books are available at special discounts when purchased in bulk quantities for businesses, associations, institutions, or sales promotions. Please call our Special Sales Department in New York at (212) 967-8800 or (800) 322-8755.

You can find Bloom's Literary Criticism on the World Wide Web at
http://www.chelseahouse.com.

Cover design by Takeshi Takahashi / Joo Young An

Printed in the United States of America
Bang BCL 10 9 8 7 6 5 4 3 2 1

This book is printed on acid-free paper.

All links and web addresses were checked and verified to be correct at the time of publication. Because of the dynamic nature of the web, some addresses and links may have changed since publication and may no longer be valid.

Contents

Editor's Note

My introduction praises *The Bluest Eye*, in agreement with Michael Wood, but by canonical standards Toni Morrison asserts that she no longer accepts.

Christopher Douglas shrewdly notes *The Bluest Eye*'s reservations about "group identity," suspicions which Morrison abandons from *Beloved* onwards.

Rather than repeatedly cite the "cultural correctness" of nearly all the remaining essayists, I will note only refreshing deviations from cant such as that by Douglas.

Debra T. Werrlein emphasizes Morrison's critique of our supposed American "ideologies of innocent childhood," after which Cat Moses interprets the "blues aesthetic" as dominating *The Bluest Eye*.

Textuality centers Carl D. Malmgren's text, while Allen Alexander discovers aspects of an African God in Morrison's novelistic vision.

Jane Kuenz locates Morrison's defense of a specific African American female subjectivity, after which Shelley Wong praises the novelist for a "liberating pedagogy."

Racism is remorselessly deconstructed by Donald B. Gibson, while Rosalie Murphy Baum compares Stephen Crane's *Maggie: A Girl of the Streets* (1893) to *The Bluest Eye*, since each shows that alcoholism can lead to family abuse.

Jennifer Gillan virtuously manifests her own multiculturalism, after which Jeffrey M. Buchanan joins those who praise Morrison as pedagogue.

Allusions in *The Bluest Eye* to Eliot's *The Waste Land* and Plato's Allegory of the Cave usefully are expounded by Thomas H. Fick, while Linda Dittmar admits to some interesting ambiguities in Morrison's first novel, but ends by affirming the supposed ideology of the book.

HAROLD BLOOM

Introduction

I

The Bluest Eye, Morrison's first novel, was published when she was thirty-nine and is anything but novice work. Michael Wood, an authentic literary critic, made the best comment on this "lucid and eloquent" narrative that I have ever seen:

> Each member of the family interprets and acts out of his or her ugliness, but none of then understands that the all-knowing master is not God but only history and habit; the projection of their own numbed collusion with the mythology of beauty and ugliness that oppresses them beyond their already grim social oppression.

Morrison herself, in an Afterword of 1994, looked back across a quarter-century and emphasized her "reliance for full comprehension in codes embedded in black culture." A reader who is not black or female must do the best he can; like Michael Wood, I have found *The Bluest Eye* to be completely lucid since I first read it, back in 1970. Like *Sula* and *The Song of Solomon* after it, the book seems to me successful in universal terms, even if one shares neither Morrison's origins nor her ideologies. *Beloved*, Morrison's most famous romance narrative, seems to me problematic, though it has reached a vast audience. A generation or two will have to pass before a balanced judgment could be rendered upon *Beloved* or Morrison's later novels, *Jazz*, *Paradise*, and *Love*. But her early phase has many of the canonical qualifications of the traditional Western literary kind that she fiercely rejects as being irrelevant to her.

What I never forget about *The Bluest Eye* is its terrifying penultimate paragraph, where the narrator censures herself and her friends for turning away from Pecola because the child's madness, engendered by the trauma of being raped by her father, Cholly, "bored us in the end":

> Oh, some of us "loved" her. The Maginot Line. And Cholly loved her. I'm sure he did. He, at any rate, was the one who loved her enough to touch her, envelope her, give something of her filled the matrix of her agony with death. Love is never any better than the lover. Wicked people love wickedly, violent people love violently, weak people love weakly, stupid people love stupidly, but the love of a free man is never safe. There is no gift for the beloved. The lover alone possesses his gift of love. The loved one is shorn, neu-tralized, frozen in the glare of the lover's inward eye.

The unhappy wisdom of this is happily free of any cultural narcissism whatsoever. Class, race, even gender do not over-determine this bleakness. Morrison's heroic survivors in *Beloved* are intended to stand up both in and against their history. Perhaps they do, but the torments they have endured also are tendentiously elaborated, because the author has an ideological design upon us, her guilty readers, white and black, male and female. The narrator of *The Bluest Eye* persuades me, where the narration of *Beloved* does not. In D. H. Lawrence's terms, I trust both the tale and the teller in *The Bluest Eye*. In *Beloved*, I do not trust the tale.

ROSALIE MURPHY BAUM

Alcoholism and Family Abuse in Maggie *and* The Bluest Eye

In 1893, Stephen Crane's *Maggie: A Girl of the Streets* depicted a young white girl and her two brothers growing up in the Bowery, with a father and mother who engage in vicious physical fights. Seventy-seven years later, in 1970, Toni Morrison's *The Bluest Eye* dramatized the plight of a black girl and her brother growing up in Lorain, Ohio, in an atmosphere of conjugal strife. In both works alcoholism plays an important role in the lives of the parents and thus of the children. But in both cases alcoholism is shown to be much more *caused* than causing.

The alcoholism occurs because of economic and cultural stress and the characters' attempts to escape that stress, but even more because of the individual and family patterns which have emerged, not necessarily to deal with this stress. It is not alcoholism itself that causes the spouse abuse and child neglect and abuse—although it is clear that alcohol affects, and even facilitates, aggressive behavior in these areas and largely determines the reactions of society to the families. The turning to alcohol by one or more members of the family is simply one mode of expression—one way of escaping stress and pain, one way of fortifying one's self-esteem. Modes of expression which appear to be innocent, virtuous, or at least neutral are shown to contribute at least equally to the destructive and complex interaction of the families. Thus, alcoholism is not presented as the cause of the problems of these families, nor as the decisive

Mosaic: A Journal for the Interdisciplinary Study of Literature, 1986 Summer; 19 (3): 91–105.

3

factor in forming children who contain within themselves the very elements which will eventually destroy them. My purpose in the following essay is to demonstrate the extent to which such a view of alcoholism is consistent with the work of many social and behavic scientists.

· · ·

On the societal and subcultural levels, as well as on the individual, small-group and situational levels, drinking behavior is influenced by cultural factors. On the societal level, for example, drinking in the United States occurs in a society which recognizes and accepts drinking for many purposes. American society is one of many in which, in Edwin M. Lemert's words, drinking is "a culture pattern, symptom of psychic stress, a symbolic protest, or a form of collective behavior (p. 568).[1] As a form of escapism (characteristic, according to Don Cahalen, Ira H. Cisin and Helen M. Crossley, of one-third of the men who drink and one-fourth of the women[2]), it can be both a symptom of stress and "a symbolic protest"; as means of compensating for loss of power—within the social structure or personal relationship—it can also be a symptom of stress and "a symbolic protest."

In addition, drunken aggressiveness is a cultural defense mechanism which serves to alleviate stress and hostility in America, and it is a defense mechanism that largely frees the aggressive drinker from guilt. The reasoning is that since alcohol releases inhibitions, the drinker may commit acts normally unacceptable to self-esteem or reputation without feeling directly responsible for these acts—as long as he can attribute their cause to alcohol. Alcohol serves as an "excuse" which is used by both the drinker and other family members in order to maintain an image of normalcy and nondeviancy to both themselves and their society. Thus, an accepted social custom—drinking—and an accepted, acknowledged result—aggression—allow the drinker to have the "time out" which Craig MacAndrew and Robert Edgerton identify as a learned behavior in which "the drunkard finds himself, if not beyond good and evil, at least partially removed from the accountability nexus in which he normally operates."[3]

According to Theodore D. Graves and Robert K. Merton,[4] such drunken aggressiveness is likely to occur more frequently in subcultures in which individuals find that strongly established societal goals are unattainable—a correlation which is hardly surprising, given the consequent stress and loss of self-esteem as well as the lack of a subculturally approved alternative defense mechanism. The tendency, too, according to David Levinson, is for "aggressive drinking behavior . . . to occur in the presence of people of lower status, perhaps as a reflection of status differentials or as a means of reinforcing those differentials."[5] Levinson also points out that "drunken aggressiveness often involves a highly ritualized set of learned behaviors" (p. 49). In fact, such ritualization can make drunken aggressiveness especially efficient as a cultural defense mechanism since it establishes rules which can control the aggression (p. 50).

On the individual, small-group and situational levels, drinking behavior is also influenced by cultural factors. The fact that aggressive behavior frequently occurs in the presence of people of lower status can of course contribute to an understanding of the large number of spouse-abuse situations which involve a high degree of alcohol abuse: forty to ninety-five percent of the cases studied by Roger Langley and Richard C. Levy, eighty-three percent by Gisela Spieker.[6] Spieker explains that an attack on a family member while intoxicated provides a feeling of "self-worth . . . frequently perceived as having 'power'"; it provides "the grounds for refusing to accept responsibility for one's own violent behavior"; and it occurs in a situation where one's behavior has "the least chance for negative consequences," a "safe zone" (p. 133).One usually is not going to lose a job or even have the police called in if one reserves one's aggression for family members. Further, Murray A. Straus suggests that cultural norms which support "a male-dominant balance of power in the family" and hence sexual inequality, which accept a high level of conflict and violence within the family structure and between siblings, and which legitimize physical punishment of the children within the family all establish the family as a base for "unintended training in violence."[7]

Building upon the work of Don Jackson and D. D. Speer, Peter Steinglass suggests that the alcoholic may be only the "labelled or identified patient, selected by the family system to express for the entire family the particular piece of disturbance represented by the symptom selected" and may thus "be protecting or stabilising a level of functioning of other family members by manifesting such clearly identifiable pathological behaviour."[8] In other words, the complementary relationship of needs, strengths and cultural values within the family system leads various members of the family to turn to alcohol to relieve stress for all members of the family and to express escapist and aggressive fantasies for all members of the family; the role of drinker is simply one in the complex process of role differentiation and in the establishing of patterns of interaction within the family system. Such an interaction helps to explain why the families of alcoholics so often remain together and makes even clearer the terrible effect such environments can have on younger children.

· · ·

The consistency between the work being done by social and behavioral scientists today on alcoholism and the portrayal by Crane and Morrison of the lives of two alcoholic families is striking, especially given the date of Crane's story. In both *Maggie* and *The Bluest Eye* cultural factors, on societal and subcultural levels, are clearly established as a major contributing cause to drinking and subsequent aggression in the home. In both works, however, the family system—created by individuals, in Morrison's novel, who are shown to have been crippled by their own childhood environments—is an equally strong contributing factor. In both works the effect of the parental violence on the children is disastrous; yet, even in the case of the children, Crane and Morrison show the complicity of the victims with their fates. There appears to be no escape in a world where victimization is inbred from generation to generation.

On a societal or subcultural level, poverty is the deadening and destructive element in the world of *Maggie*. It is a poverty of dirt, "gruesome doorways . . . dark stairways and . . . cold gloomy halls," and "long streamers of garments" fluttering from fire-escapes. It is a poverty of "loads of babies" in the street and gutter, "withered persons, in curious postures of submission to something," and ragged, quivering, weeping or fighting children.[9] Crane's details of sight, sound, smell and feeling present a sordid environment in which both the world and the characters are reduced. In such a world of hardship and stress, verbal and physical violence is the only forceful sign of life—other than tears. It is verbal and physical violence which vitalizes and sustains Maggie's parents. When Mrs. Johnson is not fighting, when "her mood" changes, all she can do is put Tommie to sleep in "an old quilt of faded red and green grandeur," a symbol of better times, and rock "to and fro upon a chair, shedding tears and crooning miserably to her two [other] children about their 'poor mother' and 'yer fader, damn 'is soul'" (p. 14).

On the individual and situational levels, Crane does not offer any information about the background of either Mrs. or Mr. Johnson although one's impression is that they both drink as a form of escape and as a reaction to feelings of powerlessness. He describes only two actual scenes of fighting between the couple, both on the same night, while at the same time creating the impression that the characteristics of these fights are definitive for the Johnsons, who are clearly engaged in just one more representative round in the battle of their lives. Crane's careful selection and arrangement of details offers an impression of blundering pantomimic figures, going through well-rehearsed and larger-than-life verbal and physical gestures of pain and protest. Thus, his very literary techniques underline the ritualistic nature Levinson identifies in much drunken behavior.

Certainly Mrs. Johnson appears to be more violent than her husband, and her violence does not depend upon an audience. Crane describes her husband and children returning home to a tenement apartment "in which a large woman was rampant" (p. 12). Whether drunkenly cleaning or cooking,

Mrs. Johnson is a heaving mass of anger, continually finding reasons in her husband's or her children's behavior to vent her anger and continually seeking escape from her grief in the bottle. Crane's fragmented descriptions of her physical characteristics are designed to emphasize her fragmented self: "massive shoulders" which heave with anger (p. 12), "immense hands on her hips," fists shaking in front of her husband's eyes (p. 13), feet "waving . . . with their dishevelled shoes near the heads of her children" (p. 14). Apparently always somewhat intoxicated, she is constantly jerking, pounding or throwing the children around and regularly howling at (but not hitting) her husband. The reason she gives for beating the children is a culturally approved one (Straus): they have been bad, and she must teach them with physical punishment.

Mr. Johnson, a man who "listlessly" plods home "with sullen eyes" (p. 9), has a much more subtle role in the family system (Steinglass) and in the permissive setting in which the couple's altercations occur. Over the years, apparently, clearly defined roles have been established by the two. A sober Mr. Johnson may roar his oath and brutally kick his son and other boys when he finds Jimmie fighting on the street, but the verbal or physical abuse in the home is his wife's territory. A drunk Mr. Johnson may have no qualms about grabbing the tin of beer which a neighbor has asked Jimmie to buy, laughingly drinking it off, and then hitting Jimmie on the head with the empty pail; but, again, the action occurs outside the home.

The sober Mr. Johnson neither abuses his children at home nor protects them from their mother's abuse in the home. He does, however, contribute to the abuse by regularly irritating his wife; he does initiate the first battle of the evening with his wife, a verbal one; and he is as active in the "lurid altercation" as she, in her drunken state, is. His role in the interaction early in the evening is to bait and enrage his wife—by assuming a stance of tranquility and imperturbability in the chaos of the home, by putting "his great muddied boots on the back part of the stove," and by initiating verbal altercations. With his wife screaming and howling at him, he looks out the window and comments unconcernedly that she really must "let up on the bot'. . . or you'll git done" (p. 13).

Thus, the roles of the two toward each other are partially ones of passive (Mr. Johnson) and active (Mrs. Johnson) aggression; but, most interestingly, neither initiates physical battle when only Mrs. Johnson is drunk. In addition, the Johnsons' drinking habits are typical of those of the families studied by Clare Wilson and Jim Orford.[10] The man drinks outside the home, in a bar, and returns home aggressive or besotted. The woman drinks regularly all day at home, seldom becoming so intoxicated that she cannot do her work around the house.

The physical battle of the evening occurs late in the evening when Mr. Johnson returns home after having gotten drunk at the neighborhood bar. At the bar, of course, he has explained lachrymosely that he gets drunk because his home is "reg'lar livin' hell" (p. 17). Thus, the earlier scene in the home offers Mr. Johnson a reason for getting drunk and his getting drunk allows the Johnsons, now both drunk, to escalate the battle they began earlier in the evening to a physical level. The proximate causes of the physical altercation stem from the well-defined roles the two play in their verbal altercations: Mrs. Johnson rages at Mr. Johnson for not controlling Jimmie's behavior, and Mr. Johnson reacts with "drunken indifference" (p. 18). But the fighting itself, now made permissible by mutual drunkenness, seems to be a perfect example of MacAndrew and Edgerton's "time-out" theory. The two seek physical release for their anger and frustration only after their drinking makes them no longer fully responsible for their actions.

When the two drunken Johnsons engage in what is apparently nightly combat, "howls and curses, groans and shrieks . . . [and the] crash of splintering furniture" permeate the tenement, while their three children cower in another room or in the outside hall. Eventually (and these battles have on occasion gone on much of the night), the two struggle to a collapse, the father's "limp body . . . across the seat of a chair," the mother's spread in the middle of the floor. The nightly ritual is over; and the terrified Maggie and Jimmie crawl out to stare at their mother's face: "inflamed and swollen from drinking," the lines of her mouth set in "vindictive hatred" (p. 18). The Johnsons do not kill each other; but the appropriate cues, responses and patterns established in their years of marriage have long ago moved beyond offering a release for their frustration, hopelessness, anger and hatred which is acceptable within the general culture. In fact, the very nature of the release they have adopted insures that they can never improve their situation or relieve their stress and frustration.

Crane does not suggest any particular, individual (in the present or past) reasons why the strongly established goals of their society are clearly beyond the reach of these two individuals; his literary intention is to give an impression of representative types. But he does clearly indicate that these representative types unwittingly comply in their own victimization. Further, he sees them and their children in a cycle of human interaction from which there is no escape. As Crane wrote in an inscription of the novel, "environment is a tremendous thing in the world and frequently shapes lives regardless."[11]

The neighbors' reactions to the Johnsons' behavior are essentially ones of acceptance. A neighbor, who offers Jimmie a haven one night, asks, "Eh, Gawd, child, what is it dis time? Is yer fader beatin' yer mudder, or yer mudder beatin' yer fader?" (p. 15). "Curious faces" appear in doorways and whisper, "Ol' Johnson's raisin' hell agin" (p. 18). The scenes of chronic drink and aggression in the Johnsons' life clearly reflect accepted subcultural norms, such drunken altercations being an acknowledged subcultural release for in-group hostility and a safety valve to alleviate stress. Even the court officials who come to know Mrs. Johnson well in her later years for both drinking and disturbing the peace regard her as a character; they grin and call her by her first name while she besieges "the bench with voluble excuses, explanations, apologies, and prayers" (pp. 24–25). The use of alcohol is clearly acceptable; its consequences are often unfortunate but understandable. Mom drinks because of the stresses of poverty and child-rearing. Dad drinks because life generally is bleak and empty and because life at home is "reg'lar livin' hell." Mom and Dad are physically violent because they are drunk. In addition, the assumptions are that the male is primarily to blame and that one of the "ter'ble" afflictions Mrs. Johnson has had to bear in life is the "disobed'ent chile" Maggie. The neighbors may be curious, but they certainly do not intrude into the private lives of a family. They come only to assist with Maggie's funeral.

The Johnsons' children are very much affected by their parents' behavior. The baby, Tommie, simply dies, going away "in an insignificant coffin, his small hand clutching a flower" (p. 20) which Maggie has stolen. But Maggie and Jimmie survive to adulthood, exhibiting typical characteristics of children growing up in such an environment. Maggie, the older, takes on what Claire Wilson describes as the familiar role of the child who assumes "a large share of housekeeping and child care"[12] and also tries to protect her younger brothers. She does not develop antisocial behavior and does not drink—daughters of alcoholics, according to N. S. Cotton, tend to become alcoholics themselves less frequently than sons[13]—but her values have been affected and she too seeks a means of escape from the reality of her life. Maggie comes to expect aggression in men, although she herself, from a deep sense of inferiority, remains passive and dependent. Thus, she is strongly attracted to Pete because of his swaggering sense of superiority, his contemptuous gaze at the world around him, and his professed prowess in regular fights with other men. She perceives that "here was the ideal man," the "supreme warrior," "a formidable man who disdained the strength of a world full of fists" (pp. 26, 27, 28). Her "spaniel-like dependence," of course, encourages Pete's "off-handedness and ease" with her (pp. 57, 58), especially once she is "ruined."

Maggie's romantic attitude toward Pete is encouraged by the theater, which offers an escape from the harsh conditions of her own life. For Maggie and the masses around her at the theater, reality for a short time becomes the "transcendental realism" of the melodramas which Pete takes her to see. Lost in plays in which dazzling heroines are rescued by heroes with "beautiful sentiments" or in which heroes living in poverty in the first act rise to "wealth and triumph in the final one," Maggie experiences both the joy within these worlds and an "ecstatic pity" (p. 36) of her own condition. Dazzled by the possibilities presented in these plays, she envisions a very ordinary opportunist like Pete as her shining "hero" and rejoices that "the poor and virtuous eventually overcame the wealthy and wicked" (p. 37) even as Pete seduces and "ruins" her. When the world of the melodramas fails her, she has nowhere to go—except to prostitution and eventually the river. In turning to sex outside of marriage with Pete, to prostitution, and eventually to suicide, Maggie, of course, offends the code of conduct of her subculture and family. Parents may drink and fight, children may be beaten—these are comprehensible, even acceptable, behaviors. But young girls may not be "ruined."

Jimmie although very different from Maggie, also displays characteristics that are, according to Wilson, typical of many children of violent alcoholics: "delinquency, truancy, aggressive behaviour, hyperactivity, and temper tantrums" (pp. 161–62). He fights savagely from an early age and quickly gains a "fair record" (p. 23) of arrests. He also begins drinking very young, thus falling into the category of those thirty-three percent of children with alcoholic parents and antisocial behavior in early life whom Cotton predicts will become heavy drinkers. Crane writes, "He became a young man of leather," with a "chronic" sneer (p. 20). The police were his enemies, "actuated by malignant impulses"; in fact, the world was primarily composed of "despicable creatures who were all trying to take advantage of him, and with whom, in defence, he was obliged to quarrel on all possible occasions" (p. 22). He craves power and, as a truck driver, a "god-driver" (p. 23), he storms through the streets, deliberately endangering vehicles and foot passengers.

After his father's death, Jimmie takes over "the vague position of head of the family" and develops a pattern with his mother not dissimilar to that which his two parents had had. He begins to stumble home late at night and reel "about the room, swearing at his relations" (p. 24) or falling asleep on the floor. His mother—her children grown and her husband dead—now drinks both at home and at saloons, from which she is often ejected for disturbances. She is ready to fight with anyone—the children of the neighborhood, other women, "the universe" itself (p. 39). And Jimmie—in his "vague position of head of the family"—offers quite the best possibility in the "safe zone" of the family. Jimmie's youth and greater strength lead to fights in which his mother is trounced. But in the process the mother and son "sway and struggle like gladiators" (p. 40) and the tenement again rocks with "a storm of crashes and curses" while "interested spectators" emerge from their apartments to enjoy the evening's entertainment. The patterns of Jimmie's adulthood are clearly set.

In Crane—usually regarded, of course, as a naturalist—none of the characters appears to have any real freedom of choice; they are victims of their environment. James Nagel argues, however, that critics like Malcolm Cowley have mistakenly regarded Maggie as a victim of "necessitarian forces."[14] He suggests that "her worldly innocence and compassion mark her as singularly free of the influences around her," both hereditary and environmental (p. 99). At the same time he notes that Maggie dies partially as a result "of her romantic dreams, of her dependency, and perhaps most of all, of her simplistic and distorted view of life." Concerned as he is with Crane's "literary impressionism," Nagel sees Maggie's death as the result of "epistemological problems of perception and interpretation" rather than of "deterministic forces beyond the control of the characters" (p. 100). I would argue, however, that the factors which form Maggie and inevitably destroy her us are cultural factors. Donald Pizer, too, suggests quite clearly that "Crane's focus in Maggie is less on the inherent evil of slum life than on the harm done by a false moral environment imposed on that life."[15] *Maggie*, to Pizer, is a novel "primarily about the falsity and destructiveness of certain moral codes" (p. 129), which are, of course, a part of the environment but are not inevitable parts of social morality. The critically entrapping environmental forces in the lives of all of the Johnsons are clearly cultural and moral factors which victimize but lie within the power of man to change.

The same is true of the Breedloves in Toni Morrison's novel. On a societal or subcultural level, poverty and racism are the destructive elements in *The Bluest Eye*. The Breedlove family lives in an abandoned store which has been divided into two rooms, with a kitchen in the back but no bath facilities except a toilet bowl. The furnishings are "anything but describable, having been conceived, manufactured, shipped, and sold in various states of thoughtlessness, greed, and indifference"; "the joylessness stank, pervading everything."[16] But it is Morrison's description of Cholly Breedlove's purchase of a new sofa which clarifies the degree of helplessness of the poor and the degrading humiliations which are part not only of their everyday life but of momentous (and presumably joyous) events like the purchase of a piece of furniture. At delivery, the fabric of the sofa across the back is split. Mr. Breedlove protests, "But I don't want no tore couch if'n it's bought new." His "pleading eyes and tightened testicles" protest. The response is simple: "Tough shit, buddy. *Your* tough shit" (p. 32). Torn fabric or not, the time payments begin.

The Breedloves, however, are not suffering only from severe poverty because of cutbacks at the plant. They are also suffering from a common cause of alcoholism among blacks[17]: societal racism, the kind of racism which makes a storekeeper look at little Pecola Breedlove with "total absence of human recognition." Pecola learns early that although "all things in her are flux and anticipation," her blackness is "static and dread." It is her blackness "that accounts for, that creates, the vacuum edged with distaste in white eyes" (p. 42). But learning early does not lessen the indignity and shock; it simply trains one not to protest. Pecola's pregnant mother listens to an older doctor explain to a group of younger doctors visiting a maternity ward that "these here women [blacks] . . . deliver right away and with no pain. Just like horses" (p. 99), before he turns with sympathy and attention to a pregnant white woman.

On a subcultural level the societal racism is aggravated by the tendency of at least some of the blacks to idealize the "sky-soft brown" (p. 49) or the "high-yellow" (p. 52). The rich Maureen Peal—"a high-yellow dream child," with long brown hair, a "summery complexion," and "sloe green eyes" (pp. 52–53)—makes the black girls "lesser. Nicer, brighter, but still lesser" (p. 61). Girls like Frieda, Pecola's friend and one of the novel's narrators, may protest the black world's emulation of the white world by dismembering her white dolls, but she cannot "destroy the honey voices of parents and aunts, the obedience in the eyes of our peers, the slippery light in the eyes of our teachers when they encountered the Maureen Peals of the world" (pp. 61–62). All she can do is experience tension: being youth and lucky, she still loves herself; but in some incomprehensible way she also knows she is judged unworthy, "lesser."

But the racism from which the Breedloves suffer operates in its most pernicious form on the individual and small-group level. The fact that Claudia and Frieda and their family are hurt but not destroyed by their poverty or color makes the point clear. The Breedloves are suffering primarily because *they* believe they are "ugly." Morrison explains, in one of the most important passages in the novel, "No one could have convinced them that they were not relentlessly and aggressively ugly. Except for the father, Cholly, whose ugliness (the result of despair, dissipation, and violence directed toward pretty things and weak people) was behavior, the rest of the family—Mrs. Breedlove, Sammy Breedlove, and Pecola Breedlove—wore their ugliness, put it on, so to speak, although it did not belong to them." The ugliness has nothing to do with color or features; it comes "from conviction, their conviction" (p. 34).

This sense of ugliness becomes the motivating force of the characters' lives. Sammy uses his ugliness to cause pain; Mrs. Breedlove uses her ugliness for martyrdom; and Pecola uses her ugliness as a shield, to hide from people. Thus, Morrison creates a world not dissimilar to Crane's, in which selection and arrangement of detail point to the unwitting complicity of the characters with the very environmental forces which victimize them. As F. D. Harper's study *Alcoholic Abuse and Black America* suggests, alcoholism is almost predictable in such a context.[18]

On the individual and small-group level, Morrison offers detailed background information on Pauline and Cholly Breedlove. Mrs. Breedlove early developed a "general feeling of separateness and unworthiness" (p. 88), which she attributed a neglected foot injury in childhood that has left her with a slight limp. She always has had a great love for order, which she has demonstrated in keeping house for her parents, for her husband in their early years when the two were deeply in love, and, in the novel, for her affluent white employers. But although the poverty and racism of her early years— not nearly as severe as that of her adult years with Cholly—have contributed to a sense of unworthiness and ugliness, Pauline's general strategy has been one of quiet acceptance colored by occasional romantic dreams.

The change in her which leads to her aggressive role in the marriage is caused by her move to a northern city where her clothes, accent and manners make her a misfit ("ugly") among the blacks; it is caused by the increased racism of the city, by her infatuation with the movies, and by her husband's "ugly" behavior. In Lorain, Ohio, Mrs. Breedlove experiences a "hateful" racism from the "white folks" which she had not experienced in Kentucky; further, she can find no place among the "Northern colored folk. . . . No better than whites for meanness. They could make you feel just as no-count, 'cept I didn't expect it from them" (p. 93). Incredibly lonely and lost, at first she turns to the movies for escape and loses herself in a world of romantic love and physical beauty, *white* physical beauty. Her own life looks bleaker and bleaker as she gazes for hours at "white men taking such good care of they women, and they all dressed up in big clean houses with the bathtubs right in the same room with the toilet" (p. 97). She tries to do her hair like Jean Harlow—until she loses a tooth and gives up trying to efface her ugliness—but cannot see her husband as Clark Gable.

Several years later, Mrs. Breedlove turns to religion and the white world as her escape from the ugliness—spiritual and physical—of her own home and family. She identifies with the virtues of the white family for whom she works—the cleanliness, order, wealth and beauty—and becomes the agent of the Lord in punishing the ugly people in her own family for their failures. She does not severely beat her children; but she screams at them, yanks, slaps and pushes them around—and not simply as a part of societally approved methods of child-raising since, in front of her own daughter, she coddles her employers' daughter. Her own children have become ugly "afterthoughts"(p. 101) of her life; no part of the order and beauty of her private white world with her employers and their "little pink-and-yellow girl" (p. 87) does she introduce into their sordid lives. Mrs. Breedlove's thinking, in fact, is very similar to that of Alice Walker's mother. Walker describes her mother as once asking her "in a moment of vicarious pride and despair," if she did not think that whites were "jest naturally smarter, prettier, better."[19]

Pauline Breedlove's role with her husband is much more aggressive than her role with her children. Because she sees herself as the Lord's caretaker of her drunken husband, she initiates the verbal and physical altercations in the home, Mrs. Breedlove always has causes for her fights—she, for example, needs Cholly to bring coal into the house and he will not get up to get it— but the real cause of the fighting is that Mrs. Breedlove is "an upright and Christian woman, burdened with a no-count man, whom God wanted her to punish" (p. 37). As Morrison explains, Mrs. Breedlove "needed Cholly's sins desperately. The lower he sank, the wilder and more irresponsible he became, the more splendid she and her task became. In the name of Jesus" (p. 38). Thus, in this couple's complex interaction, it is the spouse—whose behavior is societally and subculturally approved—who is the chief aggressor.

Pauline never ceases to remind her family that she works twelve to sixteen hours a day to support them (the responsible wage earner, but also the martyr); she is active in the church and does not drink, smoke or carouse (the conscientious Christian wife and mother, but also the avenging angel). She thinks very well of herself, "and the world itself agreed with her" (p. 102). Since Mrs. Breedlove's forms of escape—into a white world fantasy and a religious crusade—are apparently innocent, even environmentally approved, modes of expression, the world is not concerned that "the tiny, undistinguished days" of her life are "identified, grouped, and classed by these quarrels" or that the quarrels give "substance," "grandeur," "zest and reasonableness" to her life (p. 36). The degree of Pauline's anger and aggression makes it very clear that marital aggression does not depend upon alcohol. It probably does depend upon a defense mechanism, however, and Mrs. Breedlove has found justification for her aggression in her fantasies and causes.

The deprivations of Cholly Breedlove's early life were such that, despite the love of his Great Aunt Jimmy, who raised him until he was fourteen, and the friendship of an old man called Blue Jack, he is a mass of unsorted, strong emotions which often befuddle him. His mother, not "right in the head" (p. 105), abandoned him as a baby; his father never knew him; and, at fourteen, he is ridiculed by white men holding flashlights who watch him having intercourse with a young black girl. As a result, in his early teens Cholly becomes a man without bounds, a man "Dangerously free. Free to feel whatever he felt—fear, guilt, shame, love, grief, pity" (p. 125). He is free to sleep with a woman, "knock her in the head," or pick "a woman's bullet out of the calf of his leg"; he is free to drink, to kill (three white men), or to serve on a chain gang. Feeling "godlike," he is "alone with his own perceptions and appetites, and they alone interested him." The marriage to Pauline ends his freedom; and he quickly feels stifled by "the constantness, varietylessness, the sheer weight of sameness [which] drove him to despair and froze his imagination." With nothing that interests him he turns to drink: "Only in drink was there some break, some floodlight, and when that closed, there was oblivion" (p. 126).

Despite the varieties of escape which the Breedloves use—all societally acceptable ways of relieving stress, although Pauline's is clearly the strong and virtuous way, Cholly's the weak—they still need each other to deal with the frustrations and deprivations of their lives. Mr. Breedlove, "by his habitual drunkenness and orneriness," provides them both "with the material they needed to make their lives tolerable" (p. 38). And Mr. Breedlove very much needs his wife: "She was one of the few things abhorrent to him that he could touch and therefore hurt. He poured out on her the sum of all his inarticulate fury and aborted desires. Hating her, he could leave himself intact" (p. 37). His abhorrence, of course, is not simply personal, even when his wife becomes the Lord's caretaker. It is an abhorrence grounded in the deprivations, humiliations and insults of a lifetime; and the woman is an appropriate object of this abhorrence because it was a young girl who had been responsible for the terrible sexual humiliation in his youth and because she exists in a "safe zone." Mr. Breedlove appears to be the almost typical wife-beater, described by Del Martin: he is a "loser . . . angry with himself and frustrated by his life"; "helplessness, fear, inadequacy, and insecurity" gnaw at his self-esteem.[20]

The fights of the Breedloves are most frequently begun by Pauline. In fact, on those evenings when Cholly comes home too drunk to fight and simply falls into a sodden sleep, Pauline waits until the next morning to fight—a fight more terrible than the evening one would have been because it lacks "spontaneity; it would be calculated, uninspired, and deadly" (p. 35). Usually the fights occur when Cholly is very drunk, sometimes when he is hung over—which is for him, at least, a period of lessened responsibility by societal norms. The fights of the couple are highly ritualized; they have a "darkly brutal formalism that was paralleled only by their lovemaking" (p. 37). Each drunken bout of Cholly becomes the immediate cause; each bout, then, has "its own ceremonial close" (p. 36). The Breedloves have tacitly agreed not to kill each other and adjust their methods of fighting accordingly. Cholly fights his wife "the way a coward fights a man—with feet, the palms of his hands, and teeth." She fights back with frying pans, pokers and an occasional flatiron. They do not "talk, groan, or curse during these beatings. There was only the muted sound of falling things, and flesh on unsurprised flesh" (pp. 37–38).

The children's reactions to the fighting vary. Sammy's aggressive reaction is like that of Jimmie in *Maggie*. Sammy sometimes curses, sometimes leaves the house (he runs away at least twenty-seven times by the time he is fourteen), sometimes joins the fight, sometimes eggs his mother on to kill his father. Eventually, he simply leaves town.

Pecola, like Maggie, takes a passive role. She shrinks from the scene, sometimes covering herself with her quilt, wishing that one of her parents would kill the other or wishing that she herself would die. She whispers, "Don't, Mrs. Breedlove. Don't" (p. 38). It is during these periods of trying physically to shrink herself out of the horrors of her life that she develops the habit of praying to God to help her disappear. She squeezes her eyes shut and thinks parts of her body out of existence until only her eyes are left. Since she can never think her eyes out of existence, she comes to identify them with her ugliness (certainly the pictures they hold are all ugly ones) and begins to think that if she can get blue eyes her life may change.

Pecola early realizes that blue-eyed white girls are beautiful and that their lives are beautiful; in this identification she is clearly her mother's child.

When her father burns their house down, before they move to the abandoned store, she is placed by the county for a short time with Frieda's family. Pecola immediately falls in love with the Shirley Temple cup Frieda's mother gives her to drink from. She is captivated by the blue eyes and dimples and drinks three quarts of milk in one day just so she can see "sweet Shirley's face" (p. 22). Her favorite candy is Mary Janes, a candy in individual pale-yellow wrappers with a picture of a blonde, blue-eyed white girl. Pecola eats the candy, "and its sweetness is good. To eat the candy is somehow to eat the eyes, eat Mary Jane. Love Mary Jane. Be Mary Jane" (p. 43).

Pecola is not simply injured by her fantasies of the white world and by the marital abuse which is a daily part of her life, however. She, unlike the other children in Crane and Morrison, is also decisively assaulted psychologically by her mother and physically by her father. She cannot survive. Pecola lives in a day by day world in which her mother, whom she calls "Mrs. Breedlove," is called "Polly" by her employers' daughter, the little girl with the blue eyes, corn yellow hair, pink dress and pink bedroom slippers with bunny ears. Mrs. Breedlove, as she completely neglects Pecola or knocks the dirty, uncombed, ragged girl down, will not even admit to the "little pink-and-yellow girl" who the ugly black child is.

Like her assaults on her husband, Mrs. Breedlove's attacks on Pecola are not done under the influence of alcohol: they are done under the influence of the white standards of physical beauty and Pauline's identification of "physical beauty with virtue" (p. 97). All she can teach her children—when she is at home at all and can bother with them—is fear: "fear of being clumsy, fear of being like their father, fear of not being loved by God, fear of madness like Cholly's mother." All she can teach Pecola is "fear of growing up, fear of other people, fear of life" (p. 102).

The Pecola who is raped by her father is already a broken child. The drunken Cholly, seeing her washing dishes at the sink, reacts to her "young, helpless, hopeless presence." Morrison suggests many reasons for the rape: Cholly's inability to develop fatherly emotions because he had never known a parent himself; his feelings of "guilt and impotence" that he could do nothing for this whipped, burdened, miserable child; and his love, "tenderness . . . protectiveness" (p. 127). Once he touches Pecola, however, the Cholly who had been irresponsibly free for years before he married breaks out: "the doing of a wild and forbidden thing" (p. 128) excites him; the desire for her overcomes him. Consumed by hatred and tenderness—unruly, unsorted emotions of a lifetime, freed by the alcohol he has drunk—Cholly gives his daughter the final blow which drives her into insanity, although her suffering does not end with the rape (possibly two rapes). Pecola must also bear a child which dies before she can escape into insanity, living on the edge of town, flailing "her arms like a bird in an eternal, grotesquely futile effort to fly. Beating the air, a winged but grounded bird, intent on the blue void it could not reach—could not even see—but which filled the valleys of the mind" (p. 158).

There is no question that alcohol does contribute to Cholly's rape of Pecola—it frees his unruly emotions, both savage and tender—but no one could argue that alcohol *causes* the rape. Morrison's whole novel has been building to the rape scene and its consequences, Pecola's insanity. The causes of the rape run like innumerable threads through the story of the Breedlove family (the name is significant), who, as Morrison clearly shows in the novel, live in a community with other black families who are subject to many of the same environmental deprivations and frustrations but who, like Alice Walker's mother, live responsible, caring family lives. The Breedloves' lives include many of the causes of incest cited by Herschel D. Rosenzweig in his study of sexual abuse: "multiple stresses, marital disharmony or disruption, role reversals between parents and siblings . . . the evolution of inappropriate sexual activity between family members," "relatively immature and dependent" parents, frequent absence from the home of the parent of the same sex, and alcoholism.[21] Cholly and Pauline were doomed before they were adults. The same is undoubtedly true of Sammy, who has disappeared. But in Morrison, as in Crane, the most pathetic victims are the young girls who have grown up in these households.

The young black girl, Frieda, who narrates sections of the novel, however, does not allow us to see the rape simply as the natural outcome of the Breedloves' inability to deal with environmental stress and deprivation or of the disturbed family system which has emerged in an attempt simply to survive and function. She embraces Pecola, the "winged but grounded bird," within the complex system "of our town," even "of the entire country" (p. 160). Frieda sees the world as the assassin, Pecola as the scapegoat, a reading not dissimilar to Pizer's reading of *Maggie*. These young girls *are* destroyed—but they are destroyed by cultural and moral factors which an enlightened society can control. Both works also comment on the possible religious significance of the struggles of such reduced people. The omniscient narrator of *The Bluest Eye* defines the world of such victimization as one whose god is silent, whose god has forgotten that he once said, "Suffer little children to come unto me, and harm them not" (p. 143). Crane's *novella* concludes with an institutionalized Christianity—which has never given Maggie a home or been willing to shelter her after she was "ruined"—forgiving her, only once she is dead, for her sins.

Thus, not only do the works of Crane and Morrison accord with the views on alcoholism advanced by social and behavioral scientists; but these artists, writing in different centuries and describing different ethnic groups, present their "findings" in a fictional mode that perhaps best sensitizes the reading public to the causes and consequences of this problem.

NOTES

1. Edwin M. Lemert, "Alcohol, Values and Social Control," in *Society, Culture, and Drinking Patterns,* ed. David J. Pittman and Charles R. Snyder (New York, 1962), p. 568.

2. Don Cahalan, Ira H. Cisin and Helen M. Crossley, *American Drinking Practices: A National Study of Drinking Behavior and Attitudes* (New Brunswick, N.J., 1969).

3. Craig MacAndrew and Robert B. Edgerton, *Drunken Comportment: A Social Experiment* (Chicago, 1969), p. 90.

4. Theodore D. Graves, "Acculturation, Access, and Alcohol in a Tri-ethnic Community," *American Anthropologist,* LXIX (1967), pp. 306–321, and Robert K. Merton, *Social Theory and Social Structure* (New York, 1957).

5. David Levinson, "Social Setting, Cultural Factors and Alcohol-Related Aggression," in *Alcohol, Drug Abuse and Aggression,* ed. Edward Gottheil, et al. (Springfield, 1983), p. 45.

6. Roger Langley and Richard C. Levy, *Wife-Beating: The Silent Crisis* (New York, 1977); and Gisela Spieker, "What is the Link Between Alcohol Abuse and Violence?" in *Alcohol, Drug Abuse and Aggression.*

7. Murray A. Straus, "Ordinary Violence, Child Abuse, and Wife-Beating: What Do They Have in Common?" in *The Dark Side of Families,* ed. David Finkelhor, et al. (Beverly Hills, 1983), pp. 214, 231.

8. Peter Steinglass, "The Roles of Alcohol in Family Systems," in *Alcohol and the Family,* ed. Jim Orford and Judith Harwin (London, 1982), p. 131.

9. Stephen Crane, *Maggie: A Girl of the Streets,* in *Bowery Tales* (Charlottesville, 1969), p. 11.

10. Clare Wilson and Jim Orford, "Children of Alcoholics: Report of a Preliminary Study and Comments on the Literature," *Journal of Studies on Alcohol,* XXXIX (1978), pp. 121–42.

11. Crane, *Letters,* ed. R.W. Stallman and Lillian Gilkes (New York, 1960), p. 99.

12. Clare Wilson, "The Impact on Children," in *Alcohol and the Family* (London, 1982), pp. 157–59.

13. N.S. Cotton, "The Familial Incidence of Alcoholism: A Review," *Journal of Studies on Alcohol,* XL (1979), pp. 89–116.

14. James Nagel, *Stephen Crane and Literary Impressionism* (University Park, 1980), p. 99. See Malcolm Cowley, "Naturalism in American Literature," in *Evolutionary Thought in America,* ed. Stow Persons (New Haven, 1950).

15. Donald Pizer, *Realism and Naturalism in 19th-Century American Literature* (Carbondale, 1966), p. 129.

16. Toni Morrison, *The Bluest Eye* (New York, 1972), pp. 31, 32.

17. Geoffrey P. Kane, *Inner-City Alcoholism: An Ecological Analysis and Cross-Cultural Study* (New York, 1981), p. 95.

18. F.D. Harper, ed. *Alcohol Abuse and Black America* (Alexandria, 1976).

19. Alice Walker, "The Civil Rights Movement: What Good Was It?" *In Search of Our Mothers' Gardens* (New York, 1983), p. 123.

20. Del Martin, *Battered Wives* (New York, 1983), p. 46.

21. Herschel D. Rosenzweig, "Sexual Abuse: Practical Implications of Knowledge," *Unhappy Families* (Littleton, 1985), pp. 52–53, 58.

THOMAS H. FICK

Toni Morrison's "Allegory of the Cave": Movies, Consumption, and Platonic Realism in The Bluest Eye

Toni Morrison's first novel, *The Bluest Eye* (1970), is an unusually effective exploration of racism in twentieth-century America in part because of the place it gives to central legacies of Western civilization. Like Ralph Ellison, whose *Invisible Man* draws on Emerson and Whitman as well as folklore, Morrison recognizes the importance of Western literature and philosophy to the Afro-American experience in America; in some ways *The Bluest Eye* stands opposed to more hermetic work like Alice Walker's *The Color Purple*, which despite its many strengths does not come to terms with the intellectual and economic foundations of racism and whose portrayal of character and personal growth suffers accordingly.[1] Morrison's characters are more convincing and ultimately more moving than Walker's because they operate in a world shaped by a complex and sometimes repressive cultural heritage. In *The Bluest Eye* this heritage is primarily represented by T. S. Eliot's *The Waste Land* and Plato's "Allegory of the Cave" in Book VII of *The Republic*.[2] These two important moments in Western culture provide specific thematic and structural elements in the novel; in a larger sense they suggest Morrison's belief in the close relationship between intellectual traditions and particular economic and social conditions.

Eliot's contribution in *The Bluest Eye* is the more apparent because it operates on the level of imagery as well as theme and structure. In the

Journal of the Midwest Modern Language Association, 22 (1); Spring 1989: pp. 10–22. © Midwest Modern Language Association and Thomas H. Fick.

19

prologue the narrator Claudia MacTeer remembers when she and her sister Frieda planted marigold seeds in a childish rite they hoped would guarantee the health of their twelve-year-old friend Pecola's baby. If the seeds sprout, they think, the baby will thrive. But no seeds sprout, the baby dies, and Pecola spends her life "plucking her way between the tire rims and the sunflowers, between Coke bottles and milkweed, among all the waste and beauty of the world."[3] Only much later does Claudia understand that it isn't her fault, that "the entire country was hostile to marigolds that year" (160). *The Bluest Eye* is framed by the narrator's brooding recollection of a wasteland, and the seasons which title the major sections—"Autumn," "Winter," "Spring," and "Summer"—mark off a parody of rebirth and growth. In "the thin light of spring" (127) Pecola Breedlove is raped by her drunken father (a cruel sort of breeding indeed), and in summer, pregnant, she goes mad after the equivalent of Eliot's Mme Sosostris works a phony spell to give her blue eyes.

The echoes of Eliot's *Waste Land* are important for thematic and structural reasons and for what they reveal about Morrison's interest in literary tradition. The central conceptual presence in *The Bluest Eye*, however, is Plato's "Allegory of the Cave." This is initially difficult to see because the idea and image of the wasteland is everywhere directly present in the novel while Plato's allegory operates through the analogy of the cinema. Movies are the centrally destructive force in the novel not only because of the values they present—perfect white bodies and romantic love—but because of the way they present them: as flawless Archetypes above and outside the shadowy world of everyday life. For Morrison, that is, the message *and* the medium are almost equally dangerous: as we shall see, the cinema reproduces the structure of Plato's allegory in terms appropriate to a technological and capitalist society and provides the focus for an exploration of the complicity between Platonic realism, racism, and a culture of consumption. In order to understand the centrality of Platonic "realism" as it is embodied in the cinema, however, we first need to understand what personal, cultural, and artistic issues this version of realism engages.

The Bluest Eye is an angry book but it is also an orderly one, perhaps because in Afro-American literature a careful structure is frequently used to contain and shape the anger that might otherwise be construed as lack of control.[4] A reasonable place to begin, then, is with the blue eyes of the title, the blue eyes Pecola Breedlove thinks will introduce harmony and love into her fragmented and emotionally barren life. For Pecola, change has become a matter of survival: her father is a drunk, her mother's love goes to a white child, and the whole world tells her she is ugly. On the most obvious level her desire for blue eyes is a response to an ideal of beauty that takes specific form in the Shirley Temples, Hedy Lamarrs, Ginger Rogerses, and unnamed models whose blond hair, blue eyes, and white skins dominate the landscape of American life, "leaning from every billboard, every movie, every glance" (34). Blue eyes epitomize everything desirable in white American culture, but Pecola's longing for this cosmetic change expresses her deeper need to reform the world by reforming the way she sees it, a transcendental rather than existential imperative: "It had occurred to Pecola some time ago that if her eyes, those eyes that held the pictures, and knew the sights—if those eyes of hers were different, that is to say, beautiful, she herself would be different" (40).

As this quotation suggests, like many children Pecola asks questions that are disconcerting for both their naiveté and their insight. She poses one such question at the age of eleven: "'How,'" she asks Frieda and Claudia, "'do you get somebody to love you?'" (29). The children don't know, but the narrative provides a number of exemplary answers: the neighborhood whores' caustic camaraderie, her parents' desperate fights, the sterile "nesting" of bourgeois black women, and most destructively Pecola's rape by her own father.[5] But there is another question Pecola wants answered even more, for without an answer "love" has no meaning: the conditions of her own and the world's reality. This is the question she silently poses to Marie, one of the three whores who, besides Claudia and Frieda, are her only friends: "Pecola looked and looked at the women. Were they real? Marie belched, softly, purringly, lovingly" (49). Marie's answer is clear and unambiguous because its sheer physicality avoids the abstractions such a question is likely to evoke, but the primary emphasis of the passage is on sight, not sound—on the intensity of Pecola's "looking." The connection between sight and reality tells us as much about Morrison's commitment to the mode of realism as it does about Pecola. As a mode realism has been characterized by its emphasis on sight: as Jeffrey Mehlman remarks, "excellence of *vision* is the distinguishing mark of realism" and Edwin Cady finds that the principal American realists share a common concern with sight.[6] To "look and look," therefore, is to accept the world's immediate existence, as Pecola does when she accepts the whore's insistent presence, but to look with eyes other than one's own is to falsify both self and world.[7] Pecola's wish for blue eyes is not only a wish to match the ideal of the white child, it is also a rejection of right seeing, of the premises of realism for those of romance.

In fact, like many of the classic examples of realism from Flaubert's *Madame Bovary* to Clemens's *Huckleberry Finn* the themes and structure of Morrison's novel center on an explicit antagonism to the forms and motives of romance. Tom Sawyer's extravagant dedication to the conventions of romantic fiction counterpoint Huck Finn's sound heart and empirical instincts. Huck tests Tom's assertions both intentionally—for example by rubbing a lamp to see if the promised genie will show—and unintentionally by becoming involved with the real-life counterparts of Tom's fictional heroes.

The Shepherdson-Grangerford feud shows Huck that Tom's "authorities" are dead wrong when it comes to chivalric ideals: codes of honor lead to murder not glory. *The Bluest Eye* follows a similar structure of ironic counterpoint. The novel's epigraph is a "Dick and Jane" children's story that serves as an ironic commentary on the MacTeers's and Breedloves's daily lives: "Here is the house. It is green and white. . . . Here is the family. Mother, Father, Dick, and Jane live in the green-and-white house. They are very happy," and so forth. Each segment of this story is used as a section "title" to introduce its counterpart in 1940s racist America: the green and white house of Dick and Jane introduces the Breedloves's "irritating and melancholy" (30) storefront apartment; the strong and smiling father is a bitter drunk; the happy family is poor and miserable.[8] The commitment to realist discourse implied in this ironic juxtaposition is made explicit in the characterization of Pecola's friendly whores. Marie, China, and Poland "did not belong to those generations of prostitutes created in novels, with great and generous hearts, dedicated, because of the horror of circumstance, to ameliorating the luckless, barren life of men, taking money incidentally and humbly for their 'understanding.'" Instead, they are "whores in whores' clothing" (47–8).

In *The Bluest Eye,* however, the opposition between real and ideal is more profound than in *Huckleberry Finn.* The obsession with romance and chivalry that Clemens blamed on Sir Walter Scott does not depend on an alternative sense of the real, but on a belief that some actions and attitudes are better than others. Despite their literary origins, that is, notions of chivalry are thoroughly social: Tom Sawyer is not only an aficionado of pirate oaths but a consummate politician, able to read and use others' expectations and desires. Morrison, on the other hand, is interested in antithetical senses of the real, in different *ways* of locating value in the world rather than in the different values alone. The "Dick and Jane" primer is important not only because it provides a particular set of expectations of modes of behavior (as Scott provides a number of paradigmatic scenarios for Tom Sawyer) but because it locates these expectations and behaviors in a realm of immutable Archetypes—equivalent to the Platonic idea of the "real"—in contrast with which this transient world is only an imitation. Compared to the world of green and white houses, strong, smiling fathers and happy mothers, Claudia's and Pecola's world is but an "Imitation of Life," to cite the title of a movie that one character admires extravagantly.[9]

The novel centers on one successful and several unsuccessful efforts to move beyond Platonic "realism" toward an understanding and acceptance of the physical world's primacy. The first section, narrated from the young Claudia's point of view, introduces the detailed and imperfect particulars of daily life from the limited perspective of a child. Here, as in each of young Claudia's subsequent sections, typography recapitulates ontology: the right margins are "unjustified"—as ragged and as honest as the perceptions of a young girl.[10] The house is "old, cold, and green . . . peopled by roaches and mice" (12) and the first impression is of a world as starkly opposite Dick and Jane's as possible. Adults, young Claudia tells us, "do not talk to us—they give us directions. They issue orders without providing information. When we trip and fall they glance at us; if we cut or bruise ourselves, they ask us are we crazy" (12). But these are the impressions of a child; like their counterparts in the "Peanuts" comic strip the adults in *The Bluest Eye* are remote, unintelligible, and nearly invisible. Further, the uncertainty we as readers feel about the true proportions of love and neglect in Claudia's life duplicates the ambiguity mark of a world where emotions, like relationships, are mutable rather than absolute (as they are for Dick and Jane). In fact, we find out that love is not absent but "thick as Alaga syrup" (14). The adults are simply too preoccupied with scavaging coal and making ends meet to be the endlessly smiling paragons of a story book.

Unlike the monotonous rhythm of Dick and Jane's prose world, young Claudia's narrative modulates through a number of moods and ends with Pecola's question about love, a question which has been partially answered in the equivocal—because human—terms of the just-concluded section. Love is dynamic rather than static, a process rather than a magic formula. The primary focus, however, is on Claudia's commitment to right seeing—the reverse of Pecola's desire for new, impossibly blue eyes and all that they imply about value in literature as in life. Even as a child Claudia is determined to understand the "beauty, the desirability" (20) of America's cultural icons: Shirley Temple and the white dolls constructed in her image. Though fueled by hate for the icons that usurp her family's admiration, Claudia is rational and resolutely empirical in her quest for understanding. She tears apart her Christmas present of a white doll, looking for its beauty: "Remove the cold and stupid eyeball . . . take off the head, shake out the sawdust, crack the back against the brass bed rail, it would bleat still. The gauze back would split, and I could see the disk with six holes, the secret of the sound. A mere metal roundness" (21). Young Claudia is an empiricist among metaphysicians, unable to believe there is value above and beyond what can be found in the immediate world; she lays the groundwork for the older Claudia's rejection of romance for realism. For Christmas, she remembers, "I did not want. . . to possess any object. I wanted rather to feel something," and feeling is a matter of contact, of specific things and places: "The lowness of the stool made for my body, . . . the smell of lilacs, the sound of the music, and, since it would be good to have all of my senses engaged, the taste of a peach . . ." (21).

At the opposite pole from Claudia's world of sense and feeling is the celluloid world of transcendent beauty and health, Dick and Jane in the age of McLuhan. References to movies and movie stars punctuate the narrative, forming an insistent counterpoint to Claudia's quest for authenticity in experience. The MacTeers's boarder, Mr. Henry, delights in calling the young girls Greta Garbo and Ginger Rogers; Pecola drinks three quarts of milk just to see Shirley Temple's picture on the mug; black women have their hair styled like Hedy Lamarr's; Betty Grable's name looms large on theatre marquees. Movies convey an adult version of Dick and Jane's ideal world, but in *The Bluest Eye* the emphasis is not just on the particular scenes, formulae, or characters—that special hairdo or inflection—but on the medium itself. To understand the importance of the cinema, therefore, we need to consider method as well as content, the how as much as the what of its deception.

By co-opting individual sight and replacing it with the camera's apparent omniscience a movie can bestow false authority on its images and offer a nicely framed, repeatable world totally unlike young Claudia's. But it is a mistake to think of the cinema only as cultural shorthand for twentieth-century escapism; its appearance in *The Bluest Eye* serves to recall an older and more intellectually distinguished precursor. The cinema functions almost precisely like the famous cave in Plato's *The Republic*, as a brief summary of the allegory will show. Socrates asks us to imagine people living from childhood in a cave, chained by leg and neck with their backs to the only entrance. Behind them is a fire with a parapet in front of it "like the screen at a puppet-show, which hides the performers while they show their puppets over the top."[11] Objects are carried by men behind the parapet so that the fire projects the objects' shadows on the wall of the cave in front of the chained viewers. Obviously, Socrates says, the captives would think the shadows are the sole reality, and if one of the people crossing behind them spoke, the echo would make the sound seem to come from the projected shadow. He concludes, "In every way, then, such prisoners would recognize as reality nothing but the shadows of those artificial objects."[12] But the shadows are still shadows; the "real" lies outside the cave, in the immutable Archetypes represented by the objects carried between the fire and the cave wall. This allegory is an accurate though technologically unsophisticated description of the cinema: celluloid takes the place of Socrates's hand-carried objects, and a projector the place of his fire.[13] In each case the effect is the same: the screen shows the shadow of a perfect world, the "real" world of which ours is merely an imitation. But while Socrates imagines the possibility that through rigorous mathematical preparation one will be able to face the "real" (i.e., ideal) world itself, Morrison sees the very notion of a Platonic real as centrally false and destructive. The characters who measure themselves against advertisements and movies are captives not because they are ignorant of the world above and behind, but because they believe that there *is* such a world.

Pauline Breedlove is the cinema's primary victim, and her story gives shape and context to Pecola's more general tragedy. As a child in Alabama

Pauline had cultivated the pleasures of ordering her small world, but she is an artist without the means to realize her creative impulses: "She missed—without knowing what she missed—paints and crayons" (89). When her marriage to Cholly deteriorates she has little else to do but go to the movies, where she is introduced to romantic love and physical beauty, "the most destructive ideas in the history of human thought": "She was never able, after her education in the movies, to look at a face and not assign it some category in the scale of absolute beauty, and the scale was on absorbed in full from the silver screen" (97). The notion of absolute beauty commits Pauline to think of her world as a shadow, a projection of the perfect world where "'white men [take] such good care of they women, and they all dressed up in big clean houses'" (97). The consequences of Pauline's immersion in a world of absolutes are intensely personal. In order to embrace the Platonic real she must repudiate the temporal and conditional, the transient physical world whose most insistent manifestation is the body itself. Indeed, the cinema offers a neo-religious physical perfection whose ultimate source is not the Bible but a technologized Republic: "There the flawed became whole, the blind sighted, and the lame and halt threw away their crutches" (97). But in the long run the body cannot be denied, as Pauline discovers one day in the Dreamland Theatre when, coiffed like Jean Harlow, she bites into a candy bar and breaks off a rotten tooth. In contrast with the absolutes of physical beauty and romantic love the pleasures of body and emotion can only seem disappointingly transient and flawed.

The lost tooth climaxes a long process that began with a tiny spot of decay, but personal hygiene is hardly at issue here. As the narrator comments, "even before the little brown speck, there must have been the conditions, the setting that would allow it to exist in the first place" (93). In context, these conditions are social and institutional rather than narrowly hygienic: they recall the opening image of a wasteland that breeds only decay and rape. Thus while Pauline's experience in the movies can usefully be read as a general warning to dreamers it is also something more. As Marcia Westkott argues in "Dialectics of Fantasy," "Fantasy not only opposes real conditions, but also reflects them. The opposition that fantasy expresses is not abstract, but is rooted in the real conditions themselves, in concrete social relations."[14] In *The Bluest Eye* the real conditions are those of American consumer culture, the continuing "gilded age" that began after the Civil War and replaced physical slavery with other forms of mastery.[15] Try as she might, Pauline cannot be Jean Harlow, and the sense of inadequacy that comes from this failure is part of her tragedy. Even more troubling, however, is the sort of ideal that she does achieve: freedom in the 1940s means fulfilling a role that perfects the antebellum position of blacks. As her personal life falls apart she divides her time between the movies and her employer's family, where she becomes the "queen of canned vegetables," "reign[ing] over cupboards stacked high with food" (101). Her skin glows "in the reflection of white porcelain, white woodwork, polished cabinets, and brilliant copperware" (86). Finally she becomes "an ideal servant" (100), trading personal authenticity for a stereotype in the guise of an Archetype. Pauline's decline from person to "reflection" illustrates how the means of slavery have been internalized. The captive is held most obviously by her commitment to images from movies; even more fundamentally, however, she is bound by this medium's operative assumption that human existence is but an "imitation of life."

William Carlos Williams's poem "To Elsie" can help us understand the particularly American context of Pauline Breedlove's tragedy. Williams made "no ideas but in things" the battle-cry of his aesthetic program, and his prose and poetry are an extended response to the notion of Platonic realism, especially as it is worked out in twentieth-century consumer culture. He is the poet of the local and the physical, of body and place; what "depends" upon the white chickens beside the red wheelbarrow in Williams's best known poem is quite simply poetry itself. Whether dancing naked in front of the mirror ("Danse Russe"), indulging his indiscriminate nose ("Smell"), or simply eating cold plums ("This Is Just To Say") Williams is intent on recovering what we have lost pursuing abstractions. "To Elsie" is one of the clearest statements of his commitment to the immediate against the transcendental. Like Pauline Breedlove, Elsie is an exemplary rather than exceptional figure, "expressing with broken / brain the truth about us."[16] Cut off from peasant traditions, unable to see the beauty of the peasant world, she addresses herself to dreams of cheap finery,

> as if the earth under our feet
> were
> an excrement of some sky
>
> and we were degraded prisoners
> destined
> to hunger until we eat filth. . . .[17]

Like Morrison, Williams sees us as prisoners in a twentieth-century version of Plato's cave, dismissing our world as excrement while straining after a transcendent but meretricious ideal. Both believe that to free ourselves from these chains we need, like Claudia, to have "all of [our] senses engaged" (21) in the discovery of the local and immediate. But most of all we need to see straight, through our own eyes: to trust and respect the angle of vision that makes each imperfect world, and makes it valuable.

Pecola's trip to buy candy early in the novel concisely explores these needs. When Pecola sets out for Mr. Yacobowski's store she is filled with affection for herself and her immediate world: the "sweet, endurable, even cherished irritation" (40) of the coins in her shoe; the dandelions that others call ugly "because they are so many, strong, and soon" (41); the Y-shaped crack in the worn-smooth concrete so perfect for skating. These are "the familiar and therefore loved images" of her world:

> These and other inanimate things she saw and experienced. They were real to her. She knew them. They were the codes and touchstones of the world, capable of translation and possession. She owned the crack that made her stumble; she owned the clumps of dandelions. . . . And owning them made them a part of the world, and the world a part of her. (41)

But at the candy store she can't make Mr. Yacobowski see what she wants—"the angle of his vision, the slant of her finger, makes it incomprehensible to him" (42). Pecola has once again been told that the way she sees is wrong, and that her world—the immediate, the local, and the sensual—is worthless, even unreal. It is not surprising, then, that on the way home she finds the world beneath her feet has turned to excrement: she looks at the dandelions and discovers "'They *are* ugly. They *are* weeds'"; she trips on the sidewalk crack (no longer her friend) and "anger stirs and wakes in her" (43). The world has changed because Mr. Yacobowski denies her perspective, and because as a consequence Pecola, like Elsie, has been forced to deny the particular in herself—the special conditions of her own loves and hates.

As Pecola's experience suggests, *The Bluest Eye* is as critical of economic and political systems, of the underlying "concrete social relations" that generate fantasy, as it is of fantasy itself.[18] The essentially political and economic origins of Pecola's self-betrayal are represented in the exchange of the "sweet, endurable, even cherished" feel of her money—more sensation than specie—not for an equivalent feeling but for a consumable image of the ideal. Her transaction reverses the terms of Claudia's economy: feelings are exchanged for things, rather than things for feelings. Specifically, Pecola wants "Mary Janes" because each wrapper has the picture of a young girl, "blond hair in gentle disarray, blue eyes looking at her out of a world of clean comfort," and she devours the Mary Janes because to do so "is somehow to eat the eyes, eat Mary Jane. Love Mary Jane. Be Mary Jane" (43). Like the earlier milk-drinking binge (three quarts to see Shirley Temple on the mug), her action points to a confederation of the ideal with an economy of consumption. Eating Mary Janes is a strictly capitalist magic: by ingesting the product she hopes to ingest what advertising associates with it, and certainly an appeal to this magic is at the root of advertising's power.[19] In other words, the idea of a transcendent reality is no longer a matter of philosophical debate but of immediate commercial application, as the shift from cave to cinema clearly suggests. Capitalism appropriates the idea of Platonic reality in order to inspire a demand for products that is both insatiable and predictable since both qualities are essential for a smoothly functioning system. Only economic chaos can result when some want dandelions and others marigolds, when the common is as valuable as the exceptional, or when values and demand vary from region to region, class to class. Modern consumer capitalism is made possible by locating or even more commonly creating stable markets, as recent work on the institutional matrix in the publishing industry has effectively illustrated.[20] In short, in *The Bluest Eye* capitalism is presented as redefining the image of a bound and shackled audience in the "Allegory of the Cave": Socrates's observers become the captives of an economic system which appropriates the ideal in the name of profit.

In a novel concerned with racism, of course, captivity has a special resonance, and *The Bluest Eye* is profoundly concerned with the shifting forms of "slavery" in America. Slavery can be most simply defined as a commodification of the body: men become objects of commerce, as Harriet Beecher Stowe recognized when she wished to subtitle *Uncle Tom's Cabin* "The Man That Was a Thing." When we look for signs of racism in *The Bluest Eye* we are most quickly drawn to those made familiar by works like *Uncle Tom's Cabin* whose explicit message is the visible dehumanization of blacks: segregation, lynching, poor paying jobs, racial stereotyping. But even Stowe's novel deals with more than the cruder forms of Southern slavery. As Richard Slotkin demonstrates, the paternalistic slave-owning economy shared important qualities with the paternalistic factory system in the North,[21] a point Stowe also makes when she has Augustine St. Clare, her spokesperson, quote his plantation-owning brother: "'he says, and I think quite sensibly, that the American planter is "only doing, in another form, what the English aristocracy and capitalists are doing by the lower classes;" that is, I take it, appropriating them, body and bone.'"[22] Shortly after the publication of *Uncle Tom's Cabin* Herman Melville made the same connection in "The Paradise of Bachelors and the Tartarus of Maids," a powerful and topical short story which portrays the exploitation of white, unmarried women in a Northern paper mill.[23] When the balance of power definitively changed from agrarian to industrial society (and from South to North) after the Civil War, this form of economic and psychological captivity extended its domain to the Southern blacks who began to join the ranks of white workers in the North. Finally, as labor laws progressively eliminated the conditions Stowe and Melville wrote about advertising stepped in, blurring the line between "captivity" and "captivating" by internalizing the means of bondage for blacks and whites.

The journey of the Breedlove family South to North, from pre-industrial America to consumer society, recapitulates this temporal and economic change in geographic terms. The contrasting experiences of rural, Southern-reared Cholly and his Northern-born daughter are especially instructive. As an adolescent in the South Cholly is interrupted during his first sexual encounter by white hunters, who make him give a dehumanizing sexual performance at gunpoint: "'Come on, coon. Faster. You ain't doing nothing for her'" (117). But this gut-wrenching scene belongs to a polemical tradition whose very familiarity can distract us from the more subtle but related influences at work in the North—the sorts of performances and responses required of those who buy into the premises of a consumer society. The crude white masters of the South are replaced by invisible systems of mastery dedicated to maximizing profit through a process equally dehumanizing. In the sections of the novel set in Ohio, Morrison portrays Pecola's violation of self in imagery that recalls Cholly and his companion's violation at the hands of the hunters. The incident at the candy store, for example, draws its power from the conflation of sex and consumption: when Pecola eats her Mary Janes she experiences "nine lovely orgasms" (43), one for each candy. Sexual love is one of the most profound and private expressions of individuality, but for both Cholly and Pecola sex assumes a public aspect: for Cholly a spectacle, and for Pecola a form of packaged masturbation. In each case human beings are defined not in terms of their feelings but as performers and consumers respectively, and in each case the results are nearly the same: anger is displaced from its real target. When Cholly is surprised by the hunters he directs his hate not at the powerful white men, since doing so "would have consumed him, burned him up like a piece of soft coal" (119), but at his adolescent partner. Similarly, after buying the candy and tripping on the cracked sidewalk Pecola experiences a moment of cathartic anger: "There is a sense of being in anger. A reality and presence. An awareness of worth. It is a lovely surging" (43). Her anger's unspoken target is not the beloved crack but Mr. Yacobowski and all those who devalue her world; unfortunately the momentary clarity of vision, the discovery of reality and worth, cannot hold against the attraction of "blue eyes [in] a world of clean comfort" (43). Instead of turning her anger outward as Claudia does, she turns it self-destructively inward and celebrates her surrender to external definition with the orgiastic pleasures of consumption.

The story of Pecola's idealism and destruction has an unexpected but important precursor in F. Scott Fitzgerald's *The Great Gatsby*, an American classic that can help us locate *The Bluest Eye* in a long tradition of works about the American dream. Both novels focus on protagonists who at bottom believe not so much in the reality of an ideal as in the ideal nature of reality, a

Platonic reality in the service of consumption. As Nick Carraway tells us, Jay Gatsby "Sprang from his Platonic conception of himself. . . . [and] he must be about his Father's business, the service of a vast, vulgar, and meretricious beauty."[24] Race, sex, and opportunity rather than values account for his success and Pecola's failure. Despite his criminal business practices, that is, Gatsby believes in a world of absolutes where Daisy Buchanan, her voice "full of money" (120), survives in splendid and virginal youth just as he last saw her; this is a glitzy adult version of Pecola's Dick and Jane world where time, lust, and ambiguity seem to play no part. In each case the protagonist is confronted with violent proof of the world's disorder and transience. Gatsby breaks up "like glass"[25] against Tom Buchanan's brutal malice and the evidence of Daisy's imperfection; Pecola is raped by a father who has not learned how to love. One is murdered—a symbolic suicide—and the other goes mad.

In its concise duality Pecola's family name, Breedlove, summarizes the problems posed by each novel: how can one reconcile the claims of body and spirit in a secular world, how can one be in and of the world without becoming brutalized by physical impulses, enthralled by the ideal, or exploited by those who would make use of both? Cholly Breedlove shows the depth of this problem when he rapes Pecola: confused, caught between disgust and love, "he wanted to fuck her—tenderly" (128). The rape, like his name, is an oxymoron whose two terms, at least for Cholly, cannot be conjoined. But *The Bluest Eye* does not end in despair; both anger and community offer a way to redeem the waste land, although each has its own dangers.[26] Anger can provide a "sense of being" and "an awareness of worth" (43), but it becomes lethal if displaced from its rightful target: Claudia remains sane by confronting racist society directly and through her retrospective narrative, while Pecola goes mad because she fights herself. A community, on the other hand, can support and comfort, as we see in young Claudia's first section. But when Pecola's drama has played itself out this same community takes the pregnant girl as a scapegoat whose defects define their virtues; as Claudia says, "We were so beautiful when we stood astride her ugliness. Her simplicity decorated us, her guilt sanctified us, her pain made us glow with health" (159). Personal and collective health begins with the effort at self-recovery exemplified in the narrative, which is itself a shaping and refinement of Claudia's anger at the white dolls, but it ends in a recognition of human interdependency. Finally, *The Bluest Eye* asks us to consider *how* as well as *what* we see, both as individuals and as a society. The wasteland will be fully redeemed only when all its members see with their own eyes, when they are no longer held captive, like a contemporary version of Plato's audience, by the idea that "reality" is a consumable absolute, a product independent of local commitments and personal loyalties.

Notes

1. Trudier Harris, for example, argues that *The Color Purple* leaves the reader "equally skeptical about accepting the logic of a novel that posits so many changes as a credible progression for a character. Such total change of life-style, attitudes, and beliefs . . . asks more of the reader than can be reasonably expected" ("From Victimization to Free Enterprise: Alice Walker's *The Color Purple,*" *Studies in American Fiction* 14 (1986), 16.

2. Gerry Brenner has recently discussed Morrison's treatment of Western mythology in *Song of Solomon*. See *Song of Solomon*: Morrison's Rejection of Rank's Monomyth and Feminism," *Studies in American Fiction* 15 (1987), 13–24.

3. Toni Morrison, *The Bluest Eye* (New York: Pocket Books, 1970), p. 159. Future references will be cited in the text.

4. Raymond Hedin argues that anger has been problematic for black writers because of racist attributions of brutishness and lack of control. As a consequence, Hedin says, black writers have paid special attention to structure in their fiction: "Emphasis on form implicitly conveys the rationality of the writer; and that context of rationality allows him to express his anger, or the anger of his characters, without suggesting an overall lack of control" ("The Structuring of Emotion in Black American Fiction," *Novel* 16 [1982], 37). Hedin discusses *The Bluest Eye* briefly on pages 49–50. For a discussion of the novel as a female *Bildungsroman* see Joanne S. Frye, *Living Stories, Telling Lives* (Ann Arbor: University of Michigan Press, 1986), 97–102. Frye argues that "The general problem for Claudia's self-definition is a version of the conflict between submission and self-assertion, which is the problem of all female authorship" (99). But this application of Sandra Gilbert and Susan Gubar's influential thesis in *The Madwoman in the Attic* (New Haven: Yale University Press, 1979) seems less useful than Hedin's approach because it minimizes the special circumstances of black authorship in America.

5. Morrison comments that "all the time that I write, I'm writing about love or its absence" (Jane S. Bakerman, "The Seams Can't Show: An Interview with Toni Morrison," *Black American Literature Forum* 12 [1979], 60).

6. Jeffrey Mehlman, *Revolution and Repetition: Marx/Hugo/Balzac* (Berkeley: University of California Press, 1977), 124; Edwin H. Cady, *The Light of Common Day: Realism in American Fiction* (Bloomington: Indiana University Press, 1971), 5.

7. Many critics have discussed vision and the relationship between seeing, subjectivity, and objectification in *The Bluest Eye*. Frye comments that for Pecola the need "to *see,* to participate in the culture's image of what life ought to be . . . become the negation of her subjectivity" (102). Cynthia A. Davis, on the other hand, analyzes *The Bluest Eye* in terms of Sartre's Existential doctrines: "human relations revolve around the experience of 'the Look,' for being 'seen' by another both confirms one's reality and threatens one's sense of freedom" ("Self, Society, and Myth in Toni Morrison's Fiction," *Contemporary Literature* 23 [1982], 324).

8. For a concise discussion of the child's reader in *The Bluest Eye* see Phyllis Klotman, "Dick-and-Jane and the Shirley Temple Sensibility in *The Bluest Eye,*" *Black American Literature Forum* 13 (1979), 123–25.

9. Maureen Peal, the "high-yellow dream child" (52) who is everyone but Claudia and Frieda's favorite, mentions this 1934 movie starring Claudette Colbert because (in Maureen's selective synopsis) it is about a beautiful mulatto girl named Pecola who "'hates her mother 'cause she is black and ugly but then cries at the

funeral'" (57). In the movie Pecola's mother gives her pancake recipe to her white employer, who parlays it into a fortune.

10. Throughout the novel the margins reflect different narrators and points of view. The sections with ragged right margins are narrated primarily from young Claudia's point of view, although the language is the adult narrator's; sections with justified right margins are narrated by the older Claudia from an omniscient point of view. I will use "young Claudia" whenever I need to distinguish the narrator of the childhood sections from the omniscient narrator (the adult Claudia).

11. Plato, *The Republic of Plato*, trans. Francis Macdonald Cornford (1941; rpt. New York: Oxford University Press, 1967), 228.

12. Plato, 229.

13. L. Chauvois points out that in fifth- and fourth-century Greece puppet theaters formed a sort of "cinéma populaire," and that Plato's allegory of the cave is a transposition of this extremely popular form of national amusement. See L. Chauvois, "Le 'cinéma populaire' en Grèce au temps de Plato et sa projection dans l'allegorie de la 'caverne aux idées,'" *Revue Générale des Sciences Pures et Appliquées*, 74 (1967), 193–195. In the notes to his translation of *The Republic* Cornford remarks that "A modern Plato would compare his Cave to an underground cinema" (228n).

14. Marcia Westkott, "Dialectics of Fantasy," *Frontiers: A Journal of Women Studies*, 2 (1977), p. 1. Quoted in Alfred Habegger, *Gender, Fantasy, and Realism in American Literature* (New York: Columbia University Press, 1982), p. 7.

15. For a discussion of the black emigrant's experience of reification in the North see Susan Willis, "Eruptions of Funk," in *Black Literature and Literary Theory*, ed. Henry Louis Gates (New York: Methuen, 1984), 263–83.

16. William Carlos Williams, "To Elsie," in *The Collected Earlier Poems of William Carlos Williams* (New York: New Directions, 1951), 271.

17. Williams, 272–3.

18. The political thrust of Morrison's novels is apparent to every sensitive reader. As Morrison explained in a recent interview, "I am not interested in indulging myself in some private, closed exercise of my imagination that fulfills only the obligation of my personal dreams—which is to say yes, the work must be political" (Toni Morrison, "Rootedness: the Ancestor or Foundation," in *Black Women Writers [1950–1980]: A Critical Evaluation*, ed. Mari Evans [Garden City, NY: Anchor Doubleday, 1984], 343).

19. Susan Willis points out that candy is often associated with capitalism in Morrison's fiction (228n).

20. Richard H. Brodhead, *The School of Hawthorne* (New York: Oxford University Press, 1986), 48–66; Janice A. Radway, *Reading the Romance: Women, Patriarchy, and Popular Literature* (Chapel Hill: University of North Carolina Press, 1986, pp. 19–46).

21. Richard Slotkin, *The Fatal Environment: The Myth of the Frontier in the Age of Industrialization, 1800–1890* (New York: Atheneum, 1985) pp. 138–58.

22. Harriet Beecher Stowe, *Uncle Tom's Cabin*, ed. Kathryn Kish Sklar (New York: The Library of America, 1984), 269. Gillian Brown argues that "in the name of domesticity, *Uncle Tom's Cabin* attacks not only the patriarchal institution, but nineteenth-century patriarchy: not only slave traders, but the system and men that maintain 'the one great market' upon which trade depends" ("Getting in the Kitchen with Dinah: Domestic Politics in *Uncle Tom's Cabin*," *American Quarterly*, 36 [1984], p. 511).

23. For an excellent introduction to nineteenth-century American racism see Carolyn Karcher, *Shadow Over Promised Land: Slavery, Race, and Violence in Melville's America* (Baton Rouge: Louisiana State University Press, 1980), pp. 1–27.

24. F. Scott Fitzgerald, *The Great Gatsby* (New York: Charles Scribners Sons, 1925), p. 99.

25. Fitzgerald, p. 148.

26. Morrison's cautious optimism comes from a belief in the power of the local and individual; in this she resembles William Carlos Williams, who found Eliot's *The Waste Land* "the great catastrophe to our letters" because it ignored "the elementary principle of all art, in the local conditions" *(The Autobiography of William Carlos Williams* [New York: Random House, 1951], pp. 146, 174). Williams's response to Eliot is "Spring and All," a poem rooted in the sense of place. In reworking the image of the wasteland Morrison strips it of abstraction: at the end of the novel Pecola is living among very real Coke bottles, tire rims, and milkweed.

DONALD B. GIBSON

Text and Countertext in
Toni Morrison's The Bluest Eye

I . . . have no hestitation in regarding the white race as superior to all
others in beauty . . . . Human groups are unequal in beauty; and this
inequality is rational, logical, permanent, and indestructible.
>—Count Arthur de Gobineau,
>*Essay on the Inequality of the Human Races*

Along with the idea of romantic love, she [Pauline] was introduced to
another—physical beauty. Probably the most destructive ideas in the
history of human thought. Both originated in envy, thrived in insecurity,
and ended in disillusion.
>—Toni Morrison, *The Bluest Eye*

Count Joseph Arthur de Gobineau, French diplomat, ethnologist, fiction writer, bearer of the infamous reputation of "father of racism," and
a correspondent for sixteen years of Alexis de Tocqueville, wrote these
words in the early eighteen fifties. Tocqueville, as might be expected,
disagreed strongly with Gobineau's authoritarian, anti-democratic stance
and argued against the whole of such racist and reactionary thinking.[1]
We might imagine further that his counter arguments fell upon deaf ears
because Gobineau's arguments stern from very basic beliefs about human
nature, the nature of the universe, and ideas about social organization

LIT, Vol. 1, pp. 19-32. ©1989 Gordon and Breach Science Publishers S.A.

stemming from those beliefs. Gobineau's words contain implicitly the philosophical assumptions that beauty exists in and of itself, independent of human nature or Character; and it forms some part of a larger structure of the universe. Gobineau's whole system of thought seems reactive against the tide of ideas that by his time had unseated the rationalism of the Enlightenment, ushered in the American and French revolutions, and paved the way for Darwin and other thinkers who believed the world to be in process rather than fixed within established, unchangeable limits. Toni Morrison did not need to have read Gobineau to react to him, for his legacy is not only in his text but in western civilization's air. Her novel calls into question the mode of his thought and the whole authoritarian, politically reactionary system of beliefs about the nature of reality an which his and like thought is based.

Morrison's 1970 novel, for all its eloquence and beauty of expression, engages in sustained argument with modes of thought and belief explicitly stated in Gobineau's assertion above, but likewise, and perhaps more vividly presented in cultural icons portraying physical beauty: movies, billboards, magazines, books, newspapers, window signs, dolls, and drinking cups.[2] Morrison's novel deals with the most subtle implications of the general society's definition of beauty, and the novel shows us the depth and complexity of those implications. But unlike most novels that take issue with society, the novel argues with itself, clarifying rather than simplifying, uncovering and grappling with the most problematical facets of the subject, and undercutting easily held values in order to reveal complication. The novel's text is inscribed with a counter text, an oppositional discourse so intricately intertwined with text as to render it finally incapable of independent existence, transforming each by turn into the counter of the other. While text and counter text contend for dominance, the one melds into the opposite, and at midpoint between the exchange neither is independently discernible though both are present, like an optical illusion which may alternately assume one form then another, then perhaps varying degrees of both and neither depending upon the disposition of the ob- server's eye and mind.[3]

The countertextual dynamic of the novel begins with the quotation from the Dick and Jane primer, an introductory gesture, which is in fact and by implication not unlike the prefatory essay to Richard Wright's *Uncle Tom's Children*, "The Ethics of Living Jim Crow" (1938) in that it introduces what is to follow, offers evidence to comment upon and support the thematic implications of the main text, and at the same time informs the main text at each point along its course, its implications engraved within every aspect of plot, character, and description. Morrison's self-consciously epigraphical introduction, the primer text, exists as text and counter-text:

text in that it has no apparent relation to the major text but lies in the background, the mere genesis of the problem exemplified by Pecola's wanting blue eyes and exemplary, by indirection, of the causes underlying the problematical nature of the lives of the characters in its world; countertext, by turns, in that the epigraphical introduction implies one of the primary and most insidious ways that the dominant culture exercises its hegemony, through the educational system.[4] It reveals the role of education in both oppressing the victim—and more to the point—teaching the victim how to oppress her own black self by internalizing the values that dictate standards of beauty. "Don't give the girl a fishing pole," the prefatory material tells us, "teach her how to fish," teach her how to enact self-oppression while ostensibly learning to read a simple, unproblematic text. To put this in another way the act of learning to read and write means exposure to the values of the culture from which the reading material emanates. If one wants to read or write, then one must pay for the privilege. The cost of learning to read and write carries with it the necessity to submit to values beyond and other than literacy *per se*, for words do not exist independent of value. One cannot simply learn to read without being subjected to the values engraved in the text.[5]

The introduction to *The Bluest Eye* is also an enabling act, setting up, defining, and effectively writing or reinscribing the nature of what is to be written against. It is the obverse of what in the slave narrative was the act of authentication. Here the author seizes the authority of the authenticator by appropriating and subverting the role of the authenticator. That is, the authenticator's role is an authoritative role deriving its authority from socially derived power. The superiority assumed by Charles Summer and Wendell Phillips as authenticators of Frederick Douglass' *Narrative*, for example, is assumed by Morrison herself in her text. Douglass's text is authenticated by Sumner and Phillips in the *Narrative* (though he struggles mightily both literarily and historically before wresting away their implied authority). Wright authenticates his own text in "Ethics"; Morrison authenticates her text in the enabling act of her introduction. This is the less complicated aspect of Morrison's discourse in *The Bluest Eye*.[6]

The complications arise when we see that Morrison's sense of the meaning of "bluest eye" is not confined to the meaning we immediately ascribe. The text of the Dick and Jane primer, the epigraphical introduction to Morrison's narrative, is rendered by Morrison in three versions (1–3), each printed in such a way as to appear to grow less comprehensible.[7] The second version omits punctuation, decreasing the space between the lines and running the sentences together; the third omits spaces between words entirely and arbitrarily breaks words at the end of a line, even words of one syllable. The inference to be drawn is that the final version is incomprehensible. But that is not true. It is, arguably, perfectly comprehensible.[8] The difference between the first and third versions is that the third forces us to participate in the reading in a more active way by demanding that we identify individual words and supply from our own past experience of reading the first version the proper punctuation. The reader is once again, in the very act of reading, taught to read. The meaning is not, as it appears, drained away from first to final draft, but simply concentrated. The implication is that just as Pecola—and all black children—are subjected to the value scheme implied in the primer, so they have imposed upon them whole schemes of value, political, religious, moral, aesthetic, and have little or nothing to do with their actual lives. They are measured using standards they cannot possibly meet—because of genetics and economics—and are found wanting. Yet a paradox arises when we consider that Morrison organizes her text around the primer passage. The sections focusing on Pecola and her family are headed by a line or two from the primer text, the text standing in countertextual relation to the actuality of Pecola's and her family's lives. The final chapter of the novel opens with the primer lines "Look, look. Here comes a friend," and we of course recall that Pecola's friend is hallucinated, the product of her madness. But she does, after all, as the countertext has it, have her blue eyes.

The implication of the novel's structure is that our lives are contained within the framework of the values of the dominant culture and subjected to those values. We have all (there is reason to believe the author does not exclude herself nor anyone else) internalized those values, and to the extent that we have, we are instruments of our own oppression.[9] The text says we are oppressed by the values of the ruling class; the countertext says we participate in our own oppression usually to the extent of being literally the very hand or arm of that oppression.

Such a conclusion is born out by Claudia's (the sometime narrator's) relating of her response as a young child to dolls. The reader will recall her literal deconstruction of a white, blue-eyed, yellow-haired doll, an act intended as a means of discovery, and performed on the childish assumption that whatever caused the doll to appear to everyone except herself an object of great value lay within the thing itself, a reasonable assumption since she has concluded that the difference between her and the white doll is an essential, intrinsic, difference, not a superficial, extrinsic one. To discover the doll's reality by taking it apart is not to demystify it—it has not yet become mystified for her-but rather to wreak vengeance on it and to discover that the difference between her and the doll lies elsewhere than in the doll's innards.

The counter text has Claudia subsequently join those who approve of little white girls and disapprove of her.

> Adults, older girls, shops, magazines, newspapers, window signs—
> all the world had agreed that a blue-eyed, yellow-haired, pink-
> skinned doll was what every child treasured. (14)

These adults are not only white but black as well.

> What made people look at them and say "Awwwww," but not for
> me? The eye slide of black women as they approached them on the
> street, and the possessive gentleness of their touch as they handled
> them. (15)

Her antipathy towards white dolls and little white girls does not, as noted,
last forever.[10] Claudia's admission of the fact, however, turns out to be a low
keyed indictment, but devastating in its implications, of the whole scheme of
socio-political values held by the ruling classes and informing their ideology.
She fantasizes about doing the same violence to little white girls that she
does to her dolls, the closest she can come to revolt against a vicious value
scheme that threatens her very being.

> If I pinched them, their eyes—unlike the crazed glint of the baby
> doll's eyes—would enfold the pain, and their cry would not be
> the sound of an icebox door, but a fascinating cry of pain. When
> I learned how repulsive this disinterested violence was, that it was
> repulsive because it was disinterested, my shame floundered about
> for refuge. The best hiding place was love. Thus the conversion
> from pristine sadism to fabricated hatred, to fraudulent love. It
> was a small step to Shirley Temple. I learned much later to worship
> her, just as I learned to delight in cleanliness, knowing, even as I
> learned, that the change was adjustment without improvement.
> (15–16)

Claudia expresses here her understanding, a retrospective understanding and not one achieved in childhood, that social values are arbitrary, socially derived, and not existent in nature. It is not natural to have or want
blue eyes, but a society may hold such a standard and through its power—its
control of images through control of the means of the presentation of imagery, control of "magazines, newspapers, window signs," of current iconography—impress the reality of its values on those not having the wherewithal to
resist, not having the facilities to counter the assault.

But herein lies the power of Toni Morrison's argument, for she undercuts the validity of the proposition of the dominant culture that blue eyes
and cleanliness are inherently valuable by historicizing social value. Claudia

"learned" to worship Shirley Temple just as she "learned" to delight in cleanliness. The text, it is implied, is that blue eyes and cleanliness are valuable because in this society such values are imposed upon its members. The counter text reads that such values are not so much relative as arbitrary. They have no reality in and of themselves. The image of Shirley Temple as representing a standard of beauty comes about not because of anything inherent within Shirley Temple but because she exists as icon in movies and on, of all things, a common drinking cup, a trivial commercial item, that for Pecola becomes something entirely other, a chalice, a grail whose milk-white content will allow her to take in the blood of the goddess, a white blood of milk—not a red blood of wine. The milk is the blood of the goddess because it is contained within the cup. Pecola gorges herself on the blood of the goddess; she indulges an insatiable appetite. If she drinks enough white milk from the chalice, she may become like the stuff she imbibes and as well become like the image adorning the container itself. One ingests the blood of the goddess in order to become her. Pecola performs a kind of masturbatory communion, a self administered version of the ritual in which she is both priestess and communicant.[11]

This initial ritualistic act of communion prefigures a later one, later in the sequence of the book's episodes though in fact earlier in time than the communion of graham crackers and milk, bread and wine. By the time Pecola comes to live briefly with Claudia and Frieda she has already learned to indulge the rituals, the third of which (her interaction with Soaphead Church) will lead to her transformation into the creature of her desire. She devours the candy, little yellow caramels called Mary Janes, a conflation, given the immediate context of their description in the novel and the more general context of the novel's primer frame, of Christ (Mr. Jacobowski says to Pecola, "Christ. Kantcha talk?"), of the Jane of the primer, and of the Virgin Mary.[12] Pecola is an inverted Virgin Mary, however, a Virgin Mary demystified: not mysteriously and spiritually impregnated by God the father but brutally impregnated by Cholly Breedlove, the father, on the dirty floor of the kitchen of her storefront home. The offspring of this union is the Christ child, the stillborn Christ child, who is incapable of saving the world because incapable of saving himself.

The ritualistic significance of the eating of the Mary Janes and the relation to Shirley Temple, milk, communion, and sexuality are born out in Morrison's description of Pecola's experience with the candy.

> Each pale yellow wrapper has a picture on it. A picture of Mary Jane, for whom the candy is named. Smiling white face. Blond hair in gentle disarray, blue eyes looking at her out of a world of clean comfort. [Compare the primer Jane.] The eyes are petulant,

mischievous. To Pecola they are simply pretty. She eats the candy, and its sweetness is good. To eat the candy is somehow to eat the eyes, eat Mary Jane. Love Mary Jane. Be Mary Jane. Three pennies had bought her nine lovely orgasms with Mary Jane. Lovely Mary Jane, for whom a candy is named. (38)

The text is what we read of Pecola's experience; the counter text is the central mythology of the dominant culture, a mythology demystified and therefore disempowered by Morrison's analysis of the relation of the experience of specific individuals to the myth. Transubstantiation has occurred; the candy has been transformed into the body and blood of Mary Jane (Shirley Temple).[13] Lest we missed the implications of the ritual signification of Pecola's consumption of her Mary Janes, the reference to communion, to Christian mythology, and to the demystification of Christian ritual, Morrison reiterates the subtextual meaning of the Christian symbology by reference to the trinity: Pecola has three pennies; Mr. Jacobowski "scoots three Mary Janes toward her" (which mysteriously multiply into nine orgasms), "orgasms," not the spiritual transformation and renewal traditionally affected by ingestion of the host, but a suitable equivalent in the world Pecola inhabits.[14]

Morrison comments upon the episode through the first line of the next episode immediately following. One sentence after "Three pennies bought her nine lovely orgasms . . ." we read, "Three whores lived in the apartment above the Breedlove's storefront."[15] Here the text comments upon, analyzes itself. Text and countertext produce a stark indictment of the prevailing values of the dominant society. The "three whores" are named "China," "Poland," and "The Maginot Line," a commentary of its own in that the distance between the trinity (father, son and Holy Ghost) and the naturalistic fact of Pecola's purchase of penny candy is analogous to the distance between the seemingly insignificant lives of three whores in a small Midwestern town and the large-scale geopolitical and geographical dimensions of China, Poland, and The Maginot Line. The root of the analogy is Morrison's awareness in the world of this novel that no human conception, knowledge or understanding has its source outside of individual experience. The most basic myths and the broadest geopolitical conceptions have their origins in the experience of people.

The association in the text of milk and blood and the consequent evocation of the broad range of actual and mythological meanings are clearly demonstrable in the text and are not brought to it by the overimaginative analyst. In the very midst of Mrs. MacTeer's unremitting tirade against Pecola's consumption of prodigious quantities of milk, Pecola begins to menstruate—as though she is putting back into the world that which she has been accused of unjustly and unreasonably taking away. The association of

menstruation and lactation, of bleeding and feeding, is unavoidable and explicit. Mrs. MacTeer speaks:

> "Anybody need three quarts of milk to *live* need to get out of
> here. They in the wrong place. What is this? Some kind of *dairy*
> *farm?*"
> Suddenly Pecola bolted straight up, her eyes wide with terror. A
> whinnying sound came out of her mouth.
> "What's the matter with *you*?" Frieda stood up too.
> Then we both looked where Pecola was staring. Blood was running
> down her legs. Some drops were on the steps. I leaped up. "Hey.
> You cut yourself? Look. It's all over your dress." (Morrison's
> emphases 19)

Mrs. MacTeer's assault, motherly assault that it is, brings about, however,
unintentionally, the onset of Pecola's menses. It is not, Claudia tells us, the
child that the parent attacks but the condition that allows or causes the
child to appear to be a problem. It is not Pecola with whom she is angry
but the conditions that require her to be concerned about how much milk
she drinks, Pecola responds in a way Francis Bacon has seen as a response
reflective of the character of human nature.

> Whosoever hath anything fixed in this person that doth induce
> contempt hath also a perpetual spur in himself to rescue and
> deliver himself from scorn. (308)

Pecola rescues and delivers herself from scorn by giving back to the world
what she has taken away. She has consumed a natural body fluid, milk;
she gives back a natural body fluid, blood. In so doing she appeases Mrs.
MacTeer, turning her wrath not into mere tolerance but into a rarely
expressed and articulated acceptance, approval, and support.

The reality of the situation is such, however, that initiation and the potential of deliverance (in an entirely secular sense) are available for Pecola.[16]
It in any case seems so. The water has as its purpose not to drown but to
cleanse; not to inundate but to initiate. Pecola is initiated, baptized into biological female adulthood; Frieda and Claudia are detraumatized, brought
into a normalized relation to ordinary biological process.

> We could hear the water running into the bathtub.
> "You think she's going to drown her?"
> "Oh, Claudia. You so dumb. She's just going to wash her clothes
> and all."

"Should we beat up Rosemary?" [Should we react as our mother
reacted when she thought we were "playing nasty"? Does the fact
of Pecola's menstruation require the drawing of blood? Does this
situation require aggression on our parts?]
"No. [Let us emulate mother.] Leave her alone."
The water gushed, and over its gushing we could hear the music of
my mother's laughter. (22-3)

The meaning of the text at this moment lies in its playing off, one against
the other, the total childish ignorance of Claudia and Pecola, the childish half ignorance of Frieda, and the mature, woman's knowledge of Mrs.
MacTeer. From the antagonism, anger, misunderstanding and conflict of
the events leading up to this point arises a new understanding and vision, a
celebratory confluence of discordant modes. This section of the novel, you
will recall, begins with Mrs. MacTeer berating Pecola.

"Three quarts of milk. That's what was *in* that icebox yesterday.
Three whole quarts. Now they ain't none. Not a drop. I don't mind
folks coming in and getting what they want, but three quarts of
milk! What the devil does anybody need with three quarts of
milk?' (Morrison's emphasis 16)

It ends with "the music of my mother's laughing" as she bestows on Pecola
the care and comfort which may be available to the female child entering
this new stage from the female parent figure. Embedded within the text,
existing at various levels and a form of countertext, are three perspectives.
One is the perspective of the child Claudia, the nine year old who at first
hand witnesses many of the events of the novel. The second is the perspective of the significantly more mature retrospective narrator who understands
and interprets those events, events which the younger Claudia could not
possibly have understood. We see the disparity between the adult and the
child perspectives when Claudia asks whether their mother is going to
drown Pecola. Because the meaning of the section is obviously shaped, the
question could only emanate from a consciousness that knows that the question is a childish one. Hence the question betrays a consciousness that has
conceived the mind conceiving the question.[17]

The third perspective, whose existence is inferred from the existence
of the total text, the novel itself, is the author's perspective—the perspective that knows of the relation between this scene (ending with the "music" of Mrs. MacTeer's laughter) and the final episodes of the novel, sexual
intercourse visited upon the virgin Pecola by her father, the issue of that
(her stillborn child), and Pecola's ensuing madness. In other words there

lies submerged beneath "the music of my mother's laughter" a countertext, a text whose meaning we can only know retrospectively, after having read the novel. Then we know that the apparent blessing, the apparent confluence of positive meaning, value, and feeling, is only "apparent." This positive moment, one of two such moments in the novel, when Pecola relates intensely to another human being, when she is loved and accepted in a way significantly poignant to her, is mirrored on the floor of the Breedlove kitchen when Cholly, as does Mrs. MacTeer here, likewise expresses an adult, parental, sense of relatedness, concern for, and involvement with Pecola.[18] His is *another* initiation involving fluids: not clean, gushing, fresh water, but "cold, greasy dishwater."

Text and countertext are juxtaposed at the moment Pecola responds to the onset of menses, and her response is determined by the fact that she does not know what is happening to her: "her eyes [are] wide with terror." Claudia feels that something negative is occurring, that Pecola has been somehow injured: "You cut yourself." Frieda normalizes and brings the situation under control by indicating knowledge of what is occurring, naming it: "That's ministratin'."[19] Against Frieda's attempt to wrest the experience from out the chaos of ignorance, to banish fear through knowledge, Pecola pits her own specifically individualized response: "Am I going to die?"

Frieda's response to Pecola's question once again juxtaposes text and counter text, winding up the plot of the novel as though it were the mainspring of a clock whose steady and controlled release of tension will result in the ticking out of the plot. In a very significant sense the center of the novel, insofar as that center is based upon a text-countertext opposition, rests in this moment, this moment of moments, in Frieda's response to Pecola's question, a response less naive than ironic in its implications regarding Pecola's fate: "Noooo. You won't die. It just means you can have a baby!" The implication is that the ability to have a baby is a good thing. The fact is that for Pecola the countertext has it that her ability to have a baby is a curse, a curse not on women in general but on her. The implications of the interaction between Frieda and Pecola at this textual moment are teased out at the chapter's end when the question of the meaning of Pecola's potential to have a baby arises, are further explored by the three girls, however perfunctorily.

> That night, in bed, the three of us lay still. We were full of awe and respect for Pecola. Lying next to a real person who was really ministratin' was somehow sacred. She was different from us now—grown-up-like. She herself, felt the distance but refused to lord it over us.
>
> After a long while she spoke very softly, "Is it true that I can have a baby now?"

"Sure," said Frieda drowsily. "Sure you can."
"But . . . how?" Her voice was hollow with wonder.
"Oh," said Frieda, "somebody has to love you."
"Oh." (23)

This section of the novel, especially in the two passages quoted above, is the germ from which the remainder of the novel proceeds. Nearly everything that happens in Pecola's life demonstrates to the reader and to herself that nobody loves her and then finally somebody does love her and she does indeed have a baby,[20] though through a process that she neither seeks nor even could imagine. All of that is implicit in the conversation above. All unfolds, from this point on, leading inexorably to the kitchen floor of the Breedlove place and ultimately to the premature birth and the death of Pecola's child. Her insanity stands in countertextual relation to the underlying tone of these two passages. The transformation from girl to biologically mature female which seems happy and hopeful, as reflected in Claudia's and Frieda's barely concealed envy, turns horrific, "appalling," in the root sense of that word.[21] The meanings implicit in Claudia's feelings as the three lie abed that "Lying next to a real person who was really ministratin' was somehow *sacred*" (my emphasis, 28) are themselves aborted.

The chief word in the novel's text after this section is "Breedlove," Pecola's family name. "Breed" and "love" clearly exist oppositionally, in countertextual relation: "breed" is the biological phenomenon, a physiological occurrence having no affective source or consequence; "love" is a social, religious, or spiritual phenomenon, implying meaning beyond the simply phenomenal. The two definitions of relatedness are intertwined in the name. The fact of the tension brought about by the disparate meanings of the two words comprising the name, yet their having been yoked together to produce one name, replicates the character of the text itself. It is a text which ultimately does not allow us clearly to distinguish (nor does it invite awareness of the possible distinctions to be made) between the historical meanings of the words "breed" and "love." The novel at once maintains and breaks down the distinctions: the distinction between breeding and loving is a linguistic, moralistic distinction and not a distinction to be sustained by reference to any appeal to what is, to actuality. That is to say, Morrison suggests that the concepts are easily enough distinguished, but experience is not identical with our abstractions about it. Felt experience, Morrison insists, is far too complex and different in character from idea to correspond to our concepts regarding it. Specifically, our lexicon distinguishes "breed" and "love," but "love" in actuality, as experienced, may not be distinguishable from animalistic "breed," and the element of "breed" may lie inextricably buried within the experience of love.

The implications of the meaning of the family name, a name which comes to the family through Cholly ("*Charles* Breedlove," a good Anglo-Saxon name, is entombed within his full name as well as a host of other meanings), conflate in the narrative's climax, the sexual abuse of Pecola on a Saturday afternoon on the kitchen floor of the storefront the Breedloves occupy. All thematic and plot lines, the text/countertextual movement of the novel as well, converge at that particular juncture in time and space.

Cholly, during this scene, is allowed by Morrison to appropriate narrative authority insofar as he is permitted the privilege of having what occurs told from his vantage point. He does not usurp narrative authority, for his control stems entirely from the author's self-imposed limitation: she restricts herself at this point to the third person limited narration. Whatever authority Cholly possesses accrues not because it comes to him by nature, or because he is male, but because Morrison chooses to give it to him. She grants this black male a voice, and in allowing him voice, she again expresses countertextuality. There is some degree of distance between the perspective of Cholly and that of Morrison. Whereas Morrison is not Cholly, Cholly is likewise not Morrison. Yet, Morrison allows Cholly to be something other than simply evil. We know in the abstract that there are no circumstances under which a father may justifiably, knowingly have sexual intercourse with his daughter. Morrison does not tell us that what Cholly does to Pecola is all right; rather she says that what happens is very complicated, and that though Cholly is not without blame for what happens to Pecola, he is no less a victim than she.[22]

The factors motivating him on that Saturday afternoon in the Breedlove kitchen stem from the whole of his past experience, his experience as a poor, black youth, viewed by white and black oppression.[23] It is not clear where oppression begins or ends: his mother abandons him on a garbage heap, but his grandmother rescues him. Abandonment is text; rescue is counter text. The first act of oppression against him is counteracted by his grandmother. Is his abandonment an act of racial oppression? Yes, it is—however indirectly But it is also personal oppression. There cannot be any such abstraction as "oppression" if it does not find expression through the actions of specific humans. (The first act of oppression committed directly against him is his mother's abandonment.)

The entirety of his sexual life is colored by his first experience of sexual intercourse, an experience utterly intertwined with, entirely inseparable from, race. He is thoroughly humiliated by the two white hunters who threaten him with bodily harm if he does not continue sexual intercourse with Darlene. They look on bemused and contemptuous. The hatred and hostility that would be directed at the hunters under normal circumstances is displaced onto Darlene because Cholly is unable to disobey the two white men.[24] The relation between that early experience with Darlene and the later sexual encounter with Pecola is clear enough. We learn that during the episode involving Darlene and the white hunters that he "hated her" and wished he could hurt her. He hated Pecola too and wished "to break her neck." On both occasions the same "biliousness" arises within him.

As the text reads, Cholly's voice tells the unremitting, unvarnished truth of his knowledge, understanding of, and feeling about what happens in that kitchen on that Saturday afternoon. As we have it, what we see is not clearly a rape because of the circumstances surrounding it. We know exactly why Cholly responds to Pecola as he does and that fact along with others gives rise to a countertext. Had he simply felt anger toward Pecola, then the case would be more easily judged. As it is, however, he feels hostility and love; both at the same time. He does want "to break her neck," but he wants to do it "tenderly." Nothing in the tone of the text suggests that these contrary feelings are not utterly genuine. The worse is yet to come: "He wanted to fuck her—tenderly." (128)

In his drunken stupor he confuses Pecola not only with Darlene, whom he hated, but with Pauline, Pecola's mother, whom he loved. The encounter is in fact a reenactment, a reliving of his first meeting with Pauline but tinged with the experience with Darlene. The text makes that abundantly clear. The text also indicates that Morrison does not allow us as readers to get off as easily as we might if it were as clearly sexual abuse as his second attack on her is. We know what to think of fathers who fuck their daughters; perhaps we do not know so easily what to think when we learn of Cholly's thoughts at the time: "Not the usual lust to part tight legs with his own but a tenderness, a protectiveness. A desire to cover her foot with his hand and gently nibble away the itch from the calf with his teeth. He did it then, and started Pauline into laughter. He did it now." (128)

It would on the whole be easier to judge Cholly if we knew less about him and if we could isolate the kitchen floor episode from the social context in which it occurs and from Cholly's past. But we cannot; we are neither invited to nor allowed. It is especially evident that this is the case as the episode moves toward termination. We need especially to distinguish between what Morrison, as a function of the particular technical point of view at this juncture, tells us and does not tell us, Consider such a passage as this: "Following the disintegration—the falling away—of sexual desire, he was conscious of her wet, soapy hands on his wrists, the fingers clenching, but whether her grip was from a hopeless but stubborn struggle to be free, or from some other emotion, he could not tell." (128) The countertext arises from the possibilities of interpretation provoked by the technical point of view. What, in fact, *was* Pecola feeling at this point? Morrison allows myriad possibilities, among them that Pecola has now been loved, is, during the course of the act, being loved, setting out the text and countertext as in the existing shady grammatical and lexical distinction between "being loved" and "being made love to." Of course the opposite is implied as well, for her father's expression of love is by all received standards anything but that.[25] The problematic is intensified when Pecola's other self, the voice arising within her psyche when she becomes psychotic, an alter-ego, questions her response to her father's two assaults, introducing the possibility that she wanted and needed them. The text, whereas it does not imply anything like seduction on Pecola's part, at the same time allows the possibility that she is participant and not simply victim, victim and at the same moment participant.

Text/countertextual and counter/countertextual juxtaposition inform the novel throughout.[26] The portion of the primer book text beginning the scene just discussed reads: "SEEFATHERHEISBIGANDSTRONGFA-THERWILLYOUPLAYWITHJANEFATHERISSMILINGSMILEFA-THERSMILESMILE." Of course the father about to "play with" Jane, is not the inane, sterile, stereotypical stick figure of the primer text but a blood and bone human out of a different world than that of Dick and Jane, a world in fact, and in some sense unhappily, more real than theirs.

One final example of countertextuality exists in the complexity of attitude demonstrated in the novel's dialogue. Consider the array of attitudes reflected in the response of the ticket agent at the bus terminal when Cholly at fourteen seeks to buy a ticket at the rate for children twelve or younger. Cholly pretends to be twelve and though the agent hardly believes him, still he sells him the reduced rate ticket.

> "I reckon I knows a lying nigger when I sees one, but just in case you ain't, jest in case one of them mammies is really dyin' and wants to see her little old smoke before she meets her maker, I gone do it." (120)

How are we to react to this? The agent's response to Cholly is to the reader ambiguous, though not to the agent. Rattling around inside the empty shell of this racist rhetoric is a decent human impulse. But how can we separate the decency from its container? How can we not respond to the humor of the passage and how do we regard the humor in relation to the other, not humorous elements of the response? I don't think we can react simply, and I think this is Morrison's point, a point brilliantly made in a tiny corner of her edifice.

Every element of Morrison's text has its countertext. The notion of "the bluest eye," for example, suggests that her primary concern is with the culture's standard of beauty. That, as a matter of fact, is the way that this novel has been generally understood. But if this is so, what are we to do with Claudia's observations and conclusions at the novel's end?

> All of us—all who knew her—felt so wholesome after we cleaned ourselves on her. We were so beautiful when we stood astride her ugliness. [What does the word "astride" suggest here? A species of masculine dominance? Cholly's rape?] Her simplicity decorated us, her guilt sanctified us, her pain made us glow with health. (163)

The indictment of the society stands, but it is conceived far more realistically than the conception allows that erroneously contends that the racial issue involves simply black and white.[27] The novel has, as countertext, its class ramifications too. Claudia conceives of the world in terms of race alone when she deconstructs white dolls. Eventually she learns to have the regard for those dolls that her parents have. She understands the limitations of her perspective. That is, she recognizes that she is, because of her economic status, subject to the same social forces molding others. Her experience demonstrates that in a land where the bluest eye holds hegemony none of the dispossessed escapes its gaze.

Notes

1. Though Tocqueville's attitudes toward black people and slavery are somewhat problematical, he opposed slavery on moral and economic grounds. He also felt that whatever limitations slaves might possess came about because of lack of exposure to culture and not genetic causes (370–397). In a letter to Gebineau written in November 1853 after Tocqueville had read Gobineau's *Essay*, noted above, Tocqueville comments: "Thus I confess that having read your book I remain, as before, extremely opposed to these doctrines. I believe that they are probably false; I know that they are most certainly pernicious" (quoted in *Gobineau* 178).

2. Morrison has herself commented on the dialectics of her fiction: "I am not interested in indulging myself in some private, dosed exercise of my imagination that fulfils only the obligation of my personal dreams—which is to say yes, the work must be political. It must have that as its thrust. That's a pejorative term in critical circles now: if a work of art has any political influence in it, somehow its tainted. My feeling is just the opposite: if it has none, it is tainted" (quoted in *Black Women Writers*, pp. 344–345).

3. Smith in her most insightful discussion of Morrison refers to the phenomenon I describe here as Morrison's tendency to leave certain questions unresolved (124). I see what is apparently "unresolvability" as "countertextuality."

4. Jones sees the primary relation between the primer frame and the text as an ironic relation (26). Dorothy H. Lee identifies the relation between primer text and text as "counterpoint": "For each segment of the idealized picture of secure family

life, Morrison offers in counterpoint the bleak specifics of Pecola's existence" (*Black Women Writers,* p. 347).

5. This point is made by several critics, among them Ogunyemi 113, Klotman p. 124.

6. Michael Awkward first suggested a relation between the Dick and Jane epigraph and the authentication, usually by whites, of slave narratives (59). My interpretation, though similar to his, is markedly different.

7. Smith believes these passages to be rendered through Claudia (124); I think they are presented by an omniscient narrator.

8. Most critics disagree. Smith sees the final version as "virtually unintelligible" (125). Klotman (123), and Ogunyemi (113) essentially agree.

9. Other critics have made this same observation in various ways. Byerman contends that "All the blacks in the book feel insecure and even inferior because of skin tone" ("Intense Behavior" 448). Barbara Lounsberry and Grace Ann Hovet put it thusly: "In *The Bluest Eye* and the other novels, Morrison is unwilling to blame black failure entirely on outside forces or upon the hazards of minority existence" (126).

10. This point is overlooked by a number of good critics of the novel who do not take into account the fact that Claudia's deconstruction of the white dolls is but a phase of her development, that later she succumbs to those very values governing Pecola's judgment of herself. Byerman believes that the MacTeers escape the culture's judgment: "Unlike the Breedloves and the light skinned Geraldine and Maureen, they [the MacTeers] do not measure their human worth by symbols of the dominant white culture, (*Jagged Grain* 190). Weever agrees: "Her [Claudia's] revulsion protects her from the deadly seduction which claims Pecola at the end of the novel (404). House asserts the same: "Rejecting material gains which are components of success dreams, she [Claudia] dislikes artificially pretty white dolls which black children receive for Christmas" (187).

11. Byerman calls attention to the ritualistic nature of Pecola's imbibing (*Jagged Grain* 186).

12. Byerman comments on Pecola's "Christ-like" nature as seen by Claudia, seeing Pecola as a "grotesque messiah" ("Intense Behavior" pp. 451–452).

13. "Shirley Temple *is* Jane, the perfect daughter, only brought to life on the movie screen" (Mason 3).

14. De Weever interprets the eating of the candy somewhat differently: "This symbolic cannibalism is a sign of Pecola's latent instability" (406)

15. The meaning of the three prostitutes has been variously rendered. Jones identifies the three as witches of fairy tales (30–31). Ogunyemi says that "The three symbolize the helplessness of human beings in life, be it on a national, racial, or individual level. Their names evoke the helplessness of France, China, and Poland in the face of rape by more powerful forces in World War II; they evoke the helplessness of the black race raped, as it were, by the whites" (119).

16. Bakerman sees Pecola's initiation as a "failed initiation" (556).

17. Klotman's understanding of the narrative point of view differs somewhat. She feels that "Everything is told from the innocent viewpoint of childhood—Claudia as a nine-year-old. The narrative voice shifts, however, when the author wants us to have a more mature and objective view of the characters and their situations to an older Claudia, the author's persona" (123–124).

18. Klotman seems to differ: "The only tenderness she receives is from her father, in the drunken and perverse moment before he rapes her" (124).

19. Rosenberg sees this episode as demonstrating Frieda's competence in handling the "terror and mystery of that initial bleeding" (436–437). I believe it to be far more complicated than that.

20. Pecola's linking of the act of sexual intercourse and love is initiated through the conversation of the three girls quoted above. That the notion becomes a part of her belief system is born out in the conversation with her fantasized companion toward the narrative's conclusion: "If she [Mrs. Breedlove] didn't love him [Cholly], she sure let him do it to her a lot (154)." Whether, as Turner says, she "welcomes his second advance as an unaccustomed demonstration of his love" (362) seems arguable.

21. Latin "pallere," to grow pale.

22. Morrison herself expresses the concept of countertextuakity when she says of Sethe's murder of her child in *Beloved*, "She did the right thing, but she had no right to do it." Interview.

23. Byerman in an article preceding his treatment of Cholly in *Jagged Grain* sees Cholly in much the same way that I am suggesting that the whole of Morrison's novel be read: "Because we have been introduced to his way of thinking and suffering, we verge on understanding his action and sharing his confusion. Both of these responses, repulsion against the action and attraction to the actor are mutually necessary for the grotesque to work in this scene." "Intense Behavior" (451).

24. Davis says regarding this scene that in Cholly "the humiliated black male allies himself with the [other] by making the black woman the object of his displaced fury. . . . All he can do to restore his selfhood is to deny hers further" (329–330).

25. I would insist on the countertextual reading here as opposed to all other readings that see the depiction of the interaction between Cholly and Pecola as simply rape. An example of many such readings is Jones': "The most bitingly satirical example of the hatred bred by Cholly Breedlove is his violating the body of his own twelve year-old daughter Pecola, and impregnating her. All of the fiendishness of his being is epitomized in this diabolical act" (29–30).

26. Byerman identifies another text/countertextual opposition: "Pecola leaves us with an ambiguous feeling. We are sorry for her victimization, but we know that she has entered a realm where her suffering will seldom enter her consciousness." "Intense Behavior" (451).

27. Byerman concurs with this judgment: "Pecola may be the central character, but she is far from the only victim of blue eyes. 'We' individually and collectively are both victimizer and victim and, while the roles vary with each character it is also the case that the role of victimizer results from that characters own victimization by a larger society" (*Jagged Grain* 186).

WORKS CITED

Awkward, Michael. "Roadblocks and Relatives: Critical Revision in Toni Morrison's *The Bluest Eye*." In *Critical Essays on Toni Morrison*. ed. Nellie Y. McKay. Boston: G. K. Hall and Co., 1988, pp. 57–68.

Bakerman, Jane S. "Failures of love: Female Initiation in the Novels of Toni Morrison." *American Literature* 52 (1981): pp. 541–563.

Bacon, Francis. "Of Deformity," in *The Essays or Counsels, Civil and Moral of Francis Bacon.* ed. Samuel Harvey Reynolds. Oxford, 1890.

Evans, Mari, ed. *Black Women Writers (1950-1980): A Critical Evaluation.* New York: Anchor Press/Doubleday, 1984.

Byerman, Keith. *Fingering the Jagged Grain: Tradition and Form in Recent Black Fiction.* Athens: University of Georgia Press, 1985.

———. "Intense Behavior. The Use of the Grotesque in *Eva's Man* and *The Bluest Eye.*" *College Language Association Journal* 25 (1982): pp. 447–457.

Biddis, Michael D., ed. *Gobineau, Selected Political Writings.* London: Jonathan Cape, 1970.

House, Elizabeth. "The 'Sweet Life' in Toni Morrison's Fiction." *American Literature* 56 (1984): pp. 181–202.

Jones, Bessie W. and Audrey L. Vinson. The World of Toni Morrison. Dubuque, Iowa: Kendall/Hunt Publishing Co, 1985.

Klotman, Phyllis. "Dick-and-Jane and the Shirley Temple Sensibility in *The Bluest Eye.*" *Black American Literature Forum* 13 (1979): 123–125.

Lounsberry, Barbara and Grace Ann Hovet. "Flying as Symbol in Toni Morrison's *The Bluest Eye, Sula, Song of Solomon*" *College Language Association Journal* 27 (1984): pp. 119–140.

Morrison, Toni. Interview. All Things Considered. National Public Radio. WNYC, New York, 1988.

———. *The Bluest Eye.* New York: Holt, Rinehart and Winston, 1970.

Ogunyemi, Chikwenye Okonjo. "Order and Disorder in Toni Morrison's *The Bluest Eye* and *Sula.*" *Critique: Studies in Modern Fiction* 19 (1977): pp. 12–20.

Rosenberg, Ruth. "Seeds in Hard Ground: Black Girlhood in *The Bluest Eye.*" *Black American Literature Forum* 21 (1987): pp. 435–445.

Smith, Valerie. *Self-Discovery and Authenticity in Afro-American Narrative.* Cambridge, Mass., 1987.

Tocqueville, Alexis de. *Democracy in America.* Vol. 2. ed. Phillips Bradley. New York: Random House (Vintage), 1945.

Turner, Darwin. "Theme, Characterization, and Style in the Works of Toni Morrison." In Evans pp. 361–369.

Weever, Jacqueline de. "The Inverted World of Toni Morrison's *The Bluest Eye* and *Sula.*" *College Language Association Journal* 22 (1979): pp. 402–414.

SHELLEY WONG

Transgression as Poesis in The Bluest Eye

In the opening pages of *The Bluest Eye*, Toni Morrison writes that since the "why" of Pecola and Cholly Breedlove's situation is "difficult to handle, one must take refuge in how" (9). This admission, hardly the admission of a lack of technique or craft, is, instead, Morrison's admission that she is interested in, not questions of final causes, but questions of process, questions about how process comes to be shut down. Not surprisingly, then, *The Bluest Eye* opens with a tuition in closure. In a passage rendered in the style of the Dick and Jane series of primers, the novel lays bare the syntax of static isolation at the center of our cultural texts:

Here is the house. It is green and white. It has a red door. It is very pretty. Here is the family. Mother, Father, Dick and Jane live in the green-and-white house. They are very happy. See Jane. She has a red dress. She wants to play. Who will play with Jane? See the cat. It goes meow-meow. Come and play. Come play with Jane. The kitten will not play. See Mother. Mother is very nice. Mother, will you play with Jane? Mother laughs. Laugh, Mother, laugh. See Father. He is big and strong. Father, will you play with Jane? Father is smiling. Smile, Father, smile. See the dog. Bowwow goes the dog. Do you want to play with Jane? See the dog run. Run,

Callaloo 13 (1990): pp. 471–481. © The Johns Hopkins University Press.

dog, run. Look, look. Here comes a friend. The friend will play with Jane. They will play a good game. Play, Jane, play. (7)

With the exception of Jane, each character—Mother, Father, Dick (who is absent from the narrative after the first mention of his name), the dog and the cat—maintains himself in a self-enclosed unity, "each member of the family in his own cell of consciousness" (31). The short, clipped sentences accentuate their discreteness. Each of their respective actions—again, with the exception of Jane—is marked by an intransitive verb: "laugh, smile, run," and the conventional sound signatures ascribed to cats and dogs— "meow-meow" and "bowwow." While the verbs "laugh," "smile," and "run" can function as transitive verbs, they do not do so in this passage. These verbs—including "see"—are also imperatives, suggesting the presence of, though never naming, the controlling authority that directs both the reader and the characters of the story. Only Jane (and the unnamed "friend"), who "wants to play," expresses a desire, or a capacity, to engage a world beyond the self. The family is purportedly "very happy." However, the laughing and smiling, seen in the context of the characters' atomized condition, seem not to express joyful affirmation but, rather, almost scornful repudiation. They refuse to play.

In an interview, Morrison commented that she had "used the primer, with its picture of a happy family, as a frame acknowledging the outer civilization. The primer with white children was the way life was presented to black people" (LeClair 28–29). The lesson of this passage in fact goes well beyond acknowledging or presenting white bourgeois values—it goes as far as enacting the very conditions of alienated self-containment which underlie those values. We might note, for instance, that the "house" precedes the "family" in order of both appearance and discussion. In this scheme of things, human relations are preempted by property and commodity relations. The space of ownership engulfs the time of human development and fellowship. The body of human relationships is drawn into the marketplace of being, an essentially timeless space which fosters a frightening commensurability between people and units of exchange, a commensurability which renders family members falsely individualized moments of a social and material whole. In the school of bourgeois economics, the child's first lesson in cultural literacy teaches the primacy of the singular and the discrete. The lesson works against memory and history, and collapses the structure of desire and *communitas,* while simultaneously promoting the desirability of discrete repetition, the wish to be always equal to some measure of ideality divorced from one's own physical and spiritual needs.

The primer passage itself is subsequently repeated twice (though with quite another lesson in mind): the first time without punctuation or capitalization, and the second time without punctuation, capitalization, or spaces between words or sentences. Again, in an interview, Morrison offers a reason for this particular arrangement: "As the novel proceeded I wanted that primer version broken up and confused, which explains the typographical running together of words" (LeClair 29). The brevity and the apparent simplicity of this explanation belie the dynamic complexity of a formal practice. "Broken up" means broken into pieces, ceasing to exist as a unified whole. "Confused" means mixed indiscriminately, blurred, from the Latin root *confundere* meaning "to pour together." Out of this seeming contradiction, it is possible to locate a two-fold process which marks the trajectory of Morrison's narrative practice—i.e., the practice of taking apart and then pouring back together to form the ground of a new order of signification.

Formal considerations notwithstanding, some critics have read these typographical arrangements as symbolic representations of three different kinds of family situations. The first typographically "correct" version formally represents the ideal (or close to ideal) American family typified in the novel by the white Fisher family (Pauline Breedlove's employers), or the aspiring black bourgeois household of Geraldine, Louis, and Louis Junior. The second version is then associated with the family of the young narrator, Claudia MacTeer, a family admitting of some "disorder," but which "still has some order, some form of control, some love" (Ogunyemi 112). The final run-on version is said to depict the "utter breakdown of order among the Breedloves" (Ogunyemi 112).[1]

What these critics have overlooked, however, in their rush to establish thematic equivalencies, is the actuating potential of Morrison's formal textual strategies. They focus on the facts of the story but do not attend to the technique through which the story is told. The omission is problematic because while the story itself may fall within the thematic bounds of bleakness, the way in which it is told can constitute a means of resistance to both personal despair and cultural oppression. By omitting punctuation and capitalization, Morrison begins to break up—and down—conventional syntactic hierarchies, conventional ways of ordering private and public narratives.

The practical effect of this omission is to force one to reevaluate the cultural signposts which give the measure to one's life. By also omitting conventional spacing between words and sentences and breaking lines without respect for the integrity of the word, Morrison collapses those measures altogether, forcing one to pick one's way through a welter of potential signification. The progressive elimination of markers and the running together of words at once defamiliarizes and refamiliarizes the signifying terrain. In refusing the terms of the dominant culture's patterning of experience, one is in a position to restate the familiar, that is, to retrace the particular contours of one's own experience, to regain the practice of one's own narrative. This refusal of ready-made terms, and the responsibility it entails, plays itself out through other art forms, such as music—in particular, jazz. Some time ago, in answer to an interview question, the jazz pianist Thelonious Monk offered the following:

> Jazz and freedom go hand in hand. That explains it. There isn't anything to add to it. If I do add something to it, it gets complicated. That's something for you to think about. *You* think about it. *You* dig it. (Monk)

The refusal of the dominant culture's ready-made terms also challenges that culture's monopoly of meaning. The singular authority of the self-contained word threatens always to hypostatize and monopolize the very process of signification itself. As Morrison notes in conversation:

> It's terrible to think that a child with five different present tenses comes to school to be faced with those books that are less than his own language. And then to be told things about his language, which is him, that are sometimes permanently damaging. He may never know the etymology of Africanisms in his language, not even know that "hip" is a real word or that "the dozens" meant something. This is a really cruel fallout of racism. I know the standard English. I want to use it to help restore the other language, the lingua franca. (LeClair 27)

It is indeed a fallout of racism, but it is also a fallout of a way of organizing social and economic relations. It is a fallout of what one Chinese American writer has called— and called into question—a "Christian esthetic of one god, one good, one voice, one thing happening, one talk at a time," in short, an ideology and an aesthetic of authoritarian closure (Chin xxviii).

The single image of the ideal, the single meaning of the word, command either silence or mute repetition, and produce people "who know not what they do / but know that what they do / is not illegal" (Loy 127). Against a contemporary mood wherein, as Morrison notes, "everybody is trying to be 'right'" (LeClair 27), *The Bluest Eye* launches a critique of received norms of beauty and morality. The novel accomplishes this, in part, through its structural affinity with jazz, in particular, with a jazz practice which insists on overstepping conventional boundaries. Working out of an aesthetic of transgression, such music is frequently misunderstood, and mistaken for the stammered expression of past and/or present oppressions. When Theodor

Adorno condemns jazz for its perpetuation of slave rhythms, its integration of "stumbling and coming-too-soon into the collective march-step" (128), he mishears the music because he conflates "slave"—black American in bondage—with "slavish"—being imitative, submissive, or spineless. Adorno considers jazz's incorporation of slave rhythms to be black America's self-mocking responses to, and affirmation of, past and present oppressions. For Adorno, syncopation involves the "coming-too-soon" into an enforced march-step, the self-lacerating eagerness which rushes headlong into servitude. But syncopation is not always a matter of being ahead of the beat; syncopation can also involve dragging the beat, resisting the received measure by deliberately working behind the beat. While acknowledging other critics' ideas concerning the transformative power of "stumbling," Adorno nevertheless refuses to concede the idea's actuality. Had he known Monk's music, for example, he could have seen that the "stumbling," the sometimes rapid and unexpected rhythmic shifts, are not ways of reflecting or accommodating victimage but are, instead, ways of negotiating a cultural minefield. To stumble the way Monk stumbles is to recognize the constant necessity of picking one's way through that minefield, refusing to be pinned down by the enemy, to be where the enemy expects you to be, or to be caught within the range of their oppressive cultural instrumentation. It can be a terrifying freedom—the freedom to be blown apart by a careless step, by an extravagant hubris. But at the same time, "stumbling" remains one of the few honest motions left in a world that demands a collective march-step. Decrying the tendency amongst young people today to give themselves up to a totally administered existence (LeClair 28), Morrison peoples her novels with characters such as Cholly Breedlove in *The Bluest Eye* and Sula and Ajax in *Sula* who try to resist such pervasive administration:

> They are the misunderstood people in the world. There's a wildness that they have, a nice wildness. It has bad effects in a society such as the one in which we live. It's pre-Christ in the best sense. It's Eve. When I see this wildness gone in a person, it's sad. This special lack of restraint, which is a part of human life and is best typified in certain black males, is of particular interest to me. . . . Everybody knows who "that man" is, and they may give him bad names and call him a "street nigger"; but when you take away the vocabulary of denigration, what you have is somebody who is fearless and who is comfortable with that fearlessness. It's not about meanness. It's a kind of self-flagellant resistance to certain kinds of control, which is fascinating. Opposed to accepted notions of progress, the lockstep life, they live in the world unreconstructed and that's it. (Tate 125–26)

The word "unreconstructed" is crucial here, for it points up and elaborates on that two-fold process characterizing both Morrison's use of the primer passage and an analogous jazz practice. An "unreconstructed" world suggests a world that has, first of all, been taken apart and then not—or not yet—put back together in any definitive sense of a final unity. The world unreconstructed refuses the matter-of-factness with which the administered world fixes a permanent name to an object, choosing instead to remain plural and fissiparous, requiring constant naming and constant articulation. Whether that articulation evolves into the blues, jazz, or other modes of formal expression, the impulse behind it is to express the mutable extravagance of materiality and to eschew the restraining paucity of all forms of ideality. In blues and jazz, improvising becomes a way of keeping the world open to its own potentiality. Jazz articulates meaning through attention to the particulars of the moment, to the work under hand, rather than through any strict adherence to received, and preconceived, notions of the bar or the line. Musicians such as the pianist Cecil Taylor or the alto saxophonist Ornette Coleman have, in their early work, even called into question the very notion of tonal centers:

> [The resulting music is] in many cases atonal (meaning that its tonal "centers" are constantly redefined according to the needs, or shape and direction, of the particular music being played, and not formally fixed as is generally the case. . .). (Jones 226)

> [Through jazz improvisation] music and musician have been brought, in a manner of speaking, face to face, without the strict and often grim hindrances of overused Western musical concepts; it is the overall musical intelligence of the musician which is responsible for shaping the music. (Jones 227)

The improvised piece, if it is to be articulate, requires not only attention to the immediate complex of sound and feeling being worked out but, also, attention to the total field of composition, to the *"total area* of its existence as a means to evolve, to move, as an intelligently shaped musical concept, from its beginning to end" (Jones 226).

"Intelligence," I might note, takes its etymological cue from an agricultural vocabulary, from the Latin for "gleaning," the gathering together of meanings. Much of Morrison's writing comes back repeatedly to this concern with her characters' abilities to gather meaning from the ragtag details of a life. Pauline Breedlove "liked, most of all, to arrange things," but that impulse was never able to find an appropriate outlet: "she missed—without knowing what she missed—paints and crayons" (*TBE*

88–89). In Morrison's second novel, *Sula*, we find Sula Peace without a way to perform herself in the world:

> [Sula's] strangeness, her naivete, her craving for the other half of her equation was the consequence of an idle imagination. Had she paints, or clay, or knew the discipline of the dance, or strings; had she anything to engage her tremendous curiosity and her gift for metaphor, she might have exchanged the restlessness and preoccupation with whim for an activity that provided her with all she yearned for. And like any artist with no art form, she became dangerous. (121)

Similarly, for Cholly Breedlove in *The Bluest Eye*, the inability to articulate the disparate moments of a life results in a hysteria of freedom:

> The pieces of Cholly's life could become coherent only in the head of a musician. Only those who talk their talk through the gold of curved metal, or in the touch of black-and-white rectangles and taut skins and strings echoing from wooden corridors, could give true form to his life. Only they would know how to connect the heart of a red watermelon to the asafetida bag to the muscadine to the flashlight on his behind to the fists of money to the lemonade in a Mason jar to a man called Blue and come up with what all that meant in joy, in pain, in anger, in love, and give it its final and pervading ache of freedom. Only a musician would sense, know, without even knowing that he knew, that Cholly was free. Dangerously free. (125)

Cholly was free in the sense that he was not bound by responsibility (or response-ability) to anyone but himself. Having been "abandoned in a junk heap by his mother, rejected for a crap game by his father, there was nothing more to lose" (126). For Cholly, in this "godlike state" (126), the world remained unreconstructed. Having lost all measures of related-ness to others, he was free to remake, or free to not make at all, his own ties to the world. In this sense, the unreconstructed narrative of his life resembles the third primer passage where all hierarchies, all conventional ordering has been collapsed. Using the analogy of a tape recording played back at high speed, or a film shown in fast motion, the seeming absence of cultural markers requires one either to create new orders of signification or to risk losing one's way altogether. In a nation which has historically insisted upon some people "shar[ing] all the horrors but none of the privi-leges of our civilization" (Algren ix), what passes for cultural measures can, when taken up by the disinherited, quickly be revealed as a hysteria of mismeasure.

For Cholly, the inability to ground himself in new measures results in despair. Initially unfitted, by way of race and class, for the dominant culture's patterning of experience, and then fitted too tightly into the "constantness, varietylessness, [and] sheer weight of sameness" (126) of his marriage, Cholly was soon smothered by his own "inarticulate fury and aborted desires" (37). "Only in drink was there some break" (126) from the relentless routinization of body and soul. The weight of sameness, the tyranny of repetition—at home and at the mill—destroys for him the sense of time as a generative, forwarding process. The destruction, however, actually begins much earlier than his marriage. Cholly's abandonment by his parents radically disconnects him from the time of family. Later, the interruption and the frustration of his first sexual encounter by two white hunters further highlights his separation from the world of generative and reproductive time. This intrusion of the white world maintains a historical precedent in slavery. The slave trade had disrupted generative, and genealogical, time by breaking up families and by rendering family members commodities, that is, by reducing the ever-changing, ever-proliferating body to the status of exchangeable homogeneous units. Nowhere in this novel is this legacy of slavery—the disfigurement of human relationships by the marketplace—more ironically stated than in Morrison's decision to locate a family by the name of "Breedlove" in a converted (and poorly converted at that) storefront.

In the Breedloves' lives, repetition as the time of "flesh on unsurprised flesh" (38), as the copying of a static ideal, or as the submission to slave or factory time, results only in a stopped narrative, an arrested history. Pecola's rape too is, in one concrete sense, an arrested history. As Cholly moves to rape her, Pecola's "shocked body" (128) startles Cholly out of the miasma of routinized desire that was his marriage, setting in motion a "confused mixture" (128) of his memories of his first encounter with Pauline and his hatred for Darlene, the young girl who had witnessed his humiliation in front of the white hunters. Pecola's "shocked body" excites him, perhaps because it recalls for him a time before the freezing of his bodily imagination. Thus, while trying to break out of the stultifying confines of his quotidian existence by doing "a wild and forbidden thing" (128), Cholly succeeds only in copying those two earlier moments. In turning back process through raping his own daughter, Cholly breaks with and thwarts genealogical time. Within this context, their baby cannot possibly live, for nothing can issue from a stopped narrative.

The pathos of the Breedloves' lives lies in their complete alienation from each other and from the world; locked in their individual cells of consciousness, they are unable to give birth to each other, unable to bring each other into the world of generative time. In *The Bluest Eye*, Morrison allows the reader to see how the Breedloves arrive at their atomized conditions. The subsequent revelation points up how a metaphysics, a socioeconomic system, a society and a community, can interact in a mutual frenzy of blind ideality to mutilate people, particularly girls and women. The destructiveness of culturally sanctioned closures is implicit in the very title of the novel, where the "eye" is decidedly singular. There can, after all, only be one bluest eye, not a pair of eyes that are the bluest in the world, but a single eye. The impossibility of Pecola's wish is rooted in the singularity of the superlative. In order to achieve the bluest eye, she has to sacrifice the other—the result, self-mutilation. Pecola's subsequent derangement, the splitting up of her psyche and the splitting off of herself from the world, provides the only route to the superlative.

The Bluest Eye emerges as the indictment and the uncrowning of a social and economic order which upholds and implements a metaphysics of isolate unity. The world of discrete facts spawned by such a metaphysics refuses the ambivalence of the material world; it refuses to acknowledge the mutuality of material being that reveals itself in a newborn baby whose eyes "all soft and wet," are a "cross between a puppy and a dying man" (100); in a dog who coughs the "cough of a phlegmy old man" (139); in men who are dogs (15, 128); in cats who take the place of men (70); in an old woman who "yelps" like a dog (144); in a pregnant woman who "foals" (99); in a young girl who "whinnies" when she begins to menstruate (25); in all the ways that the material body asserts its transformative possibilities in an unfinished world of metamorphosis:

> The unfinished and open body (dying, bringing forth and being born) is not separated from the world by clearly defined boundaries; it is blended with the world, with animals, with objects . . . it represents the entire material bodily world in all its elements. (Bakhtin 27)

In confusing, in running together, the usually discrete states of birth and death and the discrete orders of humans and animals, Morrison breaks down the false and isolating solidity of self-contained identities and, at the same time, answers with an emphatic "No" Soaphead Church's question to God: "Is the name the real thing then? And the person only what his name says?" (*TBE* 142). In refusing the fixed identity of word and object, Morrison begins the work of decentering the logos itself. Through Soaphead's address to God, Morrison reveals the inanity at the center of the authoritarian word:

> Is that why to the simplest and friendliest of questions "What is
> your name?" put to you by Moses, You would not say, and said "I
> Am Who I Am." Like Popeye? I Yam What I Yam? Afraid you
> were, weren't you, to give out your name? Afraid they would know
> the name and then know you? Then they wouldn't fear you? (142)

One way Morrison breaks open the secretive, evasive nature of the
solitary word is by acknowledging the physicality of words themselves.
Words are not dead letters on the page but live sounds in the mouth and in
the ear. She pays careful attention to not only the connotations of words,
but also to the cadences of the language itself. Through the repetition
of words, images, and grammatical structures, she affirms and enacts
the resonance of materiality. To repeat in this way is not to yearn after
the exactness of a copy but, rather, to follow up the traces of a family
resemblance. In *The Bluest Eye*, Morrison uses the repeated phrase in much
the same way a musician uses a riff—i.e., as a way of grounding, without
prescribing, the entire composition; it is as much a point of departure as it
is a point of return. On one level, the riff bears structural affinities with the
rhetorical device of anaphora, a device which Morrison uses throughout
the novel. Anaphora literally means "a bringing again" and refers to the
practice of beginning successive sentences or clauses with the same word or
sound. Each "bringing again" of the concrete word or sound offers another
look, another hearing, another context, and another shifting around and
gathering of meanings. "Truth" is to be found, not in semantics alone, but
also in "timbre" and cadence (16).

For Morrison, language is material; language "is the thing that black
people love so much—the saying of words, holding them on the tongue,
experimenting with them, playing with them" (LeClair 27). The same could
be said of a jazz musician's relationship to the musical phrase, particularly
in the practice of the riff-solo sequence, the riff, here, being the occasion
of collective playing which launches the individual musician on his own
solo improvisation. The musician will take up the phrase and play with it,
extending it and turning it over and over again until he extracts from it all
the meaning that his own desires and questionings can call up. In Morrison's
writing, the riffing frequently takes the form of a kind of rhyming, not of
sounds necessarily (though this is often the case), but of occasions. This
rhyming manifests itself temporally and spatially. In temporal terms, the
novel is composed in such a way that it continually folds back on itself,
replaying certain themes, images, or words. When we encounter Maureen
Peal in the "Winter" section of the novel, we realize that her appearance had
in fact been prepared for in the "Autumn" section, when Pecola, savoring the
thought of eating Mary Jane candies, feels a "peal of anticipation unsettl[ing]

her stomach" (41). The sonic rhyme in "peal" signals the occasional rhyme—both the eating of the Mary Jane candies and the appearance of Maureen Peal in midwinter promise false springs. Maureen is the "disrupter of seasons" (52), and for Pecola, the Mary Janes will ultimately be the disrupters of generative time, the seasonal time of the body. The repetition also throws us forward into Pecola's later encounter with Soaphead. There, on the verge of achieving the much desired transubstantiation, of achieving the beauty and the popularity of a Maureen Peal, Pecola's stomach is unsettled by the odor of the poisoned meat and by Bob's subsequent death throes.[2]

In spatial terms, Morrison rhymes by distributing human and animal characteristics amongst her characters in such a way that the human and animal worlds are unmistakably linked through a shared materiality. When humans "nest" and dogs cough like old men, and when a "high-yellow dream child" has a "dog-tooth" and another girl "whinnies" in fear, the hierarchical boundaries between the human and the animal are no longer absolute and human pretensions to the contrary are exposed as self-delusions.

In her writing, Morrison dethrones isolate unity and, instead, articulates the connectedness of people, animals, objects, and words—in short, all the manifestations of material being. The very act of articulating—of "making [one's] own patchwork quilt of reality—collecting fragments of experience here, pieces of information there" (*TBE* 31)—becomes a means of survival. For some of Morrison's characters—such as Mrs. MacTeer and Poland, one of the three whores who live in the apartment above the Breedloves—the blues provide a means to gather and to transmute the pain of daily existence. Mrs. MacTeer, Claudia tells us, "having told everybody and everything off. . . would burst into song and sing the rest of the day," singing about "hard times, bad times, and somebody-done-gone-and-left-me times" (23–24). In his essay, "Richard Wright's Blues," Ralph Ellison writes this:

> blues is an impulse to keep the painful details of and episodes of a brutal experience alive in one's aching consciousness, to finger its jagged grain, and to transcend it, not by the consolation of philosophy but by squeezing from it a near-tragic, near-comic lyricism. (90)

Ellison's choice of the word "transcend" seems to jar against the rest of his observation, and in its place, I would insert the word "transform," for the blues do not rise above the pain but bear witness to it and make it livable. Morrison's own writing stems from a similar impulse. After Soaphead has performed Pecola's miracle, he writes a letter to God. As he prepares to do so, he reaches for a "bottle of ink [that] was on the same shelf that held the poison" (139). The juxtaposition of the ink and the poison is far from gratuitous. The literal poison on the shelf here merely underscores the novel's repeated concern with a metaphorical poisoning which works through the American culture industry's projection—from the movie screen, from Mary Jane candy wrappers, and from Shirley Temple mugs—of a single image of ideal beauty, one that is decidedly white and devoid of any "dreadful funkiness" (68). The writing-out of pain remains inseparable from the cause itself.

There are those, however, without the means to transform their experience. The criminal failure to be equal to the dominant culture's image of beauty, to be equal to any imposed measure of ideality, leaves Morrison's characters scrambling for refuge in what are often destructive alibis. When it becomes known that Cholly has raped his own daughter, and that she is pregnant as a result of it, the black community's response ranges over disgust, amusement, shock, titillation, and outrage. Their moral outrage, while purportedly based on the violation of the incest taboo, is also clearly based on the violation of culturally sanctioned standards of beauty: "Ought to be a law: two ugly people doubling up like that to make more ugly. Be better off in the ground" (148). Any child of Cholly and Pecola's was "bound to be the ugliest thing walking" (148), and it would be better, for all concerned, if the baby didn't live to remind them of their own tenuous relationship to white America's standards of beauty. The baby doesn't live. And the community's alibi, created to deflect their own complicity in its death and in Pecola's psychological death, remains intact:

> All of us—all who knew her—felt so wholesome after we cleaned ourselves on her. We were so beautiful when we stood astride her ugliness. Her simplicity decorated us, her guilt sanctified us, her pain made us glow with health, her awkwardness made us think we had a sense of humor. Her inarticulateness made us believe we were eloquent. Her poverty kept us generous. Even her waking dreams we used—to silence our own nightmares. And she let us, and thereby deserved our contempt. We honed our egos on her, padded our characters with her frailty, and yawned in the fantasy of our strength.
>
> And fantasy it was, for we were not strong, only aggressive; we were not free, merely licensed; we were not compassionate, we were polite; not good, but well behaved. We courted death in order to call ourselves brave, and hid like thieves from life. We substituted good grammar for intellect; we switched habits to simulate maturity; we rearranged lies and called it truth, seeking in the new pattern of an old idea the Revelation and the Word. (159)

"Quiet as it's kept" (9), the narrator tells us at the beginning of the novel, leaving us to anticipate the "big lie [that] was about to be told" (LeClair 28). From that moment on, the novel bears witness to the lie that is closure itself. In bearing witness, Morrison will tell the tale of "who survived under what circumstances and why" (LeClair 26). Through the telling, the dominant culture's monologue on itself will be challenged and ruptured by the lingua franca of ambivalent materiality itself. In this sense, the telling becomes a liberating pedagogy. In commenting on her function as a writer, Morrison says:

> I write what I have recently begun to call village literature, fiction that is really for the village, for the tribe . . . [my novels] ought to identify those things in the past that are useful and those things that are not; and they ought to give nourishment. (LeClair 26)

According to the tenets of an older Platonic tradition of rhetorical theory, the function of the rhetorician was to move the soul of another in order that the soul begin to move itself. In more recent terms, the American poet Charles Olson has formulated another conception of that function for the contemporary writer: "he who can tell the story right has actually not only, like, given you something, but has moved you on your own narrative" (38). In bearing accurate witness to the "big lie," Morrison has reopened the tale of the tribe, reopened for the members of her tribe and for her readers the points of entry to a private and a public narrative. Telling and freedom go hand in hand, we can hear Morrison saying—"*You* dig it."

NOTES

1. A similar reading of this primer passage can be found in Klotman, (123–125).

2. In conversation with Claudia Tate, Morrison has spoken of what I have referred to as a rhyming of occasions in terms of "omens": "you don't know what's going to happen at the time the omens occur, and you don't always recognize an omen until after the fact, but when the bad thing does happen, you somehow expected it" (Tate, 124–125).

WORKS CITED

Adorno, Theodor. *Prisms*, Trans. Samuel and Shierry Weber. Cambridge, Mass.: MIT Press, 1981.

Algren, Nelson. *Never Come Morning*, 1942. New York: Harper, 1963.

Bakhtin, Mikhail. *Rabelais and His World*, Trans. Helene Iswolsky. Bloomington: University of Indiana Press, 1984.

Chin, Frank. *The Chickencoop Chinaman/The Year of the Dragon.* Seattle: University of Washington Press, 1981.

Ellison, Ralph. *Shadow and Act.* 1953; 1964. Toronto: New American Library of Canada Limited, 1966.

Jones, LeRoi. *Blues People.* New York: Morrow Quill Paperbacks, 1963.

Klotman, Phyllis. "Dick-and-Jane and the Shirley Temple Sensibility in *The Bluest Eye.*" *Black American Literature Forum,* 13 (Winter 1979): 123–125.

LeClair, Thomas. "The Language Must Not Sweat." *New Republic,* 184 (21 March 1981): 25–29.

Loy, Mina. *The Last Lunar Baedeker.* Highlands: The Jargon Society, 1982.

Monk, Thelonious. in Martin Williams, liner notes, *The Smithsonian Collection of Classical Jazz.* Smithsonian Institute, 1953.

Morrison, Toni. *Sula,* 1973. New York: New American Library, 1982.

———. *The Bluest Eye.* New York: Washington Square Press, 1970.

Ogunyemi, Chikwenye Okonjo. "Order and Disorder in Toni Morrison's *The Bluest Eye.*" *Critique: Studies in Modern Fiction,* 19 (1977): 112–120.

Olson, Charles. *Muthologos: The Collected Lectures and Interviews,* Ed. George Butterick. 2 vols. Bolinas: Four Seasons Foundation, 1978.

Tate, Claudia, ed. *Black Women Writers at Work.* New York: Continuum, 1983.

LINDA DITTMAR

"Will the Circle Be Unbroken?"
The Politics of Form in The Bluest Eye[1]

Our metaphors of self cannot then rest in stasis, but will glory in difference and overflow into everything that belongs to us.

Deborah E. McDowell

Deborah McDowell introduces her recent essay on *Sula* with the following quotation from Henry James: "What shall we call our 'Self'? Where does it begin? Where does it end? It overflows into everything that belongs to us." My own epigraph—her concluding sentence in that same essay—reworks James's concern with "self" and "overflow" so as to highlight the mingled awe and anxiety which Toni Morrison's writing tends to elicit. McDowell's emphasis on the mediation of knowledge touches on what is at once inspirational and unsettling in Morrison's work: the verbal abundance in which this writing glories is tinged with scepticism. Its "overflow" touches off a feeling that meanings are unstable, at once elusive and in formation. In part, this effect concerns the "readerly" stance of Morrison's writing (in Barthes's sense), in that her self-reflexive narration refracts and defers meanings. In part it also concerns political issues—notably racial and sexual. In this respect, the issues of difference which McDowell identifies as operating in *Sula* are political, not just literary or personal. "Difference," it turns out, is a site of struggle which involves the material as well as theoretical consequences of ideology.

Novel: A Forum on Fiction, 23.2 (Winter 1990): pp. 137–155. Copyright NOVEL Corp. © 1990.

This converging of *difference* in its linguistic-philosophical sense (i.e. Derrida's endlessly displaced meanings) and "difference" as a political reading of abusively inegalitarian social institutions underlies the following discussion. On the one hand, Morrison's writing invokes a modernist concern with language, epistemology, and the constructed nature of art. In this respect, the ineffable quality Nelly McKay admires in her prose is not unrelated to the luminous evanescence that haunts the pages of Conrad and Faulkner, E. M. Forster and Virginia Woolf. Morrison, like them, foregrounds narrative indirection, and for her, too, this is traceable to yearnings checked by prohibition and to a will to utter checked by doubt. At the same time, McKay is right to set Morrison apart from the modernist tradition. As she notes, the ineffable quality of Morrison's writing is politically and culturally inflected through a specifically Afro-American tradition. The yearnings Morrison articulates and the prohibitions she faces are inscribed racially, as are the expressive modes she adapts from Afro-American oral, narrative, and musical traditions, notably women's culture. Ultimately, Morrison's writing insists on a double-reading which recognizes, at once, her place within the history of Western narrative in general and her place within a specifically Afro-American tradition.[2]

The following discussion applies this double-reading to Morrison's first novel, *The Bluest Eye* (1970). Though Morrison herself has commented on this book somewhat disavowingly as the novel in which she learned to write, it is a richly-crafted work that deserves study in its own right. Moreover, attention to it is useful as a paradigm for issues which come up in her subsequent novels, notably *Beloved* (1987), which is formally closer to *The Bluest Eye* and *Sula* (1973) than it is to the intervening novels—*The Song of Solomon* (1977) and *Tar Baby* (1981). My aim here is, then, to start laying the groundwork for an overview of Morrison's novels as an evolving body of work and to highlight the particular ways the formal operations of her writing function ideologically. In this respect, her novels require more than a critique of characters and plots as hypothetical instances of social actuality (Bakerman, Bishoff, Christian, Davis, Johnson, Miner, et al.). However problematic, *The Bluest Eye*'s displacing of social pathology and failed human values into the black community (a process Wallace Thurman calls "intra-racism") must be understood in relation to Morrison's craft as it guides the reception of her novel.

Seen this way, *The Bluest Eye* is not as far from *Beloved* as their plotlines might suggest. Especially in the case of a writer whose performative virtuosity so insistently determines sense, we must be careful to register the complex modulations of meaning and judgment built into her writing. As Audre Lorde puts it, the problem is that Morrison's "vigorous and evocative language which sings out like legends beneath our skin," sings of a "love that can be misshapen and frightened into hatred" (30, 29). Lorde is registering the contradictory quality of this writing, and her use of a musical trope to describe Morrison's language and the reception it elicits anticipates Morrison's subsequent comment to McKay (interview) that she is aiming for narrative procedures which, like jazz, will resist closure:

> Jazz always keeps you on the edge. There is no final chord. . . . There is something underneath that is incomplete. There is always something else that you want from the music. I want my books to be like that—because I want that feeling of something held in reserve and the sense that there is more—that you can't have it all right now.
>
> [Lena Horne and Aretha Franklin] have the ability to make you want it, and remember the want. That is a part of what I want to put in my books. They will never fully satisfy—never fully. (429)

Such withholding of closure is the essence of narrative desire—a desire knowable mainly through the medium of formal articulation, be it musical or verbal.[3]

It is Morrison's emphasis on the ineffable that beckons readers towards enthusiasm, conflict, and avoidance of conflict. The desiring state she instills in them invites all this precisely because such desire haunts and agitates, just as she intended. Readers may respond differently to the history, culture, and politics inscribed in Morrison's race, gender, and subject-matter, but the process of desiring reception she builds into her narratives forces all of them into yearning which they can either acknowledge or suppress. In part, this embattled reception simply registers her insistence on the opaque and self-referential nature of language. There is nothing humbly "transparent" and self-effacing about her style, point-of-view, and narrative structure. But this desiring reception also has to do with the fact that she sings of aberrations, and beautifully, at that. Each is important, of course, but it is only by understanding how the two interact that we gain full access to her writing.

From *The Bluest Eye* to *Beloved*, Morrison's way with words asserts itself as at once seductive and elusive. While her writing is, indeed, sensorily specific, the actual events it conveys shimmer with a suggestiveness that ultimately withholds at least as much as it gives. Her looping narrative lines, flashbacks, and anticipatory predictions similarly veil and qualify meaning.[4] The cumulative effect of all this indirection is that it encodes hesitation. Morrison's treatment of Cholly's incestuous rape of Pecola, for example, ends up foregrounding an awareness of the complexity of judgment and feeling, and this is true of *The Bluest Eye* as a whole. The construction of *Beloved* is similarly predicated

on a pattern of oblique predictions, backward loopings, and indirection, all
of which assert urgency about at once telling, judging, and suppressing that
which needs to be told. In short, the difficulty Morrison creates for her readers is not just that Cholly rapes his daughter or that Sethe kills hers, and what
these acts say about racism, slavery, poverty, and related abuses. The difficulty
is also that Morrison's rich syntax, resonant imagery, dispersed chronology,
and shifting viewpoints inscribe an ambivalent mode of reading.

In the case of Morrison, such ambivalence is neither the consequence of
empty "post-modern" flourishes nor a reflection of a modernist collapse of historical reasoning in the Lukácsian sense (Willis 96). Rather, the contradictory
claims of form and content which Morrison strives to negotiate, especially
when seen in relation to her particular ways of resisting closure, raise questions
of narrative strategy and ideology specific to her work as a black woman writer
and, by extension, to minority and female writing in general.[5] The following
discussion explores the point at which questions of form and content, art and
politics, converge in *The Bluest Eye*. My hope is that unravelling the tangled
political commitments and formal deflections of this novel will help us read all
of Morrison's fiction more complexly and alert us to ways in which narrative
form, like thematic content, is never politically neutral.

II

That *The Bluest Eye* has been criticized for being mired in the pathology
of Afro-American experience is hardly surprising. Violence, madness, and
incest are some of the extreme forms this pathology takes here, though
the racism which pushes people to such extremes is Morrison's underlying
concern. Describing a society where whiteness is the yardstick of personal
worth, where Shirley Temple and Jeanne Harlow set standards for beauty
and "Dick and Jane" readers prescribe an oppressive notion of normalcy,
where Pecola's shame at her mother's race serves as a model for self-improve-
ment,[6] where fathers deny their sons, mothers deny their daughters, and
God denies the communal prayer for the privilege of blue eyes—in such a
society, Morrison argues, marigolds cannot bloom. The marigolds are metaphoric, of course. The barrenness they signify goes beyond agriculture to
include scapegoating and intraracism, "deeply rooted in the primitive history
and prehistory of the human struggle with the environment, specifically the
struggle for agricultural maintenance symbolized by the seasons and the
marigolds" (Royster 43; Davis).

There are several problems with this metaphor: it leaves the barrenness
unaccounted for; it situates social and psychological oppression in the community that receives them (the "soil" in which the seeds were sown); it presents racism as an inescapable atavism; and it provides no means of recovery.
In fact, when one surveys the tale of inhumanity *The Bluest Eye* unfolds, it

is hard not to question the ideology of its thematics. Readers worry that the microcosm Morrison locates in her Ohio town includes few venues for anger directed beyond the black community and almost no potential for regeneration within it. Read thematically, this novel does indeed seem overwhelmingly pessimistic, given its relentless piling up of abuses and betrayals. Its formal devices partly deflect but never quite extinguish the wish for a plot-based judgment. It is the tension between the two that makes *The Bluest Eye* a problematic novel.

Morrison does not let this tension subside or drop out of view. If anything, this novel's very structure accentuates it precisely because the novel remains inconclusive to the very end. For while *The Bluest Eye* is, indeed, a brilliant orchestration of a complex, multi-formed narrative, the ideological thrust of its structure is ambiguous. Morrison orders her materials into four seasonal parts—autumn, winter, spring, and summer—but within this design nothing is simple or stable. Excerpts from a "Dick and Jane" reader serve as a framing point of reference for Claudia's ostensibly autobiographical narrative; Claudia's account frames Pecola's story; and Pecola's story, in its turn, frames the three long flashbacks which trace the stories of Pauline, Cholly, and Soaphead Church. This elaborate patterning of framing devices attenuates textual accountability. Its mediations deflect attribution, disperse sympathy and identification, and thus question judgment in ways that echo rather than counter the plot's pessimism. They pass on to readers the task of gathering the novel's parts into a signifying whole, even as their ever-shifting modulations of stance assert that the effect is doomed to remain inconclusive.

Inside this Chinese-box arrangement, an obtrusive use of varied typographies further undermines the conventions which normally efface authors' control of their story-telling. Portions of Pauline's narrative are set apart from the rest as oral history; they are italicized first-person accounts which have a distinctly spoken grammar and cadence. Cholly's and Soaphead's narratives are also foreign elements, for they are third-person accounts unattributable to Claudia or to any other dramatized narrator. The opening segment in each seasonal division has uneven right hand margins, as does Pauline's narrative in its entirety. While such margins may serve to suggest the text's informal, possibly spoken origins, the mere use of this unusual device is attention-getting, especially given its recurrent suspension and re-introduction. Such intrusion is most noticeable in the "Dick and Jane" passages, where an obtrusive and increasingly unreadable typography emphasizes their role as hostile assaults on Claudia's account. Using "found objects" in apposition to poeticized ones, these passages create an angry dialectic between documentation and fictionality and between the public domain of early childhood acculturation and the private one of personal experience.[7] Numbing the imagination with their simplifications of grammar and life, both the form and the substance of the "Dick and Jane" passages violate the integrity of the life Morrison depicts.

The overall effect of this complexly structured work is to foreground the authorial project of orchestrating a fluid, multi-voiced novel, where the parts sometimes jostle against one another, sometimes complement or blend with each other, and at all times project a dense sense of the multiplicity of narration. Since the function of the story-telling act is, as Claudia puts it, to explain, Morrison's juxtaposition of diverse voices asserts that understanding is collective. In this respect, *The Bluest Eye*'s design supplements its thematic focus on communities as sites of meaning, for it posits that meanings get constructed dialogically. [8] Maureen Peel and Geraldine, the MacTeers as well as the Breedloves, Mr. Henry and Soaphead Church, the Fishers, Hollywood, and the Maginot Line—these and others collaborate in the production of ideology within the plot. At the same time, *The Bluest Eye*'s very structure parallels the construction of meaning undertaken by its characters. Its shifting points-of-view, flashbacks, and digressions inscribe into the novel's very organization the dialogism evident in its plot. The emphasis here is on understanding and judgment as restless, dynamic, and interactive processes of meaning-production, forever open to modification and change.

This foregrounding of the unstable and constructed nature of knowledge, and of the collaborative processes which guide it, affirms the possibility of positive change. Individual characters may not participate in such change; certainly Claudia, for all her adult retrospection, provides no empowerment. But the dialogic interchange among these voices shifts the center of activity away from any one character to the readers who assemble and interpret the novel's diverse segments. Depicting and enacting ways we produce and re-produce ideology, the text reminds us that we can take charge of our future. Thus, Claudia's role as the young narrator coming of age only partly shapes the novel. Interacting with adjacent voices, she contributes to a larger process of formation. At the same time, Morrison's parcelling out of narrative authority suggests qualification. The issue is not that dialogism is inherently open-ended, but that in Morrison's writing—which is committed to a desiring openness on all levels—this open form is particularly prone to dispersal. Given that *The Bluest Eye* focuses its concern with the production of meanings on the valuation of race, gender, and social class, the danger latent in its procedures is one of ambivalence and evasion. The danger is that the pleasurable resistance to closure Morrison uses to elicit desire will also cloud our judgment.

Not surprisingly, both the hopefulness and the anxiety inherent in Morrison's treatment of the construction of meaning coexist in this novel.

Thus, while for Claudia the initiating impetus for narration is the need to account for the fact that, "Quiet as it's kept, there were no marigolds in the fall of 1941" (9), neither Claudia nor Morrison project confidence about the possibility of doing so. The narrative may originate in the need to account for this mystery, but it never fulfills its promise. "There is really nothing more to say," Claudia notes at the end of her brief introduction, "except why. But since why is difficult to handle, one must take refuge in *how*" (9). At the very outset of story-telling, Morrison already questions the act of telling—first by moving Claudia from "why" to "how," next by being vague about what she is trying to do (for "to handle" the "why" is more evasive and non-committal than "to answer" it), and finally by shifting from Claudia's first person "I" to the impersonal "one" and by admitting that the "one" is "taking refuge" in description as a substitute for explanation.[9]

Of course, this groping can be attributed to Claudia, who comes across as a still developing young person despite her seemingly powerful position as a retrospective narrator.[10] The trouble is not in Claudia's *persona*, but in Morrison's reluctance to supplement Claudia's incomplete vision forcefully. This reluctance manifests itself through Morrison's ambivalent turning to the community in which the seeds withered. For though the novel's use of a multi-voiced community affirms the rehabilitating gift of sharing and belonging, its orchestration also disperses power, deflects responsibility, and questions the efficacy of the story-telling act. It is the pleasure in voicing and the desire for its products, more than meaning, that takes over.

Morrison's use of an orchestrated narrative design belongs in a long and often dazzling tradition of experimentation, where disrupted chronology, splintered plots, decentered accountability, and disparate modes of narration can lead to a panic about the loss of center. Yet in most multi-layered narratives, and in *The Bluest Eye* alongside them, such a dismantling foregrounds reconstitution. Though putting Humpty Dumpty together again may be impossible, in that the glue joining the shards will always be visible, the process of engaging in reconstitution and, thus, in re-possession is the important recuperative activity in which such texts engage their readers. Morrison's "Dick and Jane" typography belies the text's claim to transparency, as do her leaps in chronology, in location, and in narrating viewpoints and modalities. All these devices insist on the reader's self-conscious participation in the reconstitution of the text. Of course, there are ways in which Morrison counters the disruption with stabilizing devices: she uses Claudia's narrating *persona* as a regularizing force, and she uses the inexorability and predictability of the Breedlove story (Tate) to divert readers from the text's dismantling operations to the more pressing urgency of compassion. But on the whole, *The Bluest Eye*'s disrupted construction works to undermine the text's illusionism. Instead, it elicits a reading

which subordinates the claims of realism, including the authenticating use
of narrative viewpoints, to the dynamic interaction of the parts within the
text as a whole. This dismantling design acknowledges the insufficiency of
any one voice. It posits, rather, that knowledge is constructed by the many
and that reading is a process of active re-shaping by readers.

The four-seasons organization of *The Bluest Eye* adds another complication to this already difficult patterning. For while the march of the seasons
is reassuringly predictable, it also checks the fluidity of the narrative. Here
is the novel's constant—a natural force that antedates the depicted events
by millennia, a reminder that the withering of seeds, babies, and minds in
Lorain, Ohio of 1941 fits into a much larger picture. Given the heterogene-
ity of *The Bluest Eye*'s materials, having such a regularizing force would be
a help were it not that using the seasons as a structuring device also posits
a suffocatingly cyclical design. Inherent in the notion of the seasons is the
fact that they are an annually recurring condition from which there is no escape. As a metaphor, they are a closed form, sufficient unto itself and allowing for only minor variations. Even the sequence Morrison sets up for these
seasons, starting with autumn's decline and ending with a summer edging
once again towards such a decline, accentuates the negative aspects of this
metaphor. Indeed, in Morrison's treatment, spring is a time of beatings and
the narrative section which contains Soaphead's perversion, while summer is
"a season of storms," where the mere thought of eating a strawberry bears an
uncanny resemblance to violent deflowering ("I . . . break into the tightness
of a strawberry" 146). Avoiding both the positive use of spring and summer
as symbols of renewal and the epic use of the seasons to punctuate a historical
process of struggle and change, Morrison's four-part design implies a trap.

The book's ending adds to this sense of futility. A hundred and fifty
pages after Morrison equivocates about the why and how of story-telling, she
has Claudia dismiss the strengths Claudia and others do possess:

> And fantasy it was, for we were not strong, only aggressive; we
> were not free, merely licensed; we were not compassionate, we were
> polite; not good, but well behaved. We courted death in order to call
> ourselves brave, and hid like thieves from life. We substituted good
> grammar for intellect; we switched habits to simulate maturity; we
> rearranged lies and called it truth, seeing in the new pattern of an
> old idea the Revelation and the Word. (159)

A page later Morrison uses the following paragraph to bring the book to a
close:

> And now when I see her searching for garbage—for what? The
> thing we assassinated? I talk about how I did not plant the seeds

too deeply, how it was the fault of the earth, the land, of our town. I even think now that the land of the entire country was hostile to marigolds that year. This soil is bad for certain kinds of flowers. Certain seeds it will not nurture, certain fruit it will not bear, and when the land kills of its own volition, we acquiesce and say the victim had no right to live. We are wrong, of course, but it doesn't matter. It's too late. At least on the edge of my town, among the garbage and the sunflowers of my town, it's much, much, much too late. (160)

The despair here is overwhelming. Mired in this sense of the wrong, each betrayal *The Bluest Eye* depicts, each brutalization and denial, aches with a yearning for what could have been but never came to pass. Ultimately, Morrison dodges the very questions she raises. She starts the passage accepting responsibility for assassination, even if only of an unspecified "thing," but within two lines she transfers this responsibility to a land which seems to kill "of its own volition." Depicting people as passively acquiescing in brutalizations they, presumably, never initiated, she veers from social criticism to natural disaster. Even her acknowledgement that "we were wrong" ends up linked to "it doesn't matter. It is too late." Considering that *The Bluest Eye* was written during a period of race awareness and political activism, such an ending feels particularly negative.

In fact, an overview of Morrison's work suggests an ongoing malaise in this respect. In her second novel *Sula*, the use of Shadrach, the mad prophet of self-annihilation, to frame the disintegration of Medallion's Black Bottom promises an apocalypse which never happens, and by its ending echoes the resistance to closure evident in *The Bluest Eye*:

> "All that time, all that time, I thought I was missing Jude." And the loss pressed down on her chest and came up into her throat. "We was girls together," she said as though explaining something. "O Lord, Sula," she cried, "girl, girl, girlgirlgirl."
>
> It was a fine cry—loud and long—but it had no bottom and it had no top, just circles and circles of sorrow. (149)

The Song of Solomon and *Tar Baby* avoid such open-endedness, but only by focusing on those whose wealth discolors color and whose questionable myths of levitation claim to transcend economic and political disenfranchisement. That these two novels are more simply structured and, thus, more readable on the level of chronology and narrating viewpoint makes sense, given their remove from the pressing political concerns of black communities at the time of their publication. Their relative thematic safeness, it would seem, frees them to be direct. In all these respects *Beloved* is at once a new departure and a return. Its use of history is pointedly specific and anchored in protest, but its narrative procedures once again refract chronology, point-of-view, and stylistic directness so as to highlight the mediated nature of telling and the elusive process of reception. Here, in contrast with *The Song of Solomon* and *Tar Baby,* thematic anguish seems to call forth a more elaborate strategy of deflection.

While my use of "seem" above cautions that the novels at hand may not constitute the critical mass needed for sound generalization, the correlation between thematic risk and formal strategies of deflection in Morrison's work nonetheless raises important questions about her address to readers. For though Morrison sees her formal resistance to closure as a uniquely black aesthetic mode akin to black music (McKay 1983), and though she uses it as an opportunity to free readers to tap new capabilities within themselves (e.g. compassion for Cholly, Tate), the question also arises whether some of this deflection may not have something to do with the fact that Morrison is a black woman writer whose "implied reader," to borrow Wolfgang Iser's term, is educated, middle class and not infrequently white. That is, beyond questions of Afro-American art, at issue here are also questions of address as a personal and political, not just literary, practice. In this respect, Raymond Hedin's essay, "The Structuring of Emotion in Black American Fiction," is particularly illuminating, for Hedin argues persuasively that Afro-American novelists have traditionally turned to strategies of evasion and indirection in order to suppress or disguise racial anger (35–36).

That Hedin's analysis mainly focuses on earlier writers makes historical sense, and he is right to note that even in their novels a "revolutionary threat remains, held in check but not eliminated by the structuring context of plot and character" (42). However, his reading of *The Bluest Eye* is more positive than mine. He sees its form as clarifying Morrison's anger because it brings the causes of Pecola's suffering into sharp focus. "The coherence of Morrison's vision," he writes, "and the structure which parses out its logic into repeated patterns offer the reader no solace, no refuge from Morrison's anger" (50). Hedin is right about the anger; Morrison is much more direct and unrelenting than most of her predecessors. But I question his view that she brings the causes of Pecola's suffering into sharp focus and that her narrative offers us no refuge. Morrison locates too much of Pecola's suffering in the black community, while the luminous style and predictive backward loopings with which she mediates the plot work quite deliberately to provide solace.

Beloved, in contrast, works better; it distinguishes pointedly between white brutalization of black Americans and its intra-racist carry-overs. Cincinnati's black residents may hold diverse views of Sethe and the whites who caused such massive suffering to so many blacks, but their views are clear, and they are able to join in acts of resistance and recovery in ways the residents of Medallion do not quite match. (Exceptions in *The Bluest Eye* include Aunt Jimmy's friends, the prostitutes, and church women, but only peripherally to the main plot.) Still, while thematically this novel is clearer and more optimistic, formally it nonetheless offers solace by way of narrative strategies whose mediation continues to displace the pain and anger of being defined as "other." Ben Shan's comment that "a society is molded upon its epics, and . . . imagines in terms of its created things" (39) is worth noting in this connection, precisely because it urges awareness of the ideology inscribed in the artifacts we allow to shape and unite us. When reading any work, then, we must be conscious of the ways its form, not just its theme, molds us in its own image. We must note, finally, that *The Bluest Eye* exists within the power structures which control our lives. In this respect, Ben Shan anticipates Althusser: the contradictory forces at work in Morrison's writing reflect the contradictions at work in the society out of which she writes.

III

It is Ben Shan's reminder that society imagines in terms of its created things that brings me back to the revivalist tone of my title. In part, "Will the Circle be Unbroken?" registers my interest in Morrison's use of the seasons as a value-laden construct. But the initial impulse behind this choice was musical. Alluding to the song, "Will the Circle be Unbroken?", it pays tribute to Morrison's voice. For hers is, indeed, a powerfully regenerative voice that brings out the essence beneath the surface and the heritage which defines identity. It is, indeed, a voice that tells of circles of recurrent loss, but it also displaces the pain from the realm of the physical to that of the spiritual and, thus, edges towards redemption. The impulse behind my title, then, was the need to acknowledge the voice as regenerative, even in the face of the despair inscribed in the novel's cyclical structure and wrenching plot.

Only after completing a draft of this essay did I come across Henry Dumas' story "Will the Circle be Unbroken?", which uses the same title to signify a very different meaning. Though there is considerable irony in Dumas' reversal of racist exclusionary practices ("I'm sorry, but for your own safety we cannot allow you [in]," etc.), his story concerns internal power at least as much as the social structure in which that power gets enacted. For Dumas, that power has its source in Africa's timeless heritage. It is a force— a charmed circle—that grows out of shared understanding. The "vibration" which arises from it finds its voice in jazz music in general and in a mythic afro-horn in particular:

Inside the center of the gyrations is an atom stripped of time, black. The gathering of the hunters, deeper. Coming, laced in the energy of the sun. He is blowing. Magwa's hands. Reverence of skin. Under the single voice is the child of a woman, black. They are building back the wall, crumbling under the disturbance. (114)

For both Dumas and Morrison, the voice is the source of regeneration, and for both it is the interaction of diverse voices—diverse musical instruments—that complements the power of the single voice and makes reconstitution possible.[11] Yet despite this shared emphasis on the empowering origins of Afro-American identity and on the political imperative of collective action, Morrison and Dumas head in different directions. His story uses the circle as a metaphor for an unblemished and inviolable essence, while her novel uses the seasons' cyclicality to signal a trap. His afro-horn functions as a lethal but also as a clearly regenerative symbol, while her "miracle" of blue eyes functions ambivalently. Mediated as it is through a deflecting treatment of point-of-view and narrative reliability, and placed too late in the novel to allow for adequate recuperation of deferred judgment, it edges towards articulating defeat. The extended Soaphead chapter, previously anthologized as a short story in its own right, further separates the plot's ending from what leads up to it; it disrupts Claudia's narrative just at the point where one would expect her to gain new insight. Thus, while Dumas' "Will the Circle be Unbroken?" repossesses the song, my own use of this allusion echoes but also questions the oracular opacity of Morrison's narrative strategies.

The problem with Morrison's circles is, finally, that in *The Bluest Eye* circularity functions as a structuring metaphor which runs counter to other aspects of her text. The story-line and seasonal cyclicality posit an entrapment at odds with the empowering choral organization and eloquence of her writing. Of course, cyclicality is only one organizing metaphor among several here. Alongside it is a multi-voiced orchestration which does make powerful claims for the needs of the many, cumulative reiterations which do express great anger, and a Chinese-box structure which does insist on linking the specific to its context. In all these respects design signifies and signifies constructively. At the same time, though, the fatalism inscribed in the cyclical organization of this novel cannot be denied, especially given the way Morrison foregrounds the cleavage between one season and the next. The book's format sets the seasons apart, and at the opening of each section Claudia's narrative occurs in an indeterminate present tense, as if in a-temporal space. Each opening mythologizes its materials. Each season breaks with the preceding narration, and each promises a new beginning which, the subsequent narrative shows, offers no change. The problem with this design is that it severs events from their causes and holds back the possibility of recovery. The thematic urgency the text establishes about finding ways to escape the tyranny of racist values gets undermined by uncertainty.[12]

It is especially *The Bluest Eye*'s verbal exuberance that counters the skepticism inscribed in this seasonal metaphor. Morrison's syntax belies her fatalism. Her cadences spill into long sentences in which flexible syntactical structures enact the capacity for change. Her short sentences and sentence fragments are close systems, self-sufficient, well-placed, and punchy. Her descriptive passages are rich with images, especially organic ones, which make facts resonate with latent meanings, and her mythic allusions elevate the ordinary and ascribe to the insignificant epic scope. The overall impression such writing creates is of an echoing, shimmering, reverberating experience, where each utterance initiates an ever-expanding sequence of interrelations. Note, for example, the following passage:

> They come from Mobile. Aiken. From Newport News. From Marietta. From Meridian. And the sounds of these places in their mouths makes you think of love. When you ask them where they are from, they tilt their heads and say "Mobile" and you think you've been kissed. They say "Aiken" and you see a white butterfly glance off a fence with a torn wing. They say "Nagadoches" and you want to say "Yes, I will." You don't know what these towns are like, but you love what happens to the air when they open their lips and let the names ease out. (67)

The "they" Morrison describes here are a type; they are certain "brown girls" particularized in Geraldine—a character she condemns with special anger. Yet the writing in this passage mostly beautifies these women. It is a writing that sways with their sensuous voices and caresses their nuanced gestures. Mostly it is the information which emerges later that challenges this seduction, and even then the cadences and images of Morrison's prose continue to rehabilitate the facts.

Pauline's description of her lovemaking with Cholly is one of this novel's extraordinary passages. The rainbow metaphor she assigns to orgasm is, indeed, a covenant—a broken covenant, as it turns out, given the world she and Cholly inhabit, but also a circle opened and a provisional declaration of faith. Tapping the Bible's recurrent concern with broken covenants and new possibilities for regeneration, the metaphor suggests grace. The very language Morrison uses to describe Pauline's experience inscribes this affirmation. She transmutes Pauline's tactile and visual sensations into an eroticized prose free of grammatical inhibitions and revelling in counterpointed repetitions, delays, and variations evocative of Molly Bloom's soliloquy at the end

of *Ulysses*. Linked to Pauline's orgasm, this stylistic articulation of desire
is indeed erotic. But seen in relation to the rainbow metaphor, Morrison's
style here invokes the notion of *jouissance* in its full range of associations,
at once physical and metaphysical. In this respect, *The Bluest Eye* in general and the rainbow passage in particular anticipate Alice Walker's use of
Celie in *The Color Purple* (1982) as well as the work of Toni Cade Bambara,
Ntozake Shange, and Gloria Naylor. Pauline, Celie, and others would have
been socially and linguistically disenfranchised speakers were it not for their
author's retrieving Afro-American vernacular as a medium of empowerment
that runs counter to the normalcy posited by Dick's and Jane's parents and
their dog, Spot.

In short, *The Bluest Eye* counters the muting of Pecola's voice with the
empowerment of other voices in her community. Rather than make readers
restore diachrony so as to realize a historic dialectic (Willis 96), the novel
elicits a relational, "dialogic" reading (Bakhtin).[13] To Aunt Jimmy's friends,
Morrison ascribes a conversation spanning lifetimes of struggle, where the
blending of utterances orchestrates individual experiences into a multi-layered account which parallels her own work as a novelist:

> Their voices blended into a threnody of nostalgia about pain.
> Rising and falling, complex in harmony, uncertain in pitch, but
> constant in the recitative of pain. (109)

This musicalization of experience is Morrison's theme once more when
commenting on Cholly's epic journey in search of his father:

> The pieces of Cholly's life could become coherent only in the head
> of a musician. Only those who talk their talk through the gold of
> curved metal, or in the touch of black-and-white rectangles and
> taut skins and strings echoing from wooden corridors, could give
> true form to his life. Only they would know how to connect the
> heart of a red watermelon to the asafetida bag to the muscadine to
> the flashlight on his behind to the fists of money to the lemonade
> in a Mason jar to a man called Blue and come up with what all of
> that meant in joy, in pain, in anger, in love, and give it its final and
> pervading ache of freedom. Only a musician would sense, know,
> without even knowing that he knew, that Cholly was free. (125)

Morrison's writing registers this view of music as an expressive but also
clarifying medium formally as well as thematically. Here and in numerous other passages, including Pauline's rainbow and the full Aunt Jimmy section, the
very syntax builds up sequences of repetition and variation which lead readers

through a cumulative, patterned reception akin to listening. Morrison's very writing is a performance which celebrates the free play of language and the power of the voice to utter. Finally, it is her own virtuosity that guides readers, line by line, to affirmation. Thus, when she uses the Aunt Jimmy and Cholly episodes to explore the concept of freedom, her conclusions are questionable; the freedom of old age she bestows on rural black women and the "Godlike" freedom she grants Cholly when she leaves him with nothing left to lose entail such extreme bereavement that the benefits are hardly worth having. At the same time, the writing through which Morrison lays out this proposition is so sinuous and seductive that, like the "brown girls" from Mobile, Aiken, and Newport News, she makes us want to say, "Yes, I will."

This writing just about begs to be read aloud. Its diction, rhythms, and incremental patterning almost seem propelled by sound. Repeating key words, and stringing along sentences, clauses, and phrases which share syntactical structure and which do not always group into punctuated units, this writing creates an echo-chamber effect where the very fact of reiteration becomes all powerful. This is the "verbal delirium" Patricia Yaeger sees as women writers' linguistic resistance to the despair inscribed in plots of victimization, but it is also a verbal mode rooted in Afro-American secular and religious oral traditions. Though Morrison's roots in these traditions deserve the kind of close reading which this essay cannot undertake, it is important to note this specificity (O'Shaughnessy). Like a griot, preacher, or blues singer, Morrison uses inventories and variations to make her case. The richness of her language, organized as it is into infinitely expandable sequences, suggests a wealth of possibilities and an ungovernable verbal fecundity which belie the social desolation she depicts. Such regenerative writing is not about retrieving and explaining, as *The Bluest Eye*'s opening claims, but about saying as cure. Naming her ghosts and, indeed, ours, she diminishes their power over us. Embroidering on actuality as much as China, Poland, and Miss Marie do, she makes the speaker repossess the spoken.

The power of the voice to retrieve and re-shape is the moving force of *Beloved*, too, where the entire narrative is motivated by a process of reconstitution. Though *The Bluest Eye* lacks this controlling purpose, its overall effect is similar. Claudia captures this power when she describes her mother singing the blues:

> If my mother was in a singing mood, it wasn't so bad. She would sing about hard times, bad times, and somebody-done-gone-and-left-me times. But her voice was so sweet and her singing-eyes so melty I found myself longing for those hard times, yearning to be grown without "a thin di-i-ime to my name." I looked forward to the delicious time when "my man" would leave me, when I would "hate

at evening sun go down . . ." 'cause then I would know "my
left this town." Misery colored by the greens and blues in my
; voice took all of the grief out of the words and left me with
tion that pain was not only endurable, it was sweet. (24)

Describing women's pain as not only endurable but even sweet is hardly the
lesson to teach an adolescent girl. It presupposes stasis and advocates resigna-
tion, not change. However, as Claudia sees it, it is the singing voice, and nothing else, that colors misery and cleanses out the grief. Beyond naming and
mourning, singing proves an act of resistance. Turning to a long tradition of
women's blues, it is the empowering act, not the acceptance, that is Morrison's
focus. Linking Mrs. MacTeer to Bessie Smith, she celebrates the courage and
the imagination which allow one to re-possess one's experience.

IV

The relation Morrison's poeticized voice has to the dismantling operations of
her text and the relation between this dismantled structure and the exegetic
content of her story-line are at the heart of both the trouble and the delight
her writing creates for her readers. *The Bluest Eye,* like all novels, consists of
an interrelation of narrative elements (Fowler, 123–133). Characters, story-
line, structure, images, mythic allusions, syntax, diction, and more are all
parts of a patterned whole. The way they interact constitutes a system of
knowledge which centers neither on content alone nor on pure form, but on
the interpretive transactions each text's patterning lays out for its readers. In
the case of *The Bluest Eye,* this dynamic is key to both its strengths and its
equivocations. For while this novel's story-line is distressingly naturalistic
in its sordid subject-matter and fatalism,[14] and while its seasonal cyclicality
underscores this pessimism, the choral structuring of the novel, the a-temporal and often mythologizing quality of the narrative, and the fecundity of
Morrison's writing counter the despair with affirmation. Clearly, *The Bluest
Eye* does not suffer from a simple form and content contradiction. Rather,
a close reading shows that in this text it is the free-play of the constituting
parts that leads to tensions Morrison does not resolve.

One might argue that the elusiveness at work in Morrison's writing is inherent in the nature of language, where the fact that utterances are always other than that to which they refer forever severs the gesture from its subject. In
this sense, free-play is inevitable. Signifiers will never quite correlate with the
signified. Still, while this position is not inapplicable to Morrison, it does not
fully account for the specific effects of her writing. Writing which foregrounds
"narrative desire" is always friendly to linguistically-based deconstructive and
psychoanalytic readings, and one can certainly make a strong case for readings of *The Bluest Eye* that foreground its fragile place in the symbolic order as

key to its "ineffable" quality. But Morrison's writing is too specifically Afro-American in its subject matter and form to be cut off from its cultural and political specificity. Its invocation of a rich heritage which has long been the source of power and hope for Afro-Americans requires that we cherish that in her writing which resists assimilation into a universalizing reading. Seen from this perspective, the difficulties Morrison creates for her readers register a slippage in political ideology, not the shifty nature of the signifying process.

The Bluest Eye is, in fact, a composite of different sets of values which need to be understood historically, in that it embodies both the achievement and the equivocation of the society in which it originated. It is a revolutionary novel in the ways its form assaults conventions and empowers normally disenfranchised speakers. It is a remarkable novel, too, in the ways it "sings out like legends beneath our skin," as Audre Lorde puts it. At the same time, the skepticism it evinces concerning its own revolutionary message testifies to the constraints under which it came into being. Thus, seen in terms of Roland Barthes's definition of narrative sequence as "a logical succession of nuclei bound together by a relation of solidarity" (*Image* 101), it is the wavering of solidarity here that is ideologically important. On the one hand, the dismantling operations of this text refuse to lull conservative readers into a complacent acceptance of the *status quo* and cohere formally in their complexly counterpointed patterning. On the other hand, narrative cannot be drained of referentiality, and in this novel the referentiality of both content and form is at odds with itself. As a "fugued" composition (Barthes's term), *The Bluest Eye* inspires; as a referential construct—as a guide to the practical choices we make in our daily lives—*The Bluest Eye* equivocates.

Morrison's elusive strategies suggest, finally, one balanced tenuously between faith and despair, action and entrapment. In her later fiction, these extremes move towards resolution. Especially in *Beloved,* it is the word itself—the freedom to utter and the capacity to shape imagined possibilities—that provides a redemptive vision. The fact that these extremes are laid out so distinctly in *The Bluest Eye* is useful precisely because it helps us read Morrison's subsequent novels with a clearer grasp of the relation between form and ideology. The skepticism and even pessimism of *The Bluest Eye* cannot be denied, but neither can its richness. In one sense, this dialectic is inevitable. After all, this is not a utopian novel. It is no better than the society in which it germinated. Still, the book does offer a critique of our society; it does validate anger as an appropriate response to brutalizing inequalities; and it does normalize and dignify aspects of our humanity which we often deny. Affirming the imagination's ability to repossess chaos and create coherence, Morrison colors the misery she depicts with the blues and greens of her voice. The ideological hesitations in her writing must be acknowledged, but so, too, must the message of resilience and regeneration.

Notes

1. Special thanks to Mary Helen Washington, who inspired this work and taught me about Alaga Syrup and more. Thanks also to Martha Collins, Robert Crossley, and Pancho Savery, for their close reading of drafts, and to my students Joan Medeiros, Karen Waidron, and Carolyn Barbor, for sharing their research and unpublished writing on Morrison.

2. Though Morrison rejects modernist white male influence, her textual practice reveals affinities nonetheless. This essay argues that the two strains—modernist and Afro-American—interweave in her work (Wagner).

3. This understanding of desire—at once erotic and epistemological—is indebted to the work of Roland Barthes, Julia Kristeva, Teresa De Lauretis, and Stephen Heath. Though the writing of De Lauretis and Heath concerns specifically the cinematic apparatus, both see narrative desire as a function of movement which engages us in a process of counterpointing, withholding, and retotalizing.

4. As Morrison notes in the Tate interview, "When you get to the scene where the father rapes his daughter, which is as awful a thing, I suppose, as can be imagined, by the time you get there it's almost irrelevant because I want you to look at him and see his love for his daughter" (125).

5. Morrison herself emphasizes that she is a "black woman writer" (Caldwell). Cf. Barbara Smith's discussion of Blackburn's racist casting of this terminology (171). Recent work by Dasenbrock, Cheung, Messer-Davidow, et al models the application of cross-cultural theory and criticism to the analysis of strategies of resistance and emergence in narrative.

6. Pecola is named for Peola, the "tragic mulatta" character of Stahl's film, *Imitation of Life* (1934), and Sirk's remake (1959). In Morrison's treatment, she invokes Stahl's melodrama, not Sirk's harsh irony.

7. Cf. John Dos Passos's *U.S.A.* trilogy (1930, 1932, 1936). Note McDowell's excellent discussion of private and public address in "The Changing Same."

8. The urge to retrieve a community recurs in Morrison's work, but *Sula* and especially *The Bluest Eye* emphasize place, notably the South, as essential to community, in contrast with *Beloved*, where situation defines community, or *The Song of Solomon*, which Morrison describes as a book "driven by men" (McKay 417), and *Tar Baby*'s island as a fallen Eden. In all these, communities—notably female communities—function as sites of meaning.

9. Morrison's own method of composition accounts for this pattern. As she explains to both Bakerman and McKay, she starts writing with the ending already known, and loops backwards to fill in the gaps: "I always know the endings. . . . What I don't know when I begin is how the character is going to get there. I don't know the middle" (McKay 418). The method is inspirational, not causal.

10. Royster's objection that Claudia is too obtuse and pessimistic takes her for a more controlling narrator than she actually is. Claudia covers a lot of ground, but she is not the novel's pivotal consciousness. She is a narrator, not the narrator. She is a witness, but her role as a narrator is qualified by the interaction of the novel's diverse components. Cf. Genette's distinction between internal and external focalization ("Voice" 212–262) and Valerie Smith on linguistic community.

11. The theme recurs in Afro-American literature. See especially Baldwin's "Sonny's Blues" and Bambara's "Medley" and "May Man Bovanne."

12. Morrison's cyclical design recalls the similarly dead-end organization of Genet's *The Blacks* (1958, with Maya Angelou in its first American production 1961), Albee's *The Zoo Story* (1959), Baraka's *The Dutchman* (1964), and Peter Weiss's *Marat/Sade* (1965). In all of these works, cycicality signifies entrapment and generates anger, except that in the above plays violence becomes ritualized and obsessive, while Morrison's fiction tends to transmute anger into a "song"(Lorde).

13. Cf. Maxine Hong Kingston's *The Warrior Woman* (1975), Leslie Silko's *Ceremony* (1977), Ntozake Shange's *For Colored Girls who have considered Suicide/ when the Rainbow is Enuf* (1977), and Gloria Naylor's *The Women of Brewster Place* (1980). Cheung's discussion of *The Color Purple* and *The Warrior Woman* is especially relevant here. While the above suggests a compositional mode especially congenial to women of color, its affinity to the work of Virginia Woolf, Djuna Barnes, Monique Wittig, and Kathy Acker is worth noting.

14. Cf. Emile Zola, Jack London, Frank Norris, et al. For all its gloom, naturalist fiction has always been politically embattled.

WORKS CITED

Bakerman, Jane S. "Failures of Love: Female Initiation in the Novels of Toni Morrison." *American Literature* (1981): 541–563.

———. "The Seams Can't Show: An Interview with Toni Morrison." *Black American Literature Forum* 12:2 (1978): 56–60.

Bakhtin, Mikhail. "Dostoevsky's Polyphonic Novel and Its Treatment in Critical Literature," *Problems of Dostoevsky's Poetics*. Minneapolis: Minnesota University Press, 1984: pp. 5–46.

Barthes, Roland. *The Pleasure of the Text*. New York: Hill and Wang, 1975.

———. "Introduction to the Structural Analysis of Narratives," *Image-Music-Text*. New York: Hill and Wang, 1977: pp. 79–124.

Bishoff, Joan. "The Novels of Toni Morrison: Studies in Thwarted Sensitivity." *Studies in Black Literature* 6:3 (1975): pp. 21–23.

Cheung, King-Kok. "'Don't Tell': Imposed Silences in *The Color Purple* and *The Woman Warrior*," *PMLA* 103:2 (1988): pp. 162–73.

Christian, Barbara. *Black Feminist Criticism: Perspectives on Black Women Writers*. New York: Pergamon, 1985.

Dasenbrock, Reed Way. "Intelligibility and Meaninglessness in Multicultural Literature in English," *PMLA* 102:1 (1987): pp. 10–19.

Davis, Cynthia A. "Self, Society, and Myth in Toni Morrison's Fiction," *Contemporary Literature* 23:3 (1982): pp. 323–342.

De Lauretis, Teresa. "Desire in Narrative," *Alice Doesn't: Feminism, Semiotics, Cinema*. Bloomington: Indiana University Press, 1984: pp. 103–57.

Dumas, Henry. *Ark of Bones and Other Stories*. New York: Random House, 1974.

Fowler, Roger. *Linguistics and the Novel*. New York: Methuen, 1977.

Genette, Gerard. *Narrative Discourse: An Essay in Method*. Ithaca: Cornell University Press, 1980.

Heath, Stephen. "Narrative Space," *Questions of Cinema*. Bloomington: Indiana University Press, 1981: pp. 19–75.

Hedin, Raymond. "The Structuring of Emotion in Black American Fiction," *Novel: A Forum on Fiction* 16:1 (1982): pp. 35–54.

Kristeva, Julia. *Desire In Language: A Semiotic Approach to Literature and Art*. New York: Columbia University Press, 1980 (Esp. "The Bounded Text," pp. 36–63 and "The Novel as Polylogue," pp. 159–209).

Ling, Amy. "I'm Here: An Asian American Woman's Response," *New Literary History* 19:1 (1987): pp. 151–160.

Lorde, Audre. "*Sula*/A Review," *Amazon Quarterly* 2:3 (1974): pp. 28–30.

McDowell, Deborah E. "'The Changing Same': Generational Connections and Black Women Novelists," *New Literary History* 18:2 (1987): pp. 281–302.

———. "'The Self and the Other': Reading Toni Morrison's *Sula* and the Black Female Text." *Critical Essays on Toni Morrison*, Nellie Y. McKay, Ed. Boston: G. K. Hall & Co., 1988: pp. 77–90.

McKay, Nellie. "An Interview with Toni Morrison," *Contemporary Literature* 24:4 (1983): pp. 413–429.

———. "Response to 'The Philosophical Bases of Feminist Literary Criticisms,'" *New Literary History* 19:1 (1987): pp. 161–67.

———. "Introduction." *Critical Essays on Toni Morrison*, McKay, Ed. Boston: G. K. Hall & Co., 1988: pp. 1–15.

Messer-Davidow, Ellen. "The Philosophical Bases of Feminist Literary Criticisms," *New Literary History* 19:1 (1987): pp. 65–103.

Miner, Madonne M. "Lady No Longer Sings the Blues: Rape, Madness, and Silence in *The Bluest Eye*," *Conjuring: Black Women, Fiction, and Literary Tradition*, Marjorie Pryse and H. J. Spillers, Eds. Bloomington: Indiana University Press, 1985: pp. 176–91.

Morrison, Toni. *The Bluest Eye*. New York: Pocket Books, 1972 (Holt, 1970).

———. *Sula*. New York, Knopf, 1973.

———. *The Song of Solomon*. New York: Knopf, 1977.

———. *Tar Baby*. New York: Knopf, 1981.

———. *Beloved*. New York: Knopf, 1987.

O'Shaughnessy, Kathleen. "'Life life life life': The Community as Chorus in *The Song of Solomon*." *Critical Essays on Toni Morrison*, Nellie Y. McKay, Ed. Boston: G. K. Hall & Co., 1988: pp. 125–133.

Royster, Philip M. "*The Bluest Eye*." *First World* (Winter 1977): pp. 35–44.

Shan, Ben. *The Shape of Content*. Cambridge: Harvard University Press, 1957.

Smith, Barbara. "Towards a Black Feminist Criticism," *The New Feminist Criticism: Essays on Women, Literature, Theory*, Elaine Showalter, Ed. New York: Pantheon, 1985: pp. 168–85.

Smith, Valerie, "The Quest for and Discovery of Identity in Toni Morrison's *Song of Solomon*," *Southern Review* (1985): pp. 721–32.

Tate, Claudia, Ed. "Toni Morrison" [interview], *Black Women Writers at Work*. New York: Continuum, 1983: pp. 117–31.

Wagner, Linda W. "Mastery of Narrative," *Contemporary American Women Writers*, Catherine Rainwater and William J. Scheick, Eds. Lexington: University of Kentucky Press, 1985: pp. 190–205.

Willis, Susan. "Eruptions of Funk: Historicizing Toni Morrison," *Specifying: Black Women Writing the American Experience*. Madison: University of Wisconsin Press, 1987.: pp. 83–109, 174–79.

Yaeger, Patricia. *Honey-Mad Women: Emancipatory Strategies in Women's Writing*. New York: Columbia University Press, 1988.

SHARON L. GRAVETT

Toni Morrison's The Bluest Eye:
An Inverted Walden?

When Henry David Thoreau embarked on his two-year sojourn at Walden Pond, he remarked, "it is difficult to begin without borrowing, but perhaps it is the most generous course thus to permit your fellow-men to have an interest in your enterprise. The owner of the axe, as he released his hold on it, said that it was the apple of his eye; but I returned it sharper than I received it."[1] In some ways, this passage is a graceful acknowledgment of the necessity of borrowing, whether it be to build a cabin or to write a literary work. Yet, more than that, Thoreau's choice of an axe as the implement to be borrowed reveals the two-pronged nature of his work. An axe, while a marvelous tool for construction, serves equally well for destruction. Thus, this passage not only indicates Thoreau's willingness to accept the aid of such influential neighbors as Ralph Waldo Emerson, but his desire to deny or even negate it as well.

A similar maneuver is at work in Toni Morrison's 1970 novel, *The Bluest Eye*. While Morrison's account of the black community in Lorain, Ohio seems, on the surface, far removed from Thoreau's experiences at Walden Pond nearly a hundred years earlier, a closer look reveals the striking similarities between them in both theme and structure. It indeed seems possible that Morrison has done some borrowing from her neighbor Thoreau since she shares many of his same concerns[2]; however, also like Thoreau, she uti-

West Virginia University Philological Papers, 1992; 38: pp. 201–11. © West Virginia University.

lizes her influences both constructively and destructively. Simultaneously, she updates Thoreau's message to her own era while demonstrating its ineffectualness.

Structurally, *Walden* and *The Bluest Eye* share a marked similarity; both works are arranged on the cycle of the year with each season serving as a major section. The progression of the seasons allows each author to take full advantage of the natural cycles of birth and death.[3] Thoreau records the changes in nature at Walden Pond from high summer to the frozen death of winter to rebirth in the spring and comments on how these changes mirror stages in human growth and existence. Similarly, Claudia MacTeer, the narrator of *The Bluest Eye*, sees the cycle of the year moving from the dying season of fall to fall again, which serves as an ironic counterpoint to the tale of Pecola Breedlove, who comes of age, is raped and impregnated by her father Cholly, goes mad, and loses her baby. Both authors use the seasons with their patterns and changes to comment on similar or ironic developments within the human community. However, while Walden concludes in the glorious rebirth of spring, *The Bluest Eye* ends in the blasted hopes of a life that has failed to bloom. Morrison would seem to be reversing the inherently optimistic structure of Walden, focusing instead on the death of life and hope rather than on rebirth.

This failure to come to fruition is an important theme in *The Bluest Eye* as Claudia and Frieda MacTeer, Pecola's only two friends, planted marigold seeds in the hopes that Pecola's unborn and unwanted child would live. Claudia and Frieda believed that "*if we planted the seeds, and said the right words over them, they would blossom, and everything would be all right.*"[4] The MacTeers hoped that the fecundity of one set of seeds would ensure the fecundity of another. Unfortunately, the seeds that the sisters planted with such hope never came up. This failure meant more than a loss of flowers; it also meant a loss of many of the values they wanted to find in their community such as "sincerity, truth, simplicity, faith, innocence, and the like" (Walden 164), values that Thoreau had also wanted to encourage in his community. Thoreau, too, had labored long and hard in his bean fields, "Not that I wanted to eat. . . but, perchance, as some must work in fields if only for the sake of tropes and expression, to serve as a parable-maker one day" (162). Like Claudia and Frieda, Thoreau saw the activity of planting as a metaphorical act, a hope that the virtues lacking in his society could be cultivated with the proper care.

Unfortunately for both Thoreau and the MacTeer sisters, none of them saw their seeds, or their desires, come to fruition. Thoreau laments, ". . . I am obliged to say to you, Reader, that the seeds which I planted, if indeed they were the seeds of those virtues were wormeaten or had lost their vitality, and so did not come up" (164). Claudia also mourns: "*Cholly Breedlove is dead; our innocence too. The seeds shriveled and died; her baby too*" (9). In both cases, the optimism of planting is replaced by the despair of failure. The seeds, which carried so much promise, fail to take root and grow. In this respect, *The Bluest Eye* continues the message of Walden rather than subverts it. Both works mourn the loss of innocence and hopefulness.

Not only do the seeds planted by both Thoreau and the MacTeer sisters perish in inhospitable soil, but those plants that have already taken root are not nurtured and cherished as they should be. "The finest qualities of our nature," comments Thoreau, "like the bloom on fruits, can be preserved only by the most delicate handling. Yet we do not treat ourselves nor one another thus tenderly" (6) In *The Bluest Eye*, Pecola Breedlove is the perfect example of a young plant whose rough treatment at the hands of her family and her society thwarts her continued growth. By the end of the novel, unable to cope with all the trauma in her life and the rejection by her community, Pecola "spent her days, her tendril, sap-green days, walking up and down, up and down, her head jerking to the beat of a drummer so distant only she could hear" (158).

Sensitive and vulnerable, Pecola has been so neglected and abused by those around her that she eventually retreats into madness, safe from those who had told her she was ugly and unwanted; her individuality has not been prized but scorned. There is no tolerance of the kind Thoreau counsels in *Walden:* "if a man does not keep pace with his companions, perhaps it is because he hears a different drummer. Let him step to the music which he hears, however measured or far away" (326). By the end of *The Bluest Eye*, Pecola is indeed marching to the beat of a different drummer but it is a forced rather than a voluntary march. Because her "difference" is not tolerated, she eventually is pushed totally outside of society.

In its rush to ensure conformity, society often mows down those who do not meet its rigid standards.[5] As authors, both Thoreau and Morrison seek to warn people of the dangers that such a rigid adherence to society's dictates can pose. They write to their specific communities, in Thoreau's words, in order to "wake their neighbors up."[6]

Perhaps the basic difficulty both authors see is best pinpointed in Thoreau's famous passage:

> The mass of men lead lives of quiet desperation. What is called resignation is confirmed desperation. . . . A stereotyped but unconscious despair is concealed even under what are called the games and amusements of mankind. (8)

This despair is vividly illustrated in Walden in the struggles of the individual to come to grips with the often oppressive standards of the prevailing culture. In *The Bluest Eye,* this struggle takes shape as the black community endeavors to accept the standards imposed by white society. Interestingly enough, these clashes often take place in the seemingly trivial area of the games and amusements that Thoreau had earlier identified. For example, even in the candy that she chooses, Pecola reveals her subjugation to societally imposed norms. Her favorite is a Mary Jane, not because of its taste, but because of its packaging:

> Each pale yellow wrapper has a picture on it. A picture of little Mary Jane, for whom the candy is named. Smiling white face. Blond hair in gentle disarray, blue eyes looking at her out of a world of clean comfort. . . . To cat the candy is somehow to eat the eyes, eat Mary Jane. Love Mary Jane. Be Mary Jane. (43)

Since Pecola has seen firsthand that little white girls have the acceptance, and approval of society, she seeks desperately, in any way that she can, to be close to them.

Pecola shows a similar fondness for the white movie stars who had also, garnered society's approbation. She particularly likes Shirley Temple and even drinks large quantities of milk just to see Shirley's smiling face at the bottom of her favorite mug. Pecola comes by this tendency naturally; her mother Pauline was also enamored of the movies, even going so far as trying to emulate one of her favorite movie stars. Pauline comments, *"I 'member one time I went to see Clark Gable and Jean Harlow. I fixed my hair up like I'd seen hers on a magazine. A part on the side, with one little curl on my forehead. It looked just like her. Well, almost just like"* (917). The irony of this scene is almost painful. There she sits in the movie theater, a black pregnant woman trying to look like Jean Harlow. It is just as heartbreaking to see her daughter wishing to be Mary Jane or Shirley Temple.

Pecola and Mrs. Breedlove cannot ever achieve their desires, and their pursuit prohibits them from ever appreciating their own beauty and self-worth. The notions that they imbibe from the dominant culture make it impossible for them to accept the realities of their own lives. Pauline Breedlove remembers, *"The onliest time I be happy seem like was when I was in the picture show.... White men taking such good care of they women, and they all dressed up in big clean houses with the bathtubs in the same room with the toilet. Them pictures gave me a lot of pleasure, but it made coming home hard, and looking at Cholly hard"* (97). Rather than adapt to her world, Pauline learns from the movies to reject it, and she retreats into her role as housekeeper for a wealthy white family, the Fishers. At the Fisher home, she finds the orderly but sterile life that the movies present. Rather than loving and valuing her own family, she pampers the Fisher children. She even chooses to comfort one of the Fisher children rather than Pecola when Pecola accidentally knocks a cobbler off the counter on a visit to the Fisher home. By accepting the dominant views of society, Pauline neglects the real possibilities in her own life.

Pecola, of course, convinced of her own ugliness by both her mother and society, eventually retreats into madness, finally believing that she has obtained the blue eyes for which she had prayed.[7] This predicament is exactly the one about which Thoreau was trying to warn his friends and neighbors in Concord. "For the most part," he observes, "we are not where we are, but in a false position. Through an infirmity of our natures, we suppose a case, and put ourselves into it, and hence are in two cases at the same time, and it is doubly difficult to get out" (327). This comment proves peculiarly apt for Pecola as she finds it impossible to exist both as her real self and the self society wants her to be, so she literally splits in two by the end of the novel, carrying on a conversation between her two discordant halves.[8] The cost of conformity is much too high for Pecola.

The only major characters who refuse to pay this price are the two MacTeer sisters. Claudia, in particular, serves as an appropriate narrator of the novel because she has yet to accept the idea that she should be forced to live by standards that will deny her own sense of self. Because of her youth, Claudia has escaped the forces that have already shaped adult behavior. This trait, unique to the young, is one that Thoreau had also remarked on. He points out:

> By closing the eyes and slumbering, and consenting to be deceived by shows, men establish and confirm their daily life of routine and habit every where, which still is built on purely illusory foundations. Children, who play life, discern its true law and relations more clearly than men, who fail to live it worthily, but who think they are wiser by experience, that is, by failure. (96)

Still untrained in society's mores and expectations, Claudia and Frieda have not yet succumbed to its restrictions. The most prominent example in the novel of Claudia's refusal to accept acknowledged norms is her dislike of the baby dolls that everyone else idolizes:

> Adults, older girls, shops, magazines, newspapers, window signs all the world had agreed that a blue-eyed, yellow-haired, pink-skinned doll was what every girl child treasured. "Here," they said, "this is beautiful, and if you are on this day 'worthy' you may have it." . . . . I could not love it. But I could examine it to see what it was that all the world said was lovable. (20)

Rather than playing with the dolls, Claudia dismembers them, trying to discover the secret of their attractiveness. In a similar way, Thoreau tried to dismantle the preconceptions of his society, seeking to discern what the "grossest groceries" (12) necessary to his existence were.

Throughout *The Bluest Eye*, Claudia continues to question society's values and to see their danger to herself. She understands that this valuation of foreign ideals of beauty detracts from an acknowledgment of individual beauty or self-worth. Claudia demonstrates her awareness of this understanding in her encounter with Maureen Peal, a "high yellow dream-child" (52), who embodies all the attributes valued by society. Even at her young age, Claudia realizes that ". . . Maureen Peal was not the Enemy and not worthy of such intense hatred. The *Thing* to fear was the *Thing* that made her beautiful and not us" (62).

The "thing" that made Maureen Peal beautiful was her complete assimilation into the prevailing expectations of white culture. She drank and liked white milk, her favorite film was *Imitation of Life*, and she loved Betty Grable. Significantly, Maureen was also beautiful, not only because she accepted these icons of white culture, but also because she could afford them. She has the money to buy the perfectly coordinated wardrobe and the occasional ice-cream cone after school. The dominant culture achieves and maintains its prominence because of its wealth; hence, the values it promotes tend to be monetary ones. Those unable to afford the material lifestyle society values are ruthlessly pushed aside. The Breedloves, for example, are convinced of their own ugliness because they cannot purchase the items that society considers beautiful; this preoccupation with the things that money can buy not only reminds them of their own powerlessness, but it also prevents them from focusing on things that may possess values other than monetary.

Claudia MacTeer, on the other hand, is not so absorbed in material values. For instance, while others believe they should give her lavish gifts for Christmas, Claudia thinks, "Had any adult with the power to fulfill my desires taken me seriously and asked me what I wanted, they would have known that I did not want to have anything to own, or to possess any object. I wanted rather to feel something on Christmas day" (21). Her greatest wish was not for baby dolls or candy but for feelings of family, security, warmth, and aesthetic appreciation. In this respect, Claudia is remarkably like Thoreau who treasured his neighbors' farms not because of their market value but because of the beauty they possessed: "I have frequently seen a poet withdraw, having enjoyed the most valuable part of a farm, while the crusty farmer supposed that he had got a few wild apples only" (82). Thoreau's "Economy" includes far more than a mere monetary rendering of value.

Thus, Morrison in *The Bluest Eye* continues Thoreau's tradition in *Walden* by offering a critique of her society which crushes individuals by forcing adherence to its economic and social imperatives. Also, like Thoreau, Morrison also tries to show that other ways of life are possible, in the person of Claudia MacTeer. A significant difference, however, exists between Thoreau's presentation of himself and Morrison's of Claudia. While Walden celebrates the freedom to choose a lifestyle not in conformity with the expectations of society, *The Bluest Eye* shows the dire consequences for those who cannot conform. This lack of conformity is not a choice but the result of marginalization. Despite his nonconformity, Thoreau was granted a considerable degree of latitude by his society. After all, he was white, male, and Harvard-educated; while his friends and neighbors may not have understood him, he was tolerated and free to make his own choices.

Morrison's characters, however, have no such flexibility. Their race and their gender already exclude them from many possible choices. Claudia notes, "Being a minority in both caste and class, we moved about anyway on the hem of life, struggling to consolidate our weaknesses and hang on, or to creep singly, up into the major folds of the garment" (18). Claudia's vision of her place in society differs substantially from the one that Thoreau, in a similar image, sees for himself and his readers. Imagining his work as a coat, he writes, "I trust that none will stretch the seams in putting on the coat, for it may do good service to him whom it fits" (4). While Thoreau sees himself a tailor endeavoring to fashion a different kind of coat for his reader-customers, Claudia views herself as unable to assume either of these roles in her society. Because she is black and female, she cannot choose to be different; she already is. She need go to no extreme lengths, like building her own house by a pond, to demonstrate her outcast status. Here, Morrison deconstructs the traditional American romantic belief in the power and possibility of the individual. Such prerogatives, she asserts, are blatantly unattainable for black women.

This pessimism about the potential for change accounts for the variation in the endings of *The Bluest Eye* and *Walden*. Thoreau chooses to end his account of his experiences in the spring, the season of rebirth. Even though his seeds have failed in the present, he hopes that they, like Walden Pond itself and the beautiful bug that emerges from a kitchen table years after its egg was deposited in an apple tree, will eventually come to life. He continues to believe that his seed, his work, will take hold in generations of subsequent readers and inspire them to heed his lessons. The last lines of Walden proclaim:

> I do not say that John or Jonathan will realize all this; but such is
> the character of that morrow which mere lapse of time can never

make to dawn. The light which puts out our eyes is darkness to us. Only that day dawns to which we are awake. There is more day to dawn. The sun is but a morning star. (333)

No such hope seems to exist at the end of *The Bluest Eye*. Having watched Pecola's destructive course, Claudia despairs that anything will ever change:

I talk about how I did not plant the seeds too deeply, how it was the fault of the earth, the land, of our town. I even think now that the land of the entire country was hostile to marigolds that year. This soil is bad for certain kinds of flowers. Certain seeds it will not nurture, certain fruit it will not bear, and when the land kills of its own volition, we acquiesce and say the victim had no right to live. We are wrong, of course, but it doesn't matter. It's too late. At least on the edge of my town, among the garbage and the sunflowers of my town, it's much, much, too late. (60)

The Bluest Eye does appear to invert the conclusion of *Walden*. However, such a conclusion does not do justice to the complexity of either work. Thoreau's seeming optimism at the end of *Walden* is a defiant gesture, an undefeated hope that maybe, someday, conditions could be different despite the failure of his project in the present.[9] Similarly, while Claudia despairs over the destruction of young Pecola Breedlove, her awareness of the forces that destroy Pecola and her ability to articulate them indicates that all is not lost. As long as people are able to bear witness to the failures of society and are unafraid to speak or write the truths they perceive, perhaps hope still does exist for the future(Since Claudia has survived to tell her story, maybe her seeds have not failed after all. Thus, even the endings of these two works bear more affinities than a first reading indicates.)

Morrison may indeed be a true neighbor of Thoreau's after all. While she has lived in and written about a community far different from that of nineteenth-century Concord, Massachusetts, Morrison's concerns remain quite similar. Although, in using her axe, she has not only constructed an edifice akin to Thoreau's, but, at the same time, also torn his down by showing how issues of gender and race undermine his message, yet, like the sage of Concord, Morrison truly did return his axe sharper than she borrowed it.

NOTES

1. Henry David Thoreau, *Walden, The Writings of Henry D. Thoreau*, ed. J. Lyndon Shanley (Princeton, NJ: Princeton University Press, 1988): pp. 40–41.

2. Although I have located no comparisons between Morrison and Thoreau in any of the criticism, some work is beginning to be done on her in regard to other figures in the American Renaissance. Terry Otten in *The Crime of Innocence in the Fiction of Toni Morrison* (Columbia and London: University of Missouri Press, 1989) compares Morrison to Nathaniel Hawthorne.

3. Thomas H. Fick sees the seasonal imagery as deriving from T.S. Eliot's *Waste Land*: "*The Bluest Eye* is framed by the narrator's brooding recollection of a wasteland, and the seasons which title the major sections—'Autumn,' 'Winter,' 'Spring,' and 'Summer'—mark off a parody of rebirth and growth. In 'the thin light of spring' (27) Pecola Breedlove is raped by her drunken father (a cruel sort of breeding indeed), and in summer, pregnant, she goes mad after the equivalent of Eliot's Mme. Sosostris works a phony spell to give her blue eyes" ("Toni Morrisons's 'Allegory of the Cave': Movies, Consumption, and Platonic Realism in *The Bluest Eye*, " *Journal of the Midwest Modern Language Association* 22.1 (Spring 1989): p. 10.

4. Toni Morrison, *The Bluest Eye* (New York: Washington Square Press, 1970): p. 9.

5. The dire results of such a practice are predicted in *Walden*:
Men have an indistinct notion that if they keep up this activity of joint stocks and spades long enough all will at length ride somewhere in next to no time, and for nothing, but though a crowd rushes for the depot, and the conductor shouts "All aboard!" when the smoke is blown away and the vapor condensed, it will be perceived that a few are riding, but the rest are run over,—and it will be called, and will be, "A melancholy accident." (53)

6. In the opening of *Walden*, Thoreau proclaims, "I would fain say something, not so much concerning the Chinese and Sandwich Islanders as you who read these pages, who am said to live in New England; something about your condition or circumstances in this world, in this town, what it is, whether it can be improved as well as not" (4). Similarly, Morrison directs her message to the members of her community. She told Thomas LeClair:
I write what I have recently begun to call village literature, fiction that is really for the village, for the tribe. . . . I think long and carefully about what my novels ought to do. They should clarify the roles that have become obscured; they ought to identify those things in the past that are useful and those things that are not, and they ought to give nourishment (in Thomas LeClair, "'The Language Must Not Sweat': A Conversation with Toni Morrison," *The New Republic* 21 March 1981: p. 26).

7. In *Walden*, Thoreau observes that "wherever a man goes, men will pursue and paw him with their dirty institutions, and, if they can, constrain him to belong to their desperate odd-fellow society" (71). Pauline is not the only one forced into such an odd community. Morrison also writes of the "particular brown girls" like Geraldine who adapt completely to the ways of white society and deny their own individuality, their own funkiness: "Wherever it erupts, this Funk, they wipe it away; where it crusts, they dissolve it; wherever it it drips, flowers, or clings, they find it and fight it until it dies"(68). Geraldine is so wrapped up in this battle against funkiness that she fails to see the devastating effect of her behavior on her son, who directs his anger not at his powerful mother, but at things that cannot strike back at him—him mother's beloved cat and Pecola Breedlove.

8. This double consciousness of a self that conforms to the dictates of society and one that realizes its duplicity is a staple of American literature. Thoreau

remarks that ". . . [I] am sensible of a certain doubleness by which I can stand as remote from myself as from another. However intense my experience, I am conscious of the presence and criticism of a part of me, which, as it were, is not part of me, but spectator, sharing no experience, but taking note of it" (35). Walt Whitman in "Song of Myself" similarly proclaims, "Apart from the pulling and hauling stands what I am,/Stands amused, complacent, compassionating, idle, unitary,/looks down, is erect, or bends an arm on an impalpable certainrest,/Looking down with side-curved head curious what will come next,/Both in and out of the game and watching and wondering at it" (*Leaves of Grass, Comprehensive Readers Edition, The Collected Writings of Wait Whitman*, ed. Harold W. Blodgett and Sculley Bradley [New York: New York University Press, 1965]: p. 32).

This notion of a double self also has particular relevance in the black community, as W.E.B. DuBois observes in *The Souls of Black Folk* (Chicago: A.C. McClurg & Co., 1935):

> It is a peculiar sensation, this double-consciousness, this sense of always looking at one's self through the eyes of others, of measuring one's soul by the tape of a world that looks on in amused contempt and pity. One ever feels this twoness—an American, a Negro; two souls, two thoughts, two unreconciled strivings, two warring ideas in one dark body, whose dogged strength alone keeps it from being torn asunder. (3)

9. Sherman Paul in *The Shores of America: Thoreau's Inward Exploration* (Urbana: University of Illinois Press, 1958) comments, "By 1854 the Walden experience had been altered not only by the *Journal* materials Thoreau added until the last moment but by the lengthening perspective of despair. Education by failure, determined now by conscious endeavor to find the way back to his golden age, his affirmation in *Walden* was that of one who had known the darkness but would not submit, who took instead the last refuge of optimism, the faith in faith itself"(256).

JANE KUENZ

The Bluest Eye: *Notes on History, Community, and Black Female Subjectivity*

In Toni Morrison's *The Bluest Eye*, the Breedloves' storefront apartment
is graced overhead by the home of three magnificent whores, each a tribute to Morrison's confidence in the efficacy of the obvious. The novel's
unhappy convergence of history, naming, and bodies—delineated so subtly
and variously elsewhere—is, in these three, signified most simply and most
crudely by *their* bodies and *their* names: Poland, China, the Maginot Line.
With these characters, Morrison literalizes the novel's overall conflation of
black female bodies as the sites of fascist invasions of one kind or another,
as the terrain on which is mapped the encroachment and colonization of
African-American experiences, particularly those of its women, by a seemingly hegemonic white culture. *The Bluest Eye* as a whole documents this
invasion—and its concomitant erasure of specific local bodies, histories, and
cultural productions—in terms of sexuality as it intersects with commodity
culture. Furthermore, this mass culture and, more generally, the commodity capitalism that gave rise to it, is in large part responsible—through its
capacity to efface history—for the "disinterestedness" that Morrison condemns throughout the novel. Beyond exemplifying this, Morrison's project
is to rewrite the specific bodies and histories of the black Americans whose
positive images and stories have been eradicated by commodity culture. She
does this formally by shifting the novel's perspective and point of view, a

African American Review, Volume 27, Number 3; Fall 1993: pp. 421–31. © 1993 Jane
Kuenz.

97

narrative tactic that enables her, in the process, to represent black female subjectivity as a layered, shifting, and complex reality.

The disallowance of the specific cultures and histories of African-Americans and black women especially is figured in *The Bluest Eye* primarily as a consequence of or sideline to the more general annihilation of popular forms and images by an ever more all-pervasive and insidious mass culture industry. This industry increasingly disallows the representation of any image not premised on consumption or the production of normative values conducive to it. These values are often rigidly tied to gender and are race-specific to the extent that racial and ethnic differences are not allowed to be represented. One lesson from history, as Susan Willis reiterates, is that "in mass culture many of the social contradictions of capitalism appear to us as if those very contradictions had been resolved" ("I Shop" 183). Among these contradictions we might include those antagonisms continuing in spite of capitalism's benevolent influence, along the axes of economic privilege and racial difference. According to Willis, it is because "all the models [in mass cultural representation] are white"—either in fact or by virtue of their status as "replicants . . . devoid of cultural integrity"—that the differences in race or ethnicity (and class, we might add) and the continued problems for which these differences are a convenient excuse *appear* to be erased or made equal "at the level of consumption" ("I Shop" 184). In other words, economic, racial, and ethnic difference is erased and replaced by a purportedly equal ability to consume, even though what is consumed are more or less competing versions of the same white image.

There is evidence of the presence and influence of this process of erasure and replacement throughout *The Bluest Eye*. For example, the grade school reader that prefaces the text was (and in many places still is) a ubiquitous, mass-produced presence in schools across the country. Its widespread use made learning the pleasures of Dick and Jane's commodified life dangerously synonymous with learning itself. Its placement first in the novel makes it the pretext for what is presented after: As the seeming given of contemporary life, it stands as the only visible model for happiness and thus implicitly accuses those whose lives do not match up. In 1941, and no less so today, this would include a lot of people. Even so, white lower-class children can at least more easily imagine themselves posited within the story's realm of possibility. For black children this possibility might require a double reversal or negation: Where the poor white child is encouraged to forget the particulars of her present life and look forward to a future of prosperity—the result, no doubt, of forty years in Lorain's steel mills—a black child like Pecola must, in addition, see herself, in a process repeated throughout *The Bluest Eye*, in (or as) the body of a white little girl In other words, she must not see *herself* at all. The effort required to do this and the damaging results of it are illustrated typographically in the repetition of the Dick-and-Jane story first without punctuation or capitalization, and then without punctuation, capitalization, or spacing.

Perhaps one function of the mass deployment of these stories was in fact to raise hopes for a better future in order to counteract the oppressiveness of the present and, in the process, to delimit the chance of dissatisfaction or unrest and encourage unquestioning labor at the same time. If so, it also tempts, as these tactics always do, the opposite conclusion: The comparison of their lives to Dick and Jane's seemingly idyllic ones will breed, among those unaccounted for in mass culture's representations, resentment and class consciousness instead. That this is not the result for most of the characters in *The Bluest Eye*, as it is not for most people in general, bespeaks the extent to which mass culture has made the process of self-denial a *pleasurable* experience.[1] Indeed, as I hope to show later, this process is explicitly sexual in *The Bluest Eye* and offers, particularly for women, the only occasion for sexual pleasure in the novel.

As noted above, interaction with mass culture for anyone not represented therein, and especially for African-Americans, frequently requires abdication of self or the ability to see oneself in the body of another. The novel's most obvious and pervasive instance of this is in the seemingly endless reproduction of images of feminine beauty in everyday objects and consumer goods: white baby dolls with their inhumanly hard bodies and uncanny blue eyes, Shirley Temple cups, Mary Jane Candies, even the clothes of "dream child" Maureen Peal, which are stylish precisely because they suggest Shirley Temple cuteness and because Claudia and Frieda recognize them as such. But Claudia and her sister can recognize "the *Thing* that made [Maureen] beautiful and not [them]" (62) only in terms of its *effects* on other people. Despite knowing that they are "nicer, brighter," they cannot ignore how "the honey voices of parents and aunts, the obedience in the eyes of [their] peers, the slippery light in the eyes of [their] teachers" (61–62) all pour out to the Maureen Peals of the world and not to them. From the responses of other people to girls like Maureen and others for whom Shirley Temple is the model, the sisters learn the *fact* of their own lack, variously identified as ugliness or "unworthiness," if not the essence of it. "What was the secret?" Claudia asks, "What did we lack? Why was it important? And so what?" (62)

Claudia's body, much more so than her sister's, has yet to be completely socialized in the process Frigga Haug calls "female sexualization." By this, Haug means both the production of femininity through the competent performance of feminine skills (including how to hold, move, and dress the body) and the reproduction of subordination within and on women's bodies as evidenced in the gradual "sexualization" of various body parts (for example, hair or legs) as girls mature. This process—inevitably modified, as *The Bluest*

Eye indicates, by both race and class—results in bodies that are always the site of multiple discourses circling around and ultimately comprising what we call "femininity" or, as it is generally construed, "the sexual." Claudia's confusion about the source of her failure to arouse "honey voices" and "slippery light" indicates that, though she is catching on quickly, she has yet to experience her body as the alienated entity Haug describes. She is still at the level of sensation, not prohibition or enforced definition: Instead of "asking the right questions" about her sister's near molestation, for example, Claudia wants to know what it feels like to have breasts worth touching and to have them touched (79).

The innocence of this question parallels the delight with which Claudia revels in her own body's myriad substances and smells. While women like Geraldine are quick to dispatch with "funk" wherever it "crusts" (68), Claudia is fascinated with her own body's sometimes graphically nauseating materiality: She is captivated by the menstrual blood her sister hurries to wash away; she studies her own vomit, admires the way it "[clings] to its own mass, refusing to break up and be removed" (13); she abhors the "dreadful and humiliating absence of dirt [and] the irritable, unimaginative cleanliness" (21) that accompanies it; she remembers the year recounted in the novel as a time when she and Frieda "were still in love with [themselves and] . . . felt comfortable in [their] skins, enjoyed the news that [their] senses released to [them], admired [their] dirt, cultivated [their] scars, and could not comprehend this unworthiness" (62) that distinguishes them from Maureen and is already overwhelming Pecola.

The older Claudia attributes this ease with her body to her youth and admits that she eventually succumbs to the pleasures of dominant discourse and its definitions of "femininity." Speaking of Shirley Temple, she says, "Younger than both Frieda and Pecola, I had not yet arrived at the turning point in the development of my psyche which would allow me to love her" (19). She goes on explicitly to equate "worshiping" Shirley Temple with "delighting" in cleanliness (22). *The Bluest Eye* suggests that this "development"—the sexualization of Claudia's body (changes both in it and in how she experiences it) and the simultaneous transformation of her psyche is learned and achieved through commodities like the Shirley Temple cups that proscribe appearance and behavior in accordance with the images they project. Claudia learns to "love" Shirley Temple when she learns to identify herself *as* Shirley Temple, as a complete person—limited as that is for women in our culture to some variation of "the sexual." Moreover, femininity and "the sexual" can be produced and reproduced as *commodities*, as Pecola's belief that she can simply acquire blue eyes indicates. The mass dissemination of these images of femininity in American society was and is among the primary mechanisms by which women are socialized and sexualized in this country. It is no accident that

Morrison links many of these images of properly sexualized white women to the medium of film which, in 1941, was increasingly enabled technologically to represent them and, because of the growth of the Hollywood film industry, more likely to limit the production of alternate images.

The effect of the constant circulation of the faces of, for example, Ginger Rogers, Greta Garbo, Jean Harlow, and, again, Shirley Temple is to reintroduce and exaggerate, as it does for Pauline Breedlove, "the most destructive ideas in the history of human thought" (97)—romantic love and physical beauty, each defined according to what they exclude and each destructive to the extent that they are made definitionally unavailable. After waiting out two pregnancies in the dark shadows of the silver screen, Pauline "was never able . . . [again] to look at a face and not assign it some category in the scale of absolute beauty" which she had "absorbed in full" from the movies (97). Among these faces to which she can't help but assign a predetermined value is her own, ironically made less acceptable by her Jean Harlow hairstyle because of the rotten tooth that contradicts it. In spite of the hope implicit in naming her after a fair character in a movie itself called *Imitation of Life*,[2] Pecola, too, is, according to her mother and apparently everyone else, "*ugly*'" (100). The consequences of this estimation, repeated as it is continually throughout Pecola's life, are, of course, obvious: When others—Mr. Yacobowski, her teachers, etc.—cannot or will not see her, then she ceases to be seen at all or sees herself in the iconographic images she can attain only in madness.

The horror of the industry responsible for generating and continuing these repeated, static, and unattainable images is not just that, in the process of appropriating standards of beauty and femininity for white women, it does not allow alternate images and standards to coincide—though such is certainly horrible—but that in so doing it also co-opts and transforms a history of communal and familial relationships it cannot otherwise accommodate. This co-optation was facilitated by the migration of African-Americans in the first half of this century and the end of the last to Northern, usually industrial, towns like Lorain, a process that accelerated the separation of families and friends as it removed them farther from whatever common culture existed in the rural South (Willis, *Specifying* 83–109). In the absence of a network of community members ready to step in—as Aunt Jimmy's family and friends do—and make it their business to look after each other, blacks up north who feel isolated from their past and alienated in their present are more likely to look elsewhere for self-affirming context.

As Pauline Breedlove's history bears out, the culture industry is always quick to provide its notion of what this context should be and thus assure the dependence necessary for its own continued existence, even, indeed especially, at the expense of alternate cultural forms. Although she has few fond memories of her childhood, it is her early married life in Lorain that Pauline remembers as the *"lonesomest time of my life."* She is simply not prepared for the kinds of changes wrought by her transplantation north:

> *"I don't know what all happened. Everything changed. It was hard to get to know folks up here, and I missed my people. I weren't used to so much white folks. The ones I seed before was something hateful, but they didn't come around too much. Up north they was everywhere—next door, downstairs, all over the streets—and colored folks few and far between. Northern colored folk was different too. Dicty-like. No better than whites for meanness. They could make you feel just as no-count, 'cept I didn't expect it from them."* (93)

From this seemingly fragmented and hostile community, Pauline turns to day jobs in the homes of "nervous, pretentious" people and to the movies. Her attachment to the former is due in part to the fact that at the Fishers she can exercise the artistic sensibility that otherwise cannot find expression. As a child in Alabama and especially Kentucky, Pauline "liked, most of all, to arrange things. To line things up in rows—jars on shelves at canning, peach pits on the step, sticks, stones, leaves. . . . She missed—without knowing what she missed—paints and crayons" (88–89). But it is not until her job at the Fishers that Pauline can again "arrange things, clean things, line things up in neat rows. . . . [At the Fisher's] she found beauty, order, cleanliness, and praise. . . . It was her pleasure to stand in her kitchen at the end of a day and survey her handiwork" (101). Moreover, her job with the Fishers provides her with the semblance of acceptance and community she cannot find or create in her own home and neighborhood. They have given her the nickname she never had as a child and tell small anecdotes about her. Mr. Fisher says, "'I would rather sell her blueberry cobblers than real estate'" (101). Finally, it is easier for Pauline to ignore the fact that both the name and the anecdotes are condescending and exemplative of her subordinate, and ultimately outsider, status in the Fisher household (as evidenced when Claudia feels "the familiar violence" rise at the little pink girl's question "'Where's Polly?'" [86]) than to do without the "power, praise, and luxury" (101) she finds there.

The other place she finds this "power, praise, and luxury" is, of course, the movies, and, unfortunately, it is to them that Pauline turns for help and validation rather than the few black women she has met in Lorain who, "with their goading glances and private snickers," were merely "amused" by her and her loneliness (94).[3] It is at the movies that Pauline learns to equate "physical beauty and virtue," where she "stripped her mind, bound it, and collected self-contempt by the heap." As she watches *"white men taking such good care of they women, and they all dressed up in big clean houses"* (97), Pauline finds it increasingly difficult to return to her own life and, as a result, "more and more . . . neglected her house, her children, her man" (101). Like the Dick-and-Jane story, Pauline's movies continuously present her with a life, again presumably ideal, which she does not now have and which she has little, if any, chance of ever enjoying in any capacity other than that of "the ideal servant" (101).[4] In the absence of alternate images which might validate and endorse a kind of virtue not tied to physical beauty or ones offering competing definitions of beauty itself, *and* in the absence of a network of family and friends, especially women friends, whose own lives would provide a differing model and the context in which to erect her own, Pauline succumbs to the "simple pleasure" *of* "black–and–white images projected through a ray of light" and "curtailing freedom in every way" (97).

Images projected on the screen and mass-produced items curtail freedom in other, less obvious and brutal ways as well, although the effects can be due as much to what is *not* seen or experienced as to what is. Claudia, for example, fosters a brutal hatred for her white baby dolls not just because they don't look like her but because the gift of them is supposed to replace and somehow improve upon what she would really prefer for Christmas: the *experience* of sitting "on the low stool in Big Mama's kitchen with [her] lap full of lilacs and [listening] to Big Papa play his violin for [her] alone" (21). Instead of family interaction—and the touching, playing, and ritual storytelling that might accompany it—Claudia is supposed to pretend to be the mother of this "thing" dressed in "starched gauze or lace" and sporting a "bone-cold head" (20).

Similarly, Claudia hates Shirley Temple well enough because her socks stay up, but what really gets her is the presence in the films of Bojangles. This is the outrage: the rewriting of either a historical moment (the Civil War) or interpersonal relationship (an orphaned child and benevolent older friend) with her part edited or bleached out so that those few images of African-American life afforded space on the big screen are put there not as evidence or proof of the experience itself, but as a tactic for further erasure, denial, or revisioning of just that experience. Instead of the ideologically opportune sight of an older black man "soft-shoeing it and chuckling" harmlessly, aimlessly, with a little white girl, the world should be seeing *her*, Claudia, socks around her ankles, "enjoying, sharing, giving a lovely dance thing" (19) with *her* friend, uncle, daddy Bojangles.

It does not, however, and Morrison signals the effects of these oversights—of supplanting or having supplanted both one's appearance and one's history and culture—repeatedly in *The Bluest Eye* in details of sexuality, especially women's but, as the life-stories of Cholly and Soaphead indicate, not exclusively so. Mr. Henry, for example, when first moving into the MacTeers' home, greets Claudia and Frieda with, "'You must be Greta Garbo, and you must be Ginger Rogers'" (17), thus reducing them to type in a kind of objectification which, in part, will make it easier for him later to molest Frieda. He follows this greeting with a gift of money, a gesture repeated later when he wants them out of the house so he can entertain two of the more colorful "members of [his] Bible class" (65), China and the Maginot Line. The exchange of money and the objectification of women as types converge here in such a way as to align his interaction with the two women and with Frieda and Claudia under the heading of prostitution.

The incident with Mr. Henry suggests one way the mass circulation of images of "femininity" negatively affects women in the area of sexuality by negatively affecting the attitudes and thus behavior of the people with whom they interact. *The Bluest Eye*, however, documents further the effect of those images on women themselves *on the level of the body* and in terms of how they understand and experience their own sexuality. For Pauline, for example, sexual pleasure depends entirely on the ability to "'*feel a power*'" (103) that comes from a sense of herself as desirable. In bed with Cholly, she thinks,

> *"I know he wants me to come first. But I can't. Not until he does. Not until I feel him loving me. Just me. . . . Not until I know that my flesh is all that be on his mind. . . . Not until he has let go of all he has, and give it to me. . . . When he does, I feel a power. . . . I be strong enough, pretty enough, and young enough to let him make me come." (103)*

Unfortunately, Pauline defines strength, beauty, and youth solely in the terms she's learned from film; thus, as the possibility of ever attaining them is foreclosed, so too is sexual pleasure. Confident that "'*my Maker will take care of me,*'" (104), Pauline reassures herself that "'. . . *it don't make no difference about this old earth,*'" (104), thus hoping to cash in on one dream in exchange for relinquishing another.

Sexual pleasure is no longer even a consideration for Geraldine and the other "sugar-brown girls" who have lost "the dreadful funkiness of passion . . . of nature . . . of the wide range of human emotions" (68) almost as a consequence of moving north and away from family and towns like Mobile, Aiken, and Nagadoches, whose names "make you think of love" (67) if the girls themselves do not. Geraldine's desire to eschew inappropriate manifestations of black American culture by maintaining the "line between colored and nigger" (71) and thus to effect a bland respectability is connected in her portrait with a body that can give itself only "sparingly and partially": "She stiffens when she feels one of her paper curlers coming undone from the activity of love. . . . She hopes he will not sweat—the damp may get into her hair" (69).

Geraldine's concern is focused on her hair, that part of her appearance which, along with her fair skin, she can control and adapt most easily to standards of white beauty. One is reminded at this point of Pauline and her Jean Harlow hairstyle or China who, with a flick of the wrist, converts herself from one feminine type to another: One minute she has the "surprised eyebrows" and "cupid-bow mouth" of a starlet, the next the "Oriental eyebrows" and "evilly slashed mouth" (49) of *a femme fatale*. Pecola, however, whose ugliness "came from conviction," has no such physical qualities capable of altering and thus redeeming what she and her family perceive as her "relentlessly and aggressively" ugly appearance (34). Pecola, in fact, is *all* sign: To see her body is to know already everything about her or at least everything her culture deems important about her.

The depiction of her sexuality is thus correspondingly total: Pecola gets off eating candy—nothing new here, except that, for her, orgasm takes the form of a curious transubstantiation and, ultimately, transformation: "To eat the candy is somehow to eat the eyes, eat Mary Jane. Love Mary Jane. Be Mary Jane" (43). Unlike Claudia who cannot yet, in the words of Susan Willis, "imagine herself miraculously translated into the body of Shirley Temple so as to vicariously live white experience as a negation of blackness" ("I Shop" 174), Pecola not only can, but, from this denial of self and substitution of the store-bought image, actually gets in the process "nine lovely orgasms with Mary Jane" (43). Whatever pleasurable resources Pecola's own body may harbor are available to her now—and this at the early age of eleven—only to the extent that, like her mother, she can experience them as the alienated effects of another woman's body.

Most of the time, however, she cannot do this and, rather than reconcile herself, as her mother has, to the prospect of greater glory and bigger rainbows in the next world, Pecola opts instead to make a life of her own erasure and annihilation. As her parents and brother fight in the next room, she prays to God to "'make me disappear'" and then performs the meditation to do so:

> She squeezed her eyes shut. Little parts of her body faded away. Now slowly, now with a rush. Slowly again. Her fingers went, one by one; then her arms disappeared all the way to the elbow. Her feet now. . . . The legs all at once. It was hardest above the thighs. She had to be real still and pull. Her stomach would not go. But finally it, too, went away. Then her chest, her neck. The face was hard, too. Almost done, almost. Only her tight, tight eyes were left. They were always left. (39)

The inability to make her eyes go away prompts Pecola's final disappearing act: The ugliness of her entire body is dissolved in and absolved by the blue eyes only she and her new "friend" can see. Her breakdown at the end of the novel is the last in a series of instances in which boundaries marking the space between inside and outside, self and other, sense and nonsense are broken, removed, or simply no longer perform their tasks. As the novel's prefatory Dick-and-Jane story turns from order to chaos with the gradual removal of punctuation and spacing, so too does the erasure of Pecola's body and sexuality lead to her madness and isolation.

It seems to me that it is at this point that we can begin to make sense of Morrison's notion of "disinterested violence" which she introduces first with Claudia and elaborates upon in her depiction of the three prostitutes, Cholly, and, by implication, the black community in Lorain, Ohio. After systematically destroying her baby dolls in order to "discover the dearness, to find the beauty, the desirability that had escaped [her]" (20) and then, finding this tactic unproductive, transferring "the same impulses to little white girls," Claudia "learned how repulsive this disinterested violence was, that it was repulsive because it was disinterested" (22). Michael Awkward argues that what Claudia feels is "repulsive" here is her own "failure to accept without question the standards of white America" (72), a reading which, while it has a lot of general application in the novel, seems to misdirect the focus of this passage. Claudia's self-incrimination is, it seems to me, more in response to her failure to *feel enough* for her white victims, to have the interest that would make her actions meaningful. Willis claims that Claudia's realization "that violence against whites runs the risk of being 'disinterested' . . . suggests that white people are little more than abstractions . . . [that] all are reified subjects" ("I Shop" 174). What Claudia realizes is that her violence cannot help but be disinterested, since even the little girls she thinks she wants to dismember are finally only representatives to her of the system she resents and wants to dismantle. "Disinterestedness," then, is the result of not seeing individual people and how their actions combine in ways affecting you "disinterested violence," the prelude to "adjustment without improvement" (22), is possible precisely when the specificity of bodies, places, and histories is erased, as it is by commodity culture and those living under its aegis.

Though charming in their own way, China, Poland, and the Maginot Line are also condemned in *The Bluest Eye* for just this kind of refusal to take into account difference and history:

> Except for Marie's fabled love for Dewey Prince, these women hated men, all men, without shame, apology, or *discrimination*.

They abused their visitors with scorn *grown mechanical from use*. Black men, white men, Puerto Ricans, Mexicans, Jews, Poles, whatever—all were inadequate and weak, all came under jaundiced eyes and were the recipients of their *disinterested wrath*. (47–48; emphasis added)

Neither their hatred for men and the "mechanical" violence it spawns[5] nor Marie's love for Pecola, however, has much effect on either their own standing in the community or Pecola's life. Any power moves they think they are making by indiscriminately hating all men are probably negated by the fact that they do not take into account differences in race and class, factors supremely affecting their position *vis à vis* men, especially in their profession. Their kindness to Pecola is similarly disinterested iii that, by failing to see *her* and her situation clearly, the three, in the words of Michele Wallace, "fail to understand victimization or the fact that [she] is in danger" (65).[6]

This failure is finally the community's as a whole, a fact Morrison repeatedly suggests by illustrating the extent to which as a group it too has "absorbed in full" dominant standards of value and beauty with little or no inspection of or reflection on the effects to itself or to its individual members. In her conversation with friends, Mrs. MacTeer jokes about "Aunt Julia . . . still trotting up and down Sixteenth Street talking to herself" (15). The significance of this remark is not really apparent until the depiction of Pecola's breakdown is complete, and we are presented with a similar image of Pecola "walking up and down, up and down, her head jerking to the beat of a drummer so distant only she could hear" (158). Lorain sees Aunt Julia as "'that old hag floating by in that bonnet'" whom the County will not "'take'" and whom the sight of will" 'scare the living shit out of you'" (15). One of the women attributes Aunt Julia's fate to senility, but the designation "*still* trotting" implies she has been out there a while. Their inability or refusal to make sense of her actions, to put them in context, foreshadows their eventual scapegoating of Pecola and suggests that the town has an undiagnosed and unexamined history of producing women like Pecola, that her experience—and the extremity of it—is not an isolated instance.

Morrison characterizes Cholly's disinterestedness as the condition of being "dangerously free. Free to feel whatever he felt—fear, guilt, shame, love, grief, pity. Free to be tender or violent" (125). Her depiction of him traces the source of this freedom to his loss of mother, father, community, and home and to the feeling that the history of people and events extends as far as his interest in them:

. . . Cholly was truly free. Abandoned in a junk heap by his mother, rejected for a crap game by his father, there was nothing more to

lose. He was alone with his own perceptions and appetites, and
they alone interested him. (126)

Paradoxically, this is a state that allows him to see Pecola more clearly than
probably anyone else in the book (with the exception of the adult Claudia)
and to love her in spite of what he sees, but does not allow him to interact
with her in any form other than "reactions based on what he felt at the
moment." Cholly sees his daughter washing dishes and sees also, in her
stooped frame, "an accusation" against him. Unlike others in town, though,
he sees "her young, helpless, hopeless presence" (127) and "loved her enough
to touch her, envelop her, give something of himself to her" (159) where no
one else would.

   In the four examples cited above, disinterestedness is occasioned specifically by the inability to place people and events into contexts that would flesh
out experience and thus make obvious the limitations of present actions or
beliefs. It becomes steadily more difficult for characters in *The Bluest Eye* to
do this because they are either separated from the supportive networks that
would encourage it and (or as a result) because their placement in American culture does not sanction accurate representations of what that context
would be. The result is a community of individuals who are, at times, painfully
alienated from each other as each is divided within him- or herself. Pecola's
split consciousness at the end of the novel is a literal representation of this
doubleness[7]; it affects other characters also as distortions or denials of self,
but denials and distortions approved and fostered in popular iconographic
representation.

An explicit formal project of *The Bluest Eye*, then, is to rewrite the specific stories, histories, and bodies of African-Americans which are quickly
being made invisible in commodity culture and which, if written, will make
disinterestedness and its unproductive or damaging results impossible.
Morrison acknowledges this project in so many words when she says she
wrote *The Bluest Eye* because she wanted to read the story it would tell. The
novel's shifting focus and point of view, its willingness to let different people
speak and *not* to reconcile contradictory explanations and claims where they
arise is indicative of Morrison's preference for telling all sides of Pecola's
story rather than hammering home one of them. In this, she is like other
black women writers who, according to Mae Henderson, "through their
intimacy with the discourses of other(s) . . . weave into their work competing
and complementary discourses—that seek to adjudicate competing claims
and witness concerns" (23). It would be to miss the point, then, to read *The
Bluest Eye* looking to assign blame. One of the great virtues of the book is

its capacity to empathize and to allow its readers to empathize—something not possible in the absence of history and context— with all of its characters, perhaps especially those who seem most irredeemable: Cholly, Soaphead Church, Pauline.

Finally, though, since *The Bluest Eye* and this project of representing African-Americans focuses most specifically on the histories arid bodies of black women, the novel's alternating perspective reproduces formally *their* complicated subjectivity in particular. As she shifts from young girl to older woman to black man to omniscient narrator, Morrison seems to move her examination of Pecola's life back and forth from the axis of race to that of gender. This process allows her in turn to move through the story as both insider and outsider in what Mae Henderson calls a "contestorial dialogue" involving "the hegemonic dominant and subdominant or [after Rachel Blau Du Plessis] 'ambiguously (non)hegemonic' discourses" (20). At one point Morrison writes as a black person among other black people speaking to a white audience, at others as a woman among women speaking to men. The movement between these positions allows Morrison to "see the other, but also to see what the other cannot see, and to use this insight to enrich both our own and the other's understanding" (36). Of course these categories can be separated only artificially since, as Valerie Smith notes, "the meaning of blackness in this country shapes profoundly the experience of gender, just as the conditions of womanhood affect ineluctably the experience of race" (47). By doing so here, however, Toni Morrison enables the reader to witness structurally the complexity of black female subjectivity as she writes it back into a culture whose social and economic mechanisms would otherwise try to write it out.

Notes

1. For more on this analysis of mass culture see, among many others, Adomo and Horkheimer's work in Arato and Gebhardt, Fredrick Jameson, or Tonia Modleski.

2. I take it, then, that Maureen's guess is correct, that Pauline does name Pecola after the movie's black daughter and even then getting it wrong: The daughter's name is Peola, not Pecola.

3. It is not the case, however, that the kind of community support Pauline needs is simply unavailable in Lorain. When Cholly bums their apartment, for example, Pauline's own daughter Pecola is taken in immediately by the MacTeers and, in spite of Mrs. MacTeer's raving about the amount of milk Pecola drinks, is cared for as a matter of course.

4. Morrison's reference to *Imitation of Life*, then, is quite specific and damning: Both versions of the film finally take as a given the black woman's status as servant in the white woman's household. A recent television screening of the original version was introduced optimistically as the story of two women who must "hide their friendship" by masquerading as mistress and maid. While Sirk's version problematizes as it foregrounds the story's racial thematics, it counteracts much of its own

insightfulness by concluding with an image of the fair-skinned black daughter being reincorporated into the white family, sans mama and the "problems" her definite blackness presented.

5. "On one occasion the town well knew, they lured a Jew up the stairs, pounced on him, all three, held him up by the heels, shook everything out of his pants pockets, and threw him out of the window" (48).

6. Wallace also argues that "in distinct contrast to the variety of maternal images in the book, these women neither nurture nor protect children" and that, by including them in the text, Morrison "seems to question the self-involvement of traditional modes of black female creativity, as well as [pose] a general critique of more recent feminist strategies of 'man-hating' and 'self-love'" (65). I am not sure what exactly she means by "the self-involvement of traditional modes of black female creativity," but I think the characterization of the three prostitutes is more complex and ultimately more endearing than Wallace admits. When it comes time to name who "loves" Pecola, for example, the narrator—now definitively Claudia—cites Cholly and the Maginot Line.

7. Awkward argues that Pecola's "schizophrenia" is a "coded intertext of W. E. B. Du Bois's discussion of a Black 'double consciousness' In *The Souls of Black Folk*'"(12).

WORKS CITED

Arato, Andrew, and Eike Gebhardt, eds. *The Essential Frankfurt School Reader.* New York Continuum, 1982.

Awkward, Michael. *Inspiriting Influences: Tradition, Revision, and Afro-American Women's Novels.* New York: Columbia University Press, 1989.

Hung, Frigga, ed. *Female Sexualization: A Collective Work of Memory.* Trans. Erica Carter. London: Verso, 1987.

Henderson, Mae Gwendolyn. "Speaking in Tongues: Dialogics, Dialectics, and the Black Woman Writer's Literary Tradition." Wall, pp. 16–37.

Jameson, Fredric. "Reification and Utopia in Mass Culture." *Social Text* 1 (1979): pp. 135–148.

Modleski, Tonya. *Loving with a Vengeance: Mass-Produced Fantasies for Women.* New York: Routledge, 1984.

Morrison, Toni. *The Bluest Eye.* New York: Washington Square, 1970.

Smith, Valerie. "Black Feminist Theory and Other Representations of the Other." Wall, pp. 38–57.

Wall, Cheryl A., ed. *Changing Our Own Words: Essays on Criticism, Theory, and Writing by Black Women.* New Brunswick: Rutgers University Press, 1989.

Wallace, Michele. "Variations on Negation and the Heresy of Black Feminist Creativity." *Reading Black Reading Feminist: A Critical Anthology.* Ed. Henry Louis Gates, Jr. New York: Meridian, 1990: pp. 52–67.

Willis, Susan. "I Shop Therefore I Am: Is There a Place for Afro-American Culture in Commodity Culture?" Wall, pp. 173–195.

———. *Specifying: Black Women Writing the American Experience.* Madison: University of Wisconsin Press, 1987.

ALLEN ALEXANDER

The Fourth Face: The Image of God in Toni Morrison's The Bluest Eye

Religious references, both from Western and African sources, abound in Toni Morrison's fiction, but nowhere are they more intriguing or perplexing than in *The Bluest Eye*. And of the many fascinating religious references in this novel, the most complex—and perhaps, therefore, the richest—are her representations of and allusions to God. In Morrison's fictional world, God's characteristics are not limited to those represented by the traditional Western notion of the Trinity: Father, Son, and Holy Ghost. Instead, God possesses a fourth face, one that is an explanation for all those things—the existence of evil, the suffering of the innocent and just—that seem so inexplicable in the face of a religious tradition that preaches the omnipotence of a benevolent God.

Is Morrison's introduction of this fourth face into her fiction, then, a means of depicting evil, a redesigned Satan, if you will? It is true that in Morrison's fiction the fourth face at times is portrayed as a reservoir of evil—for example, when the people of the Bottom in *Sula* believe "that the fourth explained Sula" (118), who for them is a manifestation of evil—but the fourth face is much more than a rationalization for all that ails humanity. When Morrison's references to God are taken in their totality, it becomes quite clear that her depiction of the deity is an attempt to humanize God, to demonstrate how God for her characters is not the characteristically ethereal

African American Review, Volume 32, Number; Summer 1998: pp. 293–303. © 1998 Allen Alexander.

God of traditional Western religion but a God who, while retaining certain Western characteristics, has much in common with the deities of traditional African religion and legend.[1]

Though Morrison's model of God owes much to African tradition, a major part of her portrait is dedicated to exposing how traditional Western notions about God affect her characters. If *The Bluest Eye* can in any way be characterized as an initiation story, then a major portion of a character's initiation involves discovering the inadequacy of Western theological models for those who have been marginalized by the dominant white culture. But many of Morrison's characters, unlike Richard Wright in *Black Boy* and James Baldwin's John Grimes in *Go Tell It On the Mountain*, fail to follow Baldwin's admonition in *The Fire Next Time* to recognize the religion of the white majority for what it is and to "divorce [themselves] from all the prohibitions, crimes, and hypocrisies of the Christian church" (67). In Morrison's oeuvre, the characters who blatantly attack the norms of white society—for example, Guitar Bains in *Song of Solomon*—often seem ridiculously ignorant of their own heritage (Guitar does not know the reasoning behind Malcolm X's choice of last name [160]), and consequently their philosophy retains some of white culture's worst characteristics— witness the violence and genocidal hatred of the Seven Days. Sula is a character who certainly rejects the norms of society, but it is not clear exactly which society—white or black, or both—she is rejecting. And then in *The Bluest Eye* there is the sad case of Pecola Breedlove, who falls prey to the false notions of white superiority espoused not only by the white community but also by her mother and Soaphead Church.

Though the traditional theological models of white society may adversely affect others of Morrison's characters, Pecola is by far the one character whose life seems most vulnerable to the whims of those who have bought into the Western tradition. At every turn Pecola is confronted with attitudes and images based on the myth of white superiority that reinforce her tendency toward self-hatred. When Pecola encounters Mr. Yacobowski, a white man whose religious sensibility, "honed on the doe-eyed Virgin Mary," is alien to the world she inhabits, she is struck by "the total absence of human recognition" on his face (42). But such blatant expressions of racial inequality are not limited to the white characters, who are noticeably few and far between. Geraldine, a black woman who is said to have suppressed her racial identity by getting rid of "the dreadful funkiness of passion, the funkiness of nature, the funkiness of the wide range of human emotions" in order to appease the white man's "blunted soul" (68), treats Pecola as not only a nuisance or blight, as does Mr. Yacobowski, but as a threat to the "sanitized"—i.e., anti-black—environment that she has constructed around her son. As Pecola is thrown out of Geraldine's house, she sees a portrait of an

Anglicized Jesus "looking down at her with sad and unsurprised eyes" (76), an image of a God who seems either incapable of helping her or complicit in her suffering.

With this portrait of Jesus, Morrison introduces us to one of the shortcomings of the Western model of God, namely the problem of how a supposedly omnipotent and loving God can allow the existence of evil and suffering. Morrison reintroduces this model of an inadequate God, of a deity incapable of alleviating or unwilling to rectify the injustices of human society, as she recounts Cholly Breedlove's childhood. At a church picnic, Cholly watches the father of a family raise a watermelon over his head to smash it on the ground and is impressed with the man's god-like stance, which he sees as the opposite of the unimpressive white image of God: "a nice old white man, with long white hair, flowing white beard, and little blue eyes that looked sad when people died and mean when they were bad" (106).

Although this white image of God is woefully inadequate for Cholly, who, at least during this period of his life, embraces his African heritage, it is an image to which Pauline Breedlove clings, even at the expense of her daughter's psychic well-being. Pauline, though she has not enjoyed the quasi-middle-class lifestyle that Geraldine believes is the result of having suppressed her racial identity, still looks to white society—through films produced for and religion constructed around the tastes of the white majority—to provide the guidelines for her manner of living. Her acceptance of her poverty and suffering, reflected in her belief that "*it don't make no difference about this old earth*" because "*there is sure to be a glory*" (104), echoes the teachings of slave masters, who manipulated biblical passages to stifle dissatisfaction among those they oppressed. Pauline has bought into the Western notion of linear history, an outlook that emphasizes the future and belittles the past.[2]

Pauline has also adopted the Western theological tradition of either-or thinking, of believing that the differences between good and evil, righteous and unrighteous, believer and nonbeliever, are clearly demarcated. This ethical orientation is reflected in her belief that she is "an upright and Christian woman, burdened with a no-count man, whom God wanted her to punish" (37),[3] and she rationalizes that her antipathy toward Cholly is sanctified by her God, for "Christ the Judge" demands that she make her husband pay for his transgression. Yet Pauline cannot think of "Christ the Judge" and "Christ the Redeemer" simultaneously because such a linkage does not fit the severely drawn categories of good and evil that she has inherited from the dominant white culture. To her way of thinking, "Cholly was beyond redemption" (37). Pauline's religion, built upon such a rigid and unforgiving foundation, cannot tolerate the notion that a man like Cholly could be a blend of both good and bad, that he, quite simply, could be human. Consequently, she never recognizes God's fourth face. She remains as detached from this concept as she does from her family and heritage. Pauline's belief system, whose either-or design requires its adherents to judge others, often by impossible standards, leads her to leave behind those persons, including her family members, whom she feels fail to measure up to her standards. She thus becomes an extreme individualist, a person cut loose from her cultural moorings.[4]

Though Pauline is not the only African American character in Morrison's fiction to try to mold herself in an image that she thinks will be more acceptable to white society (Jadine from *Tar Baby* and Ruth Foster from *Song of Solomon* are two obvious examples, as are Soaphead Church and Pecola in *The Bluest Eye* and Helene Wright in *Sula)*, her name, which may be a direct reference to Pauline theology, and her central role in the psychological disintegration of Pecola make her perhaps Morrison's most identifiable example of this type. And one chief reason that she so aptly fills this role is her vision of God, which is so antithetical to the fourth-face image that is more central to her heritage. Pauline's adoption of the white society's notion of an ethereal God who judges humans from an alien perspective contrasts with a strain in African American thought that has sought to put a human face on God. As Major J. Jones points out in his study *The Color of God*, this African-influenced theological outlook envisions God as "neither threat nor rival" to humans. Instead, "God is . . . the very basis or ground of the creature's fullest possible self-realization. . . . Black religious experience . . . is about being and becoming more human under God" (22).

Since this outlook suggests that one's humanity is inextricably linked to God, it follows that such an orientation would lead one to believe that perhaps the connection runs both ways, that God cannot be fully God, or at least a God to humanity, without also being in some sense human. This concept is not completely alien to Western theology, for the Christian faith itself depends on the notion of God becoming a man in the form of Jesus, but, as Jones concludes, and as Morrison suggests in her fiction, the West has lost its connection—through various factors, including, no doubt, Pauline influences on Christian theology—to this fundamental idea of a link between God and humanity. Consequently, in white society God has been molded into an otherworldly presence who, despite Christ's role as redeemer of fallen humanity, regards human weakness, in the form of sin, as something disconnected from the divine.

Within the African tradition we see a substantially different representation of God. In African folklore God is often depicted as having very human-like qualities, not only regarding his appearance but also his personality and abilities. Whereas the Western tradition pictures God as a stoical figure who demands perfection from his creation because of his own perfection, African storytellers have given God a human face, portraying him as a lovable character with a sense of humor and a streak of fallibility. Julius Lester in his renditions of traditional African folk tales characterizes God as "an amateur" (13) who is trying his best "to make the world look a little prettier" (3) but who doesn't "know what he's doing half the time" (23). This folksy God, a God who is seen not only as the creator but also as the ancestor of humanity and who consequently possesses many of the characteristics of his imperfect creation (Sawyerr 95), is a far cry from the West's omnipotent, infallible God who despises human frailty.

There is little doubt, given Morrison's characterization of Pauline, that the author sees the values of white religion as inappropriate and ultimately self-defeating guides for her African American characters. Though she does not present us with a character in *The Bluest Eye* who, like Baldwin's John Grimes, is suspicious of the trappings of white religion, including those characteristics that have been absorbed by African American Christianity, she does portray characters who embrace these trappings, such as Pauline and Geraldine, as less than admirable figures. In contrast to John Grimes, who senses that his parents' church has lost something of value because it has moved too far away from its African roots, Pauline chooses her church precisely because it is a place "where shouting [i]s frowned upon" (100), a sanctuary from the passion that she so despises. But ultimately both John and Pauline suffer from their association with these churches. John comes to regard the church as a source of darkness and oppression and thinks of God as a "monstrous heart" (217) that consumes his joy and stunts his passion for life. Pauline divorces herself from her African American heritage and in the process loses the closest manifestation of that tradition: her family. Obviously neither Baldwin nor Morrison sees a movement from an African to a Western sensibility as an appropriate step for a productive and authentic life.

The question, then, arises: How does Morrison demonstrate the qualities of an African-inspired vision of God in her fiction? Of course, no serious reader of Morrison's work would begin an analysis with the assumption that there is a simple, clear-cut answer to any question regarding her richly complex work, and her portrayal of an African religious sensibility offers no exception. Her selection of the fourth face of God image underscores her commitment to demonstrating that this sensibility is inherently attuned to the notion that God is much larger than the image to which the divine has been confined by Western theology. And a significant part of that largeness is built on the belief that God is in some way responsible—either as an active participant or a willing spectator—in the tragedies that befall human beings.

Such an idea is certainly not foreign to the Western theological tradition, which is constructed on the foundation of a Judaic faith that sees God as many things, from protector to the engine behind catastrophe. But in the Judaic tradition, there is typically a reason behind God's decision to punish humans—namely, their defiance of divine laws. In contrast to this belief that tragedy can ultimately be explained by human transgression, traditional African religions tend to understand tragedy as something that happens regardless of what humans have or have not done.

This association of God with the existence of evil is a common element among several of the many variations of traditional African religions.[5] E. Thomas Lawson notes that within the Zulu tradition evil is not seen as "an independent, autonomous power" but as a force that draws its strength from three positive powers: the God of the Sky, the ancestors, and medicine (27). K. A. Busia finds a similar belief among the Ashanti, for whom nature is populated by the "malignant spirits of fairies and forest monsters" who "are subservient to the Supreme Being, from whom ultimately they all derive their power" (qtd. in Sawyerr 100).

Within the belief systems of many African peoples God's kinship to evil far surpasses that of a source of origin. Evil not only derives its power from God but is allowed to flourish by God. Harry Sawyerr, who in the preface to his study *God: Ancestor or Creator?* stresses the difficulty of studying the African concept of God because of the vastness of the continent and the diversity of its population, nevertheless feels comfortable asserting that within African belief systems "the general well-being of man, as well as his distress, are freely attributed to God" (ix). He supports this contention with evidence from his study of the Yoruba, for whom "evil forces seem to be more subject to the ultimate control of God. They can and often do destroy human life, but not without the permission of God" (49). This notion that evil exists because God allows it to was noted over two hundred years ago by Olaudah Equiano. In his autobiography, published in 1789, Equiano recalls traditions he learned as a child in Africa, and he writes that his people believed that God "governs events, especially our deaths or captivity" (27). This same idea can be found in the work of Zora Neale Hurston, who introduced into her fiction characters like Janie and Tea Cake of *Their Eyes Were Watching God* who combine an African sensibility with a belief that "all gods dispense suffering without reason" (138). Janie and Tea Cake, caught in the destructive path of a hurricane, wonder if God "meant to measure their puny might against His" (151). And later as she watches Tea Cake suffer from a rabid dog's bite, Janie concludes that "God would do less than He had in His heart" (169).

However, there is also a strain of African belief that sees God not as the source or master of evil but as a participant in the universe's struggle against malignant forces. According to J. B. Danquah, the Akan—a cultural group which includes the Ashanti—believe that "Nana, the principle that makes for good, is himself or itself participator in the life of the whole, and is not only head" (88). Since God (Nana) is thus viewed by the Akan as a part of creation rather than as a being apart from it, they see "physical pain and evil . . . as natural forces which the Nana, in common with others of the group, has to master, dominate and sublimate" (88–89). Within this framework of belief, God and humans are part of the same community, working together, like the people of the Bottom in *Sula,* against evil, not in a futile effort to eliminate it but in order to outlast it (118).

African perspectives on the existence of evil are multiple and varied, but one idea that seems to link them is that an explanation for the presence of evil is unnecessary. Evil is a real presence in the lives of African peoples, yet it is precisely because of the weight of evil on them that they steer away from metaphysical speculations about it. As James Cone, writing from an African American Christian perspective, contends," . . . black reflections about suffering have not been removed from life but *involved* in life, that is, the struggle to affirm humanity despite the dehumanizing conditions of slavery and oppression" (183).

One African folk tale that illustrates this African belief that evil is not a riddle to be solved but a reality with which one must deal is the story of a woman who, after her family has died, goes in search of God in order to find an explanation for the tragedy that has beset her. As she searches the world for God, she encounters people who question her motives, for they contend that "'Shikakunamo [the Besetting One] sits on the back of everyone of us and we cannot shake him off!'" She ultimately fails in her quest, "'and from that day to this, say the Africans, no man or woman has solved the riddle of this painful earth'" (McVeigh 48–49).

Morrison deftly works a similar sense of tragedy into *The Bluest Eye,* though one could well argue that in her fiction it is based as much on the inadequacy of the Western model of God as on African traditions. Though there is no shortage of suffering characters in the novel, the Breedloves, like the woman troubled by Shikakunamo, or like Job in the Old Testament, seem uniquely chosen to wear the mantle of divine retribution: "It was as though some mysterious all-knowing master had given each one a cloak of ugliness to wear . . . ." The fact that they see support for the cloak "leaning at them from every billboard, every movie, every glance" is an indication of just how much what white society values has distorted their own self-image, so much so that each accepts the ugliness "without question" (34). But even though the Breedloves' pitiful circumstances seem to be largely attributable to human action, both in the form of a racist society and their own personal shortcomings, the odds are so great against them that it appears that the hands of "some mysterious all-knowing master" are holding them back, or perhaps choking the life out of them in the same way that those hands strangle the life from "a tuft of grass

[that] had forced its way up through a crack in the sidewalk, only to meet a raw October wind" (48). In the world of the Breedloves, it seems that much more than human forces are working against them, that, in fact, *the earth itself might have been unyielding*" to their survival (9).

If, then, God is, in Morrison's cosmology, the agent behind much human suffering, do her characters' attitudes suggest that they respond to their plight in a way reflective of the African sensibility toward tragedy reflected in the tale of the woman seeking Shikakunamo? This is not the case with Pauline and Pecola, both of whom approach their pain in ways more in line with the values of white culture. Pauline molds her lifestyle to correspond to what the dominant culture applauds. And Pecola withdraws into herself, "peeping out from behind the shroud very seldom, and then only to yearn for the return of her mask" (35), which she puts aside only after believing she has acquired a feature—blue eyes—that she identifies with the happiness that eludes her. Pauline and Pecola, in effect, attempt to deal with their circumstances by altering their sense of reality, not by attempting to maintain their authenticity as meaningful members of a larger community. They seem willing to exchange their personhood, and consequently their heritage, for models of themselves that only strengthen in their minds the cultural norms that make them hate their true selves.

In contrast to Pauline and Pecola, Cholly, though he is in many ways as tragic a figure as they are, seems to see the life-affirming values of his heritage, an insight that he discovers most memorably while thinking about the image of God while watching the man smash the watermelon at the church picnic:

> It must be the devil who looks like that—holding the world in his hands, ready to dash it to the ground and spill the red guts so niggers could eat the sweet, warm insides. If the devil did look like that, Cholly preferred him. He never felt anything thinking about God, but just the idea of the devil excited him. And now the strong, black devil was blotting out the sun and getting ready to split open the world. (107)

The image that Cholly relishes is one that embraces the fourth face, one that portrays God as much more than the pallid, antiseptic God envisioned by white society. Cholly's God is dynamic, complex, unpredictable, exciting, dangerous.[6]

The notion that God can be dangerous, something other than the benevolent grandfather figure that has been pre-eminent in the Western mind, might be unsettling, but Cholly appears to welcome the idea, perhaps because such an image seems much more realistic in a world that does not give the impression of being controlled by an omnipotent and loving deity. He sees this representation of God reaffirmed at his Aunt Jimmy's funeral, where "there was grief over the waste of life, the stunned wonder at the ways of God, and the restoration of order in nature at the graveyard" (113). Here, the concept of evil, of pain and suffering and those things that appear to contradict that which affirms goodness and life, is not an alien thought, nor is it something that overwhelms the funeralgoers and forces them into a state of nihilistic apathy.[7] In contrast to the Western approach to the existence of evil, which has been marked by attempts to sequester or destroy it, these people, drawing from their African heritage, feel, as Morrison herself has said about African Americans in general, "that evil has a natural place in the universe" and consequently "they are not surprised at its existence or horrified or outraged" (Parker 253).

Is there, then, no limit to the amount of evil one can tolerate without lashing out? Is not what happens to Pecola, particularly at the hands of her father and Soaphead Church, so horrific and outrageous that some response against it is necessary? For Pecola, unfortunately, there is no one to respond but herself, and her lack of response—what some might call her acceptance of her situation—cannot be attributed to the African sensibility of which Morrison has spoken. Pecola has become so disconnected from her heritage that her movement toward insanity is instead an indictment of the white cultural framework that has become her guidepost for living.

But Morrison does not intend for us to conclude that the African sensibility toward tragedy is one of complacent and powerless acceptance. To the contrary, she suggests that the correct stance for one to take with regard to tragedy is not passively to give in to its inevitability but, like the people of the Bottom in *Sula*, to be actively engaged with it so that it can be "dealt with, survived, outwitted, triumphed over" (118). Yet Pecola is ill-equipped to outwit and triumph over her tragic situation. She lacks the cultural rootedness or the intestinal fortitude to outlast the forces that work to annthilate her personhood. And in the end she accepts as her destiny the destruction of her true being in favor of an insanity-induced self-image that validates in her mind the inherent inferiority of her heritage.

The instrument that finally pushes Pecola over the edge is Soaphead Church, a character who not only rejects his African heritage but who also relinquishes his identity as a human being in favor of the self-generated delusion that he is in some sense a god. He is a hater of humanity, a self-professed misanthrope whose "disdain for people" ironically "led him into a profession designed to serve them," that of a "Reader, Adviser, and Interpreter of Dreams" (130). However, he "serves" others not out of a spirit of generosity but because of a selfish desire to assert his power over the innocent and weak. Into the lair of this preyer on humanity walks Pecola, who stands little chance of withstanding Soaphead. Instead of sexually molesting her, as he has been fond of doing to other girls, Soaphead assaults her psyche, taking from her any knowledge of her true identity.

But is Soaphead totally to blame for Pecola's demise? From his seemingly peculiar perspective he is not, but is his view of the world really all that unique? It would be easy to conclude, given Morrison's consistently negative appraisal of Western theological models, that Soaphead, who is easily Morrison's most detestable character in a novel that is replete with them, represents the worst side of white religion. Such a conclusion makes even more sense when one considers how Soaphead, following the path the West has laid down for God, severs himself from humanity. In this sense he could be seen as an allegorical figure. But Morrison is much too complex a writer to introduce such an obviously allegorical character into her work, and there is evidence in the text that suggests that Soaphead, far from being solely a human likeness of the white God, actually embraces a theological perspective that is not far removed from that of the fourth-face notion of African tradition. Like the people of the Bottom, he believes that, "since decay, vice, filth, and disorder were pervasive, they must be in the Nature of Things," that "evil exist[s] because God had created it." But he also departs from the African perspective, rejecting the notion that evil is part of God's nature and instead believing that the deity "made a sloven and unforgivable error in judgment: designing an imperfect universe" (136). His adoption of this idea suggests that he still embraces the Western notion of dualism, the belief that good and evil exist as separate forces. His explanation for the existence of evil, then, is not far removed from that of Western theologians who have struggled with the apparently contradictory notion that evil exists in spite of the presence of an omnipotent and benevolent God. Yet Morrison, ever conscious of complicating Soaphead's character, once again undercuts any idea that we might have regarding his one-to-one connection to any theological tradition, revealing that he sees God as something less than omnipotent, as a power so weak and incompetent that "Soaphead suspected that he himself could have done better" (136).

In the final analysis Soaphead's theology is schizophrenic, leaping back and forth between Western and African traditions, between different notions of the physical and metaphysical. His perspective is thus an anticipation of what will happen to Pecola, whose idea of self will teeter on the edge between reality and a reality-induced fantasy, a delusion that may have been locked into place by Soaphead but one for which the community surrounding her—her family and friends and the messages thrust at her by white society—is also culpable. Pecola becomes the ultimate tragic figure, who, in the words of Claudia MacTeer, took "all of our waste which we dumped on her and which she absorbed" (159). In this sense she becomes a

Christ figure, one who takes on the ugliness (sin) of the world around her and consequently absolves others of their feelings of inferiority (guilt). But Morrison's final image of God is an aborted one: Unlike Christ, there is no resurrection for Pecola. In her world, "it's much, much, much too late" to keep hope alive (160).[8]

Although there is no clear affirmation of life in *The Bluest Eye*, the possibility of hope, though it seems far removed from the lives of the characters, remains for those who can rediscover the value of their heritage and reject the notion that they can succeed only if they adopt the norms of white society. The experiences of Pauline and Pecola suggest that it is impossible for a character to adapt to white society without also sacrificing one's true self. In order to adapt, both Pauline and Pecola have to embrace the Western concept of dualism—of believing that life is divisible, that good is distinguishable from evil, that the past, present, and future are disconnected. The failure of these two characters to retain their authenticity, to be who they truly are, suggests "that half a reality is insufficient for anyone" (Lepow 364).

In contrast to the efforts of Pauline and Pecola to separate themselves from their heritage, there are characters who seem to have an understanding that their lives in the past and the present have value. For example, the three prostitutes—China, Poland, and Miss Marie—who live above the Breedloves offer a counterpoint to Pauline, showing Pecola that their lives, no matter how much they are despised by others, have meaning because the women define themselves rather than relying on the judgments of outsiders. They make no pretensions about being anything other than "whores in whores' clothing" (48) and thus provide Pecola with a contrast to her mother, who tries to change who she is in order to fit white society's dictates. Whereas Pauline has done her best to squelch her own and her daughter's taste for the passion of life, the prostitutes, with their large appetites for the sensual, whether it be in the form of sex or food, show Pecola that the physical is a realm to be embraced rather than shunned. Marie makes even the disgusting seem beautiful to Pecola, who witnesses her belching "softly, purringly, lovingly" (49). That love might be associated with such physical crudeness is an idea that Pecola could never have gotten from her mother. And it is Pecola's failure to embrace the image Marie provides that ultimately makes her susceptible to Soaphead's trap, for he exploits her tendency to divorce physical reality from her identity.

Much like the prostitutes, Mr. and Mrs. MacTeer seem largely unconcerned with fulfilling any roles prescribed by outside influences. They do not pamper their children the way that Pauline, trying to emulate the whites for whom she works, pampers "the little girl in pink" (87). Mrs. MacTeer often speaks harshly to her daughters, but Claudia realizes that "love, thick and dark as Alaga syrup" (14), fills her home. Their father also proves his love through actions rather than words, standing as "Vulcan guarding the flames" of the home fires (52). Though Claudia and Frieda do not always understand the words of their parents, they understand "the edge, the curl, the thrust of their emotions" (16). Unlike Pecola, who must face Pauline's and Soaphead's acts of deception, Claudia and Frieda have the advantage of living with adult role models who place more value on action than image. Mr. and Mrs. MacTeer are soundly grounded in reality. Consequently, they are not drawn to the false ideals peddled by Hollywood and Madison Avenue which so distort Pauline's self-image.

Cholly, though there are aspects of his character that put him "beyond the reaches of human consideration" (18), has experienced and appreciated the value of his heritage through individuals like Aunt Jimmy. He provides Pecola with yet another alternative to her mother, acting as a physical foil to Pauline's movement toward an image-driven existence. When Pecola recalls the sound of her parents making love, she remembers being appalled by Cholly's groans, yet as "terrible as his noises were, they were not nearly as bad as the no noise at all from her mother" (48–49). As imperfect as Cholly is, he is still more genuine than Pauline. His rape of Pecola is reprehensible, but he does not rape her mind the way that Pauline and Soaphead do. Claudia senses that Cholly really loves Pecola: "He, at any rate, was the one who loved her enough to touch her, envelop her, give something of himself to her" (159). The fact that this one gift given to Pecola is in reality a sexual assault on her body underscores just how horribly brutal her life is.

But perhaps the character who holds the most promise for living an authentic existence is Claudia, whose telling of the story is a sign in itself that she has come to recognize the value of rediscovering the past. It is Claudia, after all, who seems to be most in touch with reality, for she is the one who reconstructs it for the reader. Claudia understands that those who try to measure their world with black-and-white scales and to find easy solutions to the drudgery of daily life are doomed to lose not only their grounding in their heritage but also their grounding in reality. Ultimately, the price such a person pays is the loss of one's self. When Claudia observes her parents, she recognizes that their authenticity is not based on the literal meaning of the words they speak but in the way they are spoken: "Sometimes their words move in lofty spirals; other times they take strident leaps, and all of it is punctuated with warm-pulsed laughter— like the throb of a heart made of jelly" (16). The story she gives us is not one that allows us to march straight toward the truth, for such a path would oversimplify a world that is so full of evil and so far beyond explanation that it need not be explained—it can only be "dealt with, survived, outwitted, triumphed over" (*Sula* 118). Claudia's narrative, which has a circular and, some might say, elusive quality to it, is in itself a reflection of the image that is so central to her heritage: the fourth face of God.

NOTES

1. Any serious student of Western and African religions knows that the conceptualizations of God within fairly similar theological traditions can differ dramatically. My intent in this essay is not to examine the competing models within closely related traditions but to explore how Morrison presents the differences between general models of two distinctly different traditions: the Western and the African.

Though my study is limited to the images of God present in *The Bluest Eye*, other studies have dealt with this topic in relation to some of Morrison's other novels. See Vashti Crutcher Lewis for a comparison of Shadrack's role in *Sula* to that of "a divine river spirit" or "a West African Water priest who represents and speaks for a river god" (92). See Janice M. Sokoloff for an examination of Eva Peace's god-like role in *Sula*. And see Lauren Lepow for an exploration of Valerian's role in *Tar Baby* as "the image of a white man's god" (368) and an analysis of the religious connotations of Son's name.

2. Maxine Lavon Montgomery has made this same point with regard to the people of the Bottom in *Sula*, arguing that "Western linear history" is "a distorted version of reality that keeps the townsfolk reaching out in vain for a future that persistently eludes their grasp" (128).

3. Patricia Hunt discusses *Sula's* parabolic qualities, which she sees as part of Morrison's critique of either-or thinking.

4. As Trudier Harris has pointed out, Pauline's separation from the African American community is underscored by her "attachment to the rich white family for which she works in Ohio when they assign her a nickname—Polly" (20). Harris contends that Pauline's acceptance of the nickname is a subversion of the tradition of nicknaming that has been a central feature of the African American community.

5. Though most scholars argue that African traditional religions tend to associate evil with God in some way, at least one writer, Gwinyai H. Muzorewa, concludes that "African traditional religion holds that all good comes from God and that evil was not created by God" (19).

6. The contrasting images of a white and a black God envisioned by Cholly are part of a larger pattern of inversion present throughout the novel. See Jacqueline de Weever for a discussion of this pattern in *The Bluest Eye* and *Sula*.

7. According to John S. Mbiti, in many African religions God "is brought into the picture primarily as an attempt to explain what is otherwise difficult for the human mind" (45). In contrast to Western religious traditions, within which the existence of evil is typically blamed on the sinful nature of humans and a spiritual being who stands in conflict with a benevolent God, practitioners of African religions tend not to divorce God from the problem of evil.

8. Pecola's symbolic connection to Christ and her failure to triumph over her circumstances is illustrative of Morrison's drive to stress the failure of white theological models for her African American characters. Deborah Guth has uncovered

this same theme in *Beloved,* in which "the hostile dialogic interaction between" Christian symbols and the circumstances of African American characters "leads to a total polarization that exposes the terrible inadequacy of the Christological model to contain or clarify the teleology of black historic reality" (90).

Works Cited

Baldwin, James. *Go Tell It on the Mountain.* 1953. New York: Dell, 1985.
———. *The Fire Next Time.* 1962. New York: Dell, 1988.
Cone, James H. *God of the Oppressed.* San Francisco: Harper, 1975.
Danquah, J. B. *The Akan Doctrine of God: A Fragment of Gold Coast Ethics and Religion.* 2nd ed. London: Frank Cass, 1968.
de Weever, Jacqueline. "The Inverted World of Toni Morrison's *The Bluest Eye* and *Sula.*" *CLA Journal 22* (1979): pp. 402-14.
Equlano, Olaudah. *The Life of Olaudah Equiano.* 1789. London: Dawsons of Pall Mall, 1969.
Guth, Deborah. "'Wonder what God had in mind': *Beloved's* Dialogue with Christianity." *Journal of Narrative Technique* 24.2 (1994): pp. 83-97.
Harris, Trudier. *Fiction and Folklore: The Novels of Toni Morrison.* Knoxville: University of Tennessee Press, 1991.
Hunt, Patricia. "War and Peace: Transfigured Categories and the Politics of *Sula.*" *African American Review* 27 (1993): pp. 443–59.
Hurston, Zora Neale. *Their Eyes Were Watching God.* 1937. New York: Harper, 1990.
Jones, Major J. *The Color of God: The Concept of God in Afro-American Thought.* Macon: Mercer University Press, 1987.
Lawson, E. Thomas. *Religions of Africa: Traditions in Transformation.* San Francisco: Harper, 1984.
Lepow, Lauren. "Paradise Lost and Found: Dualism and Edenic Myth in Toni Morrison's *Tar Baby.*" *Contemporary Literature* 28 (1987): pp. 363–377.
Lester, Julius. *Black Folktales.* New York: Grove, 1969.
Lewis, Vashti Crutcher. "African Tradition in Toni Morrison's *Sula.*" *Phylon* 48 (1987): pp. 91-97.
Mbiti, John S. *African Religions and Philosophy.* 2nd ed. Oxford: Heinemann, 1989.
McVeigh, Malcolm J. *God in Africa: Conceptions of God in African Traditional Religion and Christianity.* Cape Cod: Claude Stark, 1974.
Montgomery, Maxine Lavon. "A Pilgrimage to the Origins: The Apocalypse as Structure and Theme in Toni Morrison's *Sula.*" *Black American Literature Forum* 23 (1989): pp. 127–137.
Morrison, Toni. *The Bluest Eye.* 1970. New York: Washington Square Press, 1972.
———. *Song of Solomon.* 1977. New York: Plume, 1987.
———. *Sula.* 1973. New York: Plume, 1982.
Muzorewa, Gwinyai H. *The Origins and Development of African Theology.* Maryknoll: Orbis, 1985.
Parker, Bettye J. "Complexity: Toni Morrison's Women—An Interview Essay." *Sturdy Black Bridges: Visions of Black Women in Literature.* Ed. Roseann P. Bell, Parker, and Beverly Guy-Sheftall. New York: Anchor, 1979: pp. 251–257.
Sawyerr, Harry. *God: Ancestor or Creator?* London: Longman, 1970.
Sokoloff, Janice M. "Intimations of Matriarchal Age: Notes on the Mythical Eva in Toni Morrison's *Sula.*" *Journal of Black Studies* 16 (1986): pp. 429–34.

CAT MOSES

The Blues Aesthetic in Toni Morrison's
The Bluest Eye

> The blues aesthetic is an ethos of blues people that manifests itself in
> everything done, not just in the music. (ya Salaam 2)

Readers of Toni Morrison's first novel, *The Bluest Eye*, are often so over-
whelmed by the narrative's emotional content—the child Pecola's incestuous
rape, ensuing pregnancy, and subsequent abandonment by her community
and descent into madness—that they miss the music in this lyrically "songified" narrative.[1] Morrison has stated that her narrative "effort is to be *like*
something that has probably only been fully expressed perhaps in music . . ."
("Interview" 408). *The Bluest Eye* is the genesis of her effort "to do what the
music did for blacks, what we used to be able to do with each other in private and in that civilization that existed underneath the white civilization"
(Morrison, "Language" 371). The catharsis and the transmission of cultural
knowledge and values that have always been central to the blues form the
thematic and rhetorical underpinnings of *The Bluest Eye*. The narrative's
structure follows a pattern common to traditional blues lyrics: a movement
from an initial emphasis on loss to a concluding suggestion of resolution of
grief through motion. In between its initial statement of loss and its final

African American Review, Volume 33, Number 4; Winter 1999: pp. 623–637. © 1999
Cat Moses.

emphasis on movin' on, *The Bluest Eye* contains an abundance of cultural wisdom. The blues lyrics that punctuate the narrative at critical points suggest a system of folk knowledge and values that is crucial to a young black woman's survival in the 1930s and '40s and which supports Claudia's cathartic role as storyteller. The lyrics also illustrate the folk knowledge and values that are *not* transmitted to Pecola—information without which she cannot survive as a whole and healthy human being.

In traditional blues songs, the singer is the subject, the *I* who tells her (or his) own story. In *The Bluest Eye*, however, Claudia tells Pecola's story. Except for a few fragmented lines of dialogue, Pecola remains silent within Claudia's narrative. Much of the critical discourse on the novel has focused on the relationship between voice and empowerment, and on the problematics of a narrative that silences its dispossessed protagonist while seeking to empower the dispossessed and to critique power relations. This essay addresses the apparent contradiction between *The Bluest Eye's* silenced protagonist and its traditionally African American equation of voice with empowerment by situating Claudia's narrative voice within African American oral traditions and a blues aesthetic. I posit Claudia as the narrative's blues subject, its bluest "I" and representative blues figure, and Pecola as the abject *tabula rasa* on which the community's blues are inscribed. I assert that, rather than singing Pecola's blues, Claudia "sings" the community's blues. Claudia bears witness, through the oral tradition of testifying, to the community's lack of self-love and its transference of this lack onto the abject body of Pecola.

In the first section below, I address the initial reference to a specific blues song in the novel by discussing the lyrics and structure of "The St. Louis Blues" as representative of traditional blues. I then lay the foundation for a discussion of *The Bluest Eye* as a blues narrative. In the ensuing section, I build upon this foundation to discern a female blues subjectivity in *The Bluest Eye*, a subjectivity constructed through African American oral traditions and embodied in the three whores' speech, song, and laughter, and in Claudia's narrative voice. Finally, I position Claudia's subjectivity within a blues aesthetic and her voice within the oral tradition of testifying.

The earliest reference to a specific blues in *The Bluest Eye* follows the scene in which Mrs. MacTeer harangues the girls after Pecola consumes what Mrs. MacTeer deems more than her share of the milk in the refrigerator, and it precedes the narrative of Pecola's first menstruation. This reference to the blues, then, forms a bridge between childhood (the milk consumption represents Pecola's effort to consume—and become—Shirley Temple) and womanhood. The blues to which Claudia refers exemplify the cultural knowledge and values transmitted orally to Claudia that ease and assist her transition into womanhood—folk wisdom that is not conveyed to Pecola. The blues are first represented in the text in Claudia's reminiscence about the Saturdays when her "mother was in a singing mood." Claudia recalls snatches of lyrics from "hard times" songs her mother frequently sings, including the phrase "hate to see that evening sun go down," a reference to one of the earliest recorded and most popular blues songs, "St. Louis Blues," by W. C. Handy (25).

Musicians from the early twentieth century to the present have revised, improvised, and recorded Handy's classic, whose lyrics convey a wealth of folk knowledge and cultural values. Hearing her mother sing the blues, Claudia finds herself

> longing for those hard times, yearning to be grown without "a thin di-ime to my name." I looked forward to the delicious time when "my man" would leave me, when I would "hate to see that evening sun go down "'cause then I would know "my man has left this town." Misery colored by the greens and blues in my mother's voice took all the grief out of the words and left me with a conviction that pain was not only endurable, it was sweet. (25-26)

The lyrical language in which Claudia describes her mother's singing is suggestive of the sweet and cathartic tone of traditional blues. The tone and the positive spectrum of emotion she describes as the colors of her mother's voice are more powerfully affecting than the pain signified by the words. Morrison tells us that music was one of "the most prominent elements" in her own early life ("Interview" 396). Her mother was a singer, and her home was filled with the seductive blues yearning that Claudia describes, a yearning at the emotional center of the "St. Louis Blues" and *The Bluest Eye.*

In referring to the "St. Louis Blues," Morrison has chosen a blues that registers all of the central concerns of *The Bluest Eye.* Both the song and the novel exhibit a lyrical progression from an initial statement of loss to a concluding statement of resolve to move on, literally and figuratively. The song opens on the traditional blues note of loss or lack: The speaker's man has left her with an empty bed, and consequently she hates to see the lonely nighttime come. The song then proceeds immediately, in the second verse, to the suggestion of resolution through the motion nearly always implied in the blues: "Feelin' tomorrow lak I feel today / I'll pack mah trunk, an' make mah getaway."

Houston Baker writes that the notion of resolution of earthly problems through motion is implied in the *sound* of the blues:

> The dominant blues syntagm in America is an instrumental imitation of *train-wheels-over-track-junctures*. The sound is the "sign," as it were, of the blues, and it combines an intriguing melange of phonics: rattling gondolas, clattering flatbeds, quilling whistles, clanging bells, rambling boxcars, and other railroad sounds. . If desire and absence are driving conditions of blues performance, the amelioration of such conditions is implied by the onomatopoeic *training* of blues voice and instrument.[2]

Baker adds that, "even as [the blues] speak of paralyzing absence and ineradicable desire, their instrumental rhythms suggest change, movement, action . . ." (8). This observation certainly applies to the "St. Louis Blues," a traditional twelve-bar blues augmented with an eight-bar bridge and an additional twelve-bar blues. Its rhymed couplets, most of them obeying strict iambic pentameter, develop a complex iteration of cultural values and direct a black audience to sources of support and sustenance in times of trouble.

Like many other blues, the "St. Louis Blues" suggests a literal as well as a tropological resolution through motion: The speaker announces her intent to board a train and seek her lover who has left for St. Louis, invoking cultural wisdom that may be interpreted in literal as well as figurative terms. She suggests that looking up a friend employed by the railroad lines is the first step toward a way out of troubled times (verse seven). This is excellent practical advice in a time period when the railroads employed large numbers of black men in some of the better-paying, service-oriented positions in the urban North. For black people negotiating the route of the Great Migration, from the Jim Crow South to the urban North, friends on the railroad line were indispensable. A friend on the railroad could be a poor person's only ticket to ride. In figurative terms this verse suggests that there *is* a way out of troubled times and that this way out involves forming and relying on a close-knit community and making one's needs known. It also suggests that the two-timing man may not be the speaker's only love interest ("mah ol' frien', Jeff / Gwine to pin mahself close to his side / If I flag his train, I sho can ride"), and that women can give as well as they get in the field of intimate intrigues. Figuratively, in referring to the train, the song suggests to the listener's imagination the sound of the train, echoed in the sound of the blues, and at this juncture of sound and reference to sound, the promise of motion and change is magnified and enhanced.

James McPherson, in *Railroad: Trains and Train People in American Culture*, notes that to nineteenth-century

> backwoodsmen, Africans, and recent immigrants—the people who comprised the vernacular segment of society . . . the [steam engine locomotive] might have been loud and frightening, but its whistle

and its wheels promised movement. And since a commitment to
both freedom and movement was the basic premise of democracy,
it was probable that such people would view the locomotive as a
challenge to the integrative powers of their imaginations. (6)[3]

Claudia tells the reader twice that Mrs. MacTeer is "all the time singing
about trains and Arkansas" (98). Claudia, with her keen sense of justice,
hears freedom and democracy in what Houston Baker would call the
"*trained*" sound of her mother's singing voice. The Saturdays on which her
mother does not sing are "lonesome, fussy, soapy days. Second in misery only
to those tight, starchy, cough-drop Sundays, so full of 'don'ts' and 'set'cha
self downs'" (25). The singing Saturdays are full of possibility; her mother's
"voice so sweet and her singing-eyes so melty" (25) stir her imagination and
yearning, and leave her with a sense of "conviction" (26) that sustains her in
times of trouble.

The singing subject of the "St. Louis Blues" is a female,[4] and in verse
seven she yearns for the sense of dominion, motion, and freedom represented
by the masculine railroad line ("If I flag his train, I sho can ride"). The tone
and tenor of Claudia's narrative express a similar longing. In employing the
"St. Louis Blues" to provoke and represent Claudia's yearning, Morrison inverts traditional notions of the masculine and the feminine and claims for
Claudia some of the "masculinity" that she will later claim for Sula. The notion that there is always somewhere else to go when hard times hit, and a way
to get there, sustains Claudia. The only somewhere else for Pecola to go is
insane. The poverty of her imagination, an imagination which has not been
nurtured by the blues or any other source of cultural sustenance, is reflected
in the destitution of the Breedlove home.

The traditional progression from cathartic statement of loss to an-
nouncement of the intent to achieve resolution through motion is accomplished in the first two verses of the "St. Louis Blues." The remaining eight
verses that Claudia would have become familiar with through her mother's
repeated performances affirm cultural values essential to her growth and development—and the growth and development of any young, black, working-class person. The third verse of the song iterates a theme that is central
to this novel and that runs throughout the body of Morrison's work: The
glitz of beauty industry consumer products that reify light skin and straight
hair— the make-up and fashion apparel ruined in the rain on Hagar's fatal
shopping spree in *Song of Solomon*, for example—can be both powerful and
powerfully misleading. Verse three argues that it is not the St. Louis woman
who has stolen the speaker's man, it is "diamon' rings . . . / powder an' . . .
store-bought hair." The St. Louis woman is not present in this verse; rather,
her presence is suggested solely by the reified products with which she adorns

herself. Verse four of the "St. Louis Blues" recapitulates the song's initial sense of loss. It echoes the soulless emptiness that the speaker asserts (in the third verse) lies beneath the St. Louis Woman's patina of beauty and success. In *The Bluest Eye*, Maureen Peal is more a conglomeration of signifying products—"patent-leather shoes with buckles . . . sweaters the color of lemon drops . . . a brown velvet coat trimmed in white rabbit fur, and a matching muff"—than a presence (62). Her surname may be read as Morrison's signifying on the word *peel* to emphasize 'skin,' 'rind,' 'patina,' or 'husk.'

The last two verses of the "St. Louis Blues" relate cultural values absolutely crucial to Claudia's survival and Pecola's downfall, and speak to the sensitive issue at the emotional center of *The Bluest Eye:* caste prejudice, or intraracism based upon skin tone. Verse nine describes the sought-after man as "stovepipe brown" and links his desirability to his dark-toned skin; and verse ten inverts the caste hierarchy that has filtered down from the dominant white culture into Lorain's black community, a caste hierarchy that privileges light skin, blue eyes, and European features and that is embodied in Maureen Peal. The speaking subject of the "St. Louis Blues" constructs a striking visual image of the desired man as "Blacker than midnight, teeth lak flags of truce / Blackest man in de whole St. Louis." She then employs this image in a direct inversion of the dominant caste hierarchy, closing the verse with a popular aphorism, passed down through generations of African Americans, that assigns the highest aesthetic value to the darkest skin: "Blacker de berry, sweeter is de juice. . . . "While Claudia is regularly serenaded—on Saturdays, when her mother was in a singing mood—with this concise, confident, and lyrical deconstruction of the Shirley Temple aesthetic, Pecola is rejected by Pauline, who embraces the "corn-yellow"-haired child of her white employers. One of the novel's more chilling scenes, rivaled in emotional content only by the rape scene, is the one in which Pauline slaps Pecola for accidentally overturning the blueberry cobbler, throws her out of the house, and then tenderly embraces the white Fisher child, who calls her by her first name (Pecola must call her mother "Mrs. Breedlove" [107–109]). Clearly, Pauline has internalized the notion that black is not beautiful. Pecola and the dark berries in the bubbling cobbler with which she is associated are objects to be swept out of the way as Pauline rushes to embrace the rich white child.

Claudia's defiance of and Pecola's internalization of the Shirley Temple aesthetic are illustrated in the Maureen Peal "six-finger-dog-tooth-meringue-pie" episode (61–73). In rejecting Maureen and "calling her out of her name," Claudia rejects the intraracism implicit in the privileging of Maureen's "high yellow dream" complexion and her "two lynch ropes" of long brown hair (62). Pecola desires what Claudia rejects: light skin, straight hair, blue eyes, and the social status they represent. Claudia's defiance is a learned and nurtured defiance, encouraged by a severe but loving mother who sings to her on Saturdays.) Pecola internalizes the caste aesthetic that the "St. Louis Blues" mediates against; an aesthetic that Morrison argues has insidiously infiltrated not only families like the Breedloves but whole communities.

Claudia tells us that she comes to embrace this aesthetic tentatively, reluctantly, and consciously. As Inger-Anne Softing notes, "Claudia is the only character in this novel who consciously makes an attempt at deconstructing the ideology of the dominant society. This is seen in her dismembering of the dolls" (90). Describing her gradual awareness that her violent dismembering of white baby dolls was unacceptable, Claudia speaks of a conversion "from pristine sadism to fabricated hatred to fraudulent love. . . . I learned much later to worship [Shirley Temple], just as I learned to delight in cleanliness, knowing, even as I learned, that the change was adjustment without improvement" (23). This awareness of her reluctant capitulation to intraracism seems remarkable in a child. It is almost certainly the observation of the adult Claudia, who is engaged in the act of remembering and interpreting her childhood. Still, it is noteworthy that the child Claudia seems to stand alone in her critique of a "master" aesthetic that is internalized by nearly everyone in her community, from the adults who give the gift of white baby dolls and Shirley Temple cups, to Geraldine, to the bully boys who taunt Pecola and whose words Maureen Peal repeats: "'Black and ugly black e mos'" (73).

Morrison has stated that her purpose in writing the novel was to "peck away at the gaze that condemns" Pecola's blackness as ugly ("Afterword" 210); Morrison critiques the "racial self-loathing" implicit in the community's valorization of Maureen Peal and the peel/skin color/caste hierarchy that she represents. Whereas Maureen Peal and Shirley Temple serve as icons of the destructive reification of caste and whiteness, respectively, the "St. Louis Blues" singing subject recognizes the vapidity beneath the husk of powder, rings, and store- bought hair. Claudia, too, even as a child, recognizes the self-loathing inherent in the condemning gaze, and the blues wisdom that fills the house on Claudia's mother's singing Saturdays has fostered this recognition. Thus, Morrison implies that the MacTeers have retained a connection to ancestral knowledge essential to survival in their current situation, a connection lost to the Breedloves.

The Breedloves follow a trajectory away from the values of the black, poor, rural South and toward values that serve the interests of a privileged, white upper-middle class and of capitalism itself. This trajectory serves to instill in the Breedloves' own family a sense of worthlessness and lack. Morrison makes it clear that Cholly and Pauline Breedlove, and particularly Pauline, were once connected to a community that embodied the cultural values expressed in the blues. In Pauline's italicized narrative fragments concerning her girlhood in the rural South, she recalls a delicious yearning and pleasure associated not with consumer products but with community and with the associated fruits of the earth[5]:

> *When I first seed Cholly I want you to know it was like all the bits of color from that time down home when us chil'ren went berry picking after a funeral and I put some in the pocket of my Sunday dress, and they mashed up and stained my hips. My whole dress was messed with purple, and it never did wash out. Not the dress nor me. I could feel that purple deep inside me. And that lemonade Mama used to make when Pap came in out the fields. It be cool and yellowish. . . . And that streak of green the June bugs made on the trees the night we left from down home. All of them colors was in me.* (115)

Pauline's use of the word *colors* to name an abstract emotional yearning recalls the blues yearning instilled in Claudia by the sound of her mother's voice. The above passage is, in essence, Pauline's blues, and it expresses a longing for home and community and a choice to move on, to "go down to the crossroads," as Robert Johnson put it in his historic blues, and head north. In lyrically expressing a longing for the rural Southern community that revolved around church ("Sunday dress") and ritual ("berry picking," "funeral"), Pauline accomplishes what the blues singer accomplishes: She recreates that which is lost and for which she longs, transforming lack into poetry. Unfortunately, the transformation is temporary and exists only in her memory. Pauline's narrative traces her movement toward the white bourgeois values represented by the Hollywood films that seduce her, and by the flawless home of the Fishers. The lure of the material supplants her memories of community, even though she can never hope to possess what she longs for.

Pauline seeks acceptance and success in terms defined by a white power structure that excludes her, whereas Claudia possesses an altogether different understanding of social structures. She seems intuitively to understand a central tenet of blues wisdom embodied in the "St. Louis Blues": Seek alternative forms of knowledge and understanding within the community, not in the white power structure. These forms are represented by the song's reference to the "gypsy,"[6] a figure who has a long history in African American literature and oral culture.[7]

The "gypsy" fortune teller or root doctor figure is negatively personified in *The Bluest Eye* by Soaphead Church. Claudia understands that Soaphead Church may reside within the community, but he is not of the community. She seems instinctively to understand that Church despises blackness and lives in thrall to a value system that excludes him. Because Claudia is part of the community, she is privy to information circulated orally about Church's "nasty" habit of molesting young girls. But Pecola, because she is treated as an outcast, is not privy to this knowledge. She sees in Church an outcast like herself, living on the fringes of the community, and in her first visit to him she is made to understand that he despises blackness just as she despises her own blackness. Pecola visits Church hoping for some magic, but Morrison twists the root doctor/fortune teller figure into a self-loathing, obsessive-compulsive child molester in order to underscore the dangerous nature of the only alternative sources of knowledge and succor available to children like Pecola, whose families and communities are not looking out for their well-being.

The cultural values and knowledge embodied in the blues and transmitted orally to Claudia enable her to develop what would much later come to be called a black aesthetic.8 Claudia does not, however, passively absorb this body of cultural knowledge and draw strength from it. She not only hears the blues, but she listens to and, more importantly, "sings" the blues. Indeed, the blues define her storytelling voice and style. Claudia is a blues subject engaged in what Kalamu ya Salaam calls the act of "reclaiming the black blues self."

As a singing subject, Claudia has some talented and versatile models in *The Bluest Eye*. Mrs. MacTeer and Poland serenade the reader with only a few lines, but these lines constitute a rich variety of blues expression that reflects the range of techniques Claudia employs as a blues narrator. Like Mrs. MacTeer singing the "St. Louis Blues" and Pauline reconstructing the rural South in blues prose, Poland transforms lack into poetry:

> I got blues in my mealbarrel
> Blues up on the shelf
> I got blues in my mealbarrel
> Blues up on the shelf
> Blues in my bedroom
> 'Cause I'm sleeping by myself. (51)

The transformation of lack, loss, and grief into poetic catharsis is the constitutive task of the blues singer, and it is the labor that Claudia accomplishes in narrating *The Bluest Eye*. Central to the transmogrification of lack into poetry in Poland's "Mealbarrel Blues" is an assertion of subjectivity: In singing to affirm not having (blues, not meal, fill the mealbarrel), Poland establishes a desiring self. In desiring, she exists, and in naming her desire, she acts to fulfill it.

In the act of naming the blues (which Poland does five times in the verse above, in every line but the last), she calls down the power of *Nommo*, defined by Angela Y. Davis as a "West African philosophical concept . . . 'the magic power of the word' . . . the very basis of music" (6). In naming the blues, Poland activates the catharsis that holds the promise of ameliorating the blues. Davis goes on to assert that, in keeping with the tradition of *Nommo*, black women blues artists historically have shaped and interpreted a female blues subject who yearns for freedom. She emphasizes that the yearned-for freedom is not to be confused with Western notions of symbolic freedom; rather, given the material conditions of blues production, freedom must be understood first as literal—ownership of one's body—and, later (in history), as material—control over the means of production, and freedom from poverty, discrimination, debt, and disenfranchisement. Davis asserts that the sexual desire expressed in African American women's blues lyrics is a "camouflaged dream of a new social order" (14). It is also an assertion of women's control over their bodies.

When a woman is living in desperate material conditions, with nothing but the blues in her pantry, her body is all that she owns and controls; thus, assertion of ownership and control is a courageous political statement. Women blues singers from Ma Rainey to Koko Taylor have boldly and boastfully asserted their sexuality. When Mr. Henry molests Frieda and Frieda explains to Claudia the nature of his transgression, Claudia attempts to insert her voice into this tradition, and Morrison emphasizes the humor and naïveté in the guileless child's attempt. Claudia enthusiastically asks, "'Really? How did it feel?'" (99). She then asks if it didn't feel good, and displays an innocent jealousy at Mr. Henry's choosing Frieda instead of her, aligning herself with the blues singer who complains of an empty bed.

The three whores embody the blues singer's assertion of sexuality, desirability, and ownership of their bodies. Nowhere in the novel is this clearer than in the paragraph describing their laughter:

> All three of the women laughed. Marie threw back her head. From deep inside, her laughter came like the sound of many rivers. . . . China giggled spastically. Each gasp seemed to be yanked out of her by an unseen hand jerking an unseen string. Poland, who seldom spoke unless she was drunk, laughed without sound. When she was sober, she hummed mostly or chanted blues songs, of which she knew many. (52–53)

Inger-Anne Softing writes that Poland, in addition to carrying "on the old tradition of blending the sweet and the sad," introduces into the text "true carnival laughter . . . nonauthoritarian and nonhierarchical" (88). Softing points out that all three of the whores in *The Bluest Eye* laugh with their whole bodies, from the depths of being, constituting "true carnivalesque" in "a novel which, on the whole, is not filled with the liberating force of laughter" (88). The whores' laughter is the quintessential blues utterance: It wells up from within, with the force and rhythm of a freight train, and it erupts into pure catharsis. It is a public communication of emotions that are both private and shared.

Although the blues typically feature a first-person singular subject, and exhibit a concern "with the problems and/or experiences of the individual" (Southern 335), Davis observes in women's blues a "public communication of private troubles" that "allows for the development of a collective social consciousness within the black population" (14–15). Houston A. Baker, Jr., describes the blues as "an anonymous (nameless) voice issuing from the black (w)hole" (5). Poland's "Blues in my bedroom / 'Cause I'm sleeping by myself" may be read as a sensual and a political expression of collective need. Her "Mealbarrel Blues" conflates the language of sexual desire and the desire for freedom from poverty.

The conflation of material lack and sexual desire is humorously developed, in storytelling rather than singing form, in exchanges between Marie and China as China attempts to insert herself into the legend of John Dillinger. Marie and China enact a tradition that blends call-and-response, an erotic blues sensuality, and tongue-in-cheek humor—signifying. Miss Marie responds to Pecola's earnest " 'How come they [men] all love you?'" with, "'What else they gone do? They know I'm rich and good lookin'.'" Marie proceeds to tell a tall tale of how she came to be rich, the story in which she claims to be the mysterious Lady in Red who turned John Dillinger in to the "F. B. and I." China responds with guffaws and interrupts Marie's story, first with questions mimicking Pecola's earnestness ("'Yeah. . . . Where you get it from?'"), then with affirmations ("'We *know* that'"), and finally with goading insults, to which Marie responds playfully and aggressively:

> "I was little and cute then. No more than ninety pounds, soaking wet."
> "You ain't never been soaking wet," China said.
> "Well you ain't never been dry. Shut up. . . . (53)

China hoots, "'She makin' like she's the Lady in Red that told on John Dillinger. Dillinger wouldn't have come near you lessen he was going hunting in Africa and shoot you for a hippo'" (54).

China and Marie engage in the black vernacular tradition of signifying, which Geneva Smitherman defines as "the verbal art of insult in which a speaker humorously puts down, talks about, needles—that is, signifies on— the listener" (118). Signifying has been enacted in musical forms from blues to rap; it is a component of some of the earliest recorded blues, and it has remained a staple in the blues repertoire. Pecola hears Poland singing, and she listens to China signifying on Marie's story, but she lacks the cultural knowledge necessary to understanding. She is exiled from the collective consciousness; it is as though she doesn't speak the language of the blues, although she most certainly *lives* the blues. Although she is close in age to Claudia and Frieda, she lacks Claudia's sense of irony and humor and both sisters' mastery of language.

Throughout the novel, Claudia's observations are guided by a sharp-edged humor. Her narrative is characterized by the adaptive laughing-to-keep-from-crying perspective that is central to the blues and that Bernard Bell, in his study of the African American novel, terms "double vision." Some of the most humorous moments in *The Bluest Eye* occur in the scenes following Frieda's molestation by Mr. Henry. Claudia and Frieda's unwitting play on the meaning of *ruined* and their misinterpretation of vague and confusing adult speech leads them to believe that the only cure for the ruination that has been wrought on Frieda by Mr. Henry is for Frieda to become an alcoholic. Their youthful logic and the examples of China and Poland lead them to conclude that drinking whisky will prevent Frieda from getting fat, the ruinous result, they believe, of molestation. When Claudia and Frieda signify on Maureen Peal and play a child's version of the dozens when Maureen goads them, Pecola "fold[s] into herself, like a broken wing," because she is ashamed and lacks the double vision necessary to participation in this ritual (73).[9] Listening to China and Marie signifying, Pecola misses the humor and the innuendo; she responds with guileless earnestness: "'You rich, Miss Marie?'" (53); "'But what about the money?'" (54). Her responses to the whores' language play foreground her focus on the lack and need ("'rich . . . ? . . . money?'") that always marks the first verse(s) of a blues song—in this case it is material, a material desire, later reified in her desire for blue eyes. But Pecola's development as a blues subject stops at the first verse: She is entirely defined and consumed by lack. It is as though she is entrapped in the opening lines of a blues song; her character is never developed, as blues subjectivity is always developed, to the point of agency.

In Maxine Hong Kingston's *The Woman Warrior*, the narrator's mother explains "'the difference between mad people and sane people'": "'Sane people have variety when they talk-story. Mad people have only one story that they talk over and over'" (159). By the closing pages of *The Bluest Eye*, Pecola has only one story, the story of her beautiful blue eyes. Her identity is hopelessly fragmented; and, as Madonne Miner notes, "tragically, even when combined, [Pecola and her 'imaginary friend'] do not compose one whole being. . . . she no longer exists as a reasonable human being" (181). Claudia's voice gathers strength as Pecola fragments. Guided by a blues aesthetic, Claudia constructs a wealth of stories and a variety of perspectives from which to interpret her childhood experiences and Pecola's story. Even as a child, Claudia subverts the consumer culture and the outside gaze that seek to impose impossible standards of beauty on her community; she subsumes the master narrative into a blues narrative.

Central to Claudia's narrative style is the oral tradition of testifying. Geneva Smitherman defines this oral tradition that came out of the traditional black church as "a ritualized form of black communication in which the speaker gives verbal witness to the efficacy, truth and power of some experience in which all blacks have shared" (58). She adds that "to testify is to tell the truth through story"; testifying is not "plain and simple commentary but a dramatic narration and a communal reenactment of one's feelings and experiences" (150) Testifying is a tradition which, like call-and-response, is rooted in African American religious practice and can be traced to West African song and speech. The testifying utterance is a chronicle initiated by an individual— a registering of emotion rather than an outpouring of emotion in response to a call. In *Song of Solomon*, when Pilate stalks into the church at Hagar's funeral and calls out "'Mercy'" and Reba sings out "'I hear you,'" and they continue in this vein, singing back and forth, "*In the nighttime. / Mercy / In the darkness. / Mercy . . . ,*" they are performing call-and-response (317). Moments later, in the same scene, when Pilate repeats, "'My baby girl,'" as she gazes into the coffin, and then speaks these three words to the audience, she is testifying. Yvonne Atkinson observes that the emotional impact of this scene is the result of the layering of call-and-response and testifying, and that the layering of these two and of other residually oral forms throughout Morrison's fiction is central to her artistry.

The accomplished blues singer blends these two oral forms, as does Claudia in *The Bluest Eye*. When she offers up Pecola's story, she is testifying to the community's failings and the community's unspoken desire, which Pecola vocalizes. Morrison places Claudia in a position similar to that of Pilate gazing into the coffin. Claudia is gazing, in the novel's final pages, at Pecola picking among the garbage, and she turns her gaze outward toward the reader and testifies that Pecola is the site of inscription of a communal shame. This act of testifying is a narrative act that is central to Morrison's work. Morrison asserts that her

> work bears witness and suggests who the outlaws were, who survived under what circumstances and why. . . . All that is in the fabric of the story in order to do what the music used to do. The

> music kept us alive, but it's not enough any more. Whenever I feel
> uneasy about my writing, I think: what would be the response of
> people in the book if they read the book? That's my way of staying
> on track. Those are the people for whom I write. ("Language"
> 371)

Inherent in testifying is the assumption of commonalties between the testifying subject and her audience (Atkinson). Claudia skillfully bridges the
dramatic distance she has constructed as a blues narrator—just as Morrison
bridges that distance as a blues writer—and she assumes crucial commonalties with the community she speaks from, to, and about, critiquing it firmly
but lovingly and absolving its guilt and shame.

Throughout *The Bluest Eye*, Claudia sets herself up as an individual
who questions the community's tastes and judgments and often finds them
suspect; but she is not outside of or in opposition to the community—she
critiques the community from within. Morrison places her in a call-and-
response dialectic with a community chorus.[10] The traditional blues singer
did not speak for the community, but she did speak *from* the community. As
Giles Oakley puts it,

> Many black people would have been . . . offended by the idea
> that the blues singer "spoke" for them, in much the same way
> that others would reject the spokesmanship of the preacher.
> Nevertheless, there did exist what almost amounted to a blues
> community. Its significance was in the process of communal
> creation and participation in a shared culture. . . . the idea that the
> blues were an expression of deeply felt emotions made the music
> more than simply entertainment. (47)

In addition to Claudia's voice, we hear Pauline's, an omniscient narrator's,
and fragments of dialogue representing nearly every quarter of the community, from the three whores to Geraldine and Junior to Soaphead Church
to unidentified gossips. Claudia develops an individual voice that taps into
the community's repressed racial self-hatred and its deeply concealed guilt at
displacing that self-hatred onto Pecola. Hers is not what Robert Cataliotti
calls "a traditional country blues, which were most frequently performed by
solo artists." The country blues was thought of and enacted, for the most
part, as a masculine tradition. Claudia's blues are what Cataliotti and others
before him have termed a "Classic Blues . . . performed by a female singer
with accompaniment provided by a pianist, possibly augmented by a small
instrumental combo. Nonetheless, the singer certainly remained the dominant personality in the performance" (75). Claudia's is the dominant voice

in the novel, and Frieda frequently responds in the affirmative to Claudia's blues "call," as do Mrs. MacTeer's and Poland's blues and China's signifying. They are the blues chorus that mediates against the buzzing of voices that condemns Pecola.

The playwright August Wilson has said that the blues provide "a way of processing information about Black life, particularly information about the nobility . . . the beauty . . . and the resiliency of Black life." Claudia's embodiment of the blues aesthetic enables her to "process" precisely the "information" to which Wilson refers. *The Bluest Eye* does not appear to be a novel about beauty and nobility; it seems largely bereft of these elements. Even marigolds fail to grow in this fictional world.

"Beauty" is a deeply problematic concept in Morrison's work. In fact, the omniscient narrator of *The Bluest Eye* asserts that "physical beauty" and romantic love "are probably the most destructive ideas in the history of human thought" (122)[11] As Morrison interrogates a master narrative of beauty, her blues aesthetic lends structure, style, and form to the interrogation. The emphasis in Claudia's blues narrative is on resiliency, and the resiliency she develops as a blues subject allows her to appreciate the beauty and the nobility even in a community that fails its most destitute resident. At the novel's close, after blame has been assigned ("we were not strong, only aggressive; we were not free, merely licensed; we were not compassionate, we were polite; not good, but well behaved" [205]) and limited absolution granted ("I even think now that the soil of the entire country was hostile to marigolds that year"), Claudia is able to look "among the garbage . . . of [her] town" and focus, in the novel's final line, on beauty: "sunflowers" (206).

Morrison constructs Claudia as a blues subject: sensuous, brutally honest, poetic, ironically humorous, and adept at call-and-response, signifying, and testifying. She learns to sing from her mother, and her blues is *The Bluest Eye*. Her storytelling mode is a blues mode in its sensuality, honesty, lyricism, ironic distance, humor, dialectic with the community, and open-endedness. Blues narratives, like blues lyrics, never end on a closed note, and *The Bluest Eye* is no exception. At the end of a "typical" blues there is affirmation, as there is in "St. Louis Blues" (of the beauty in blackness), and there is movement, or a statement of intent to move, but there is no closure, no neatly wrapped-up ending.[12]

The subjects of blues narratives achieve, by their narratives' close, an ironic distance—and often a physical distance—from the lack and loss expressed in the narratives' beginnings. Indeed, the construction of ironic distance and open-endedness is a primary function of the blues, which codify a means of resistance to oppression and a call to "move on" up and out. Claudia's blues narrative may be understood as a sustained signifying on the master aesthetic of physical beauty and the racial self-loathing that this master aesthetic produces. Hers is a complex and polyvocal signifying, involving a call-and-response dialectic with her community. Claudia could not carry on this dialectic, could not "sing" this blues without first living the blues. As Janie in Hurston's *Their Eyes Were Watching God* puts it, "'It's uh known fact. . . . you got tuh *go* there tuh *know* there'" (183). Claudia's narrative traces a trajectory from the childhood experience and naming of lack—her community's lack of a sense of the intrinsic beauty of blackness and hence its scapegoating of the Breedloves and of Pecola, in particular—to a sense of resolution through movement.

At the novel's close, Claudia claims membership in the community ("my town"), but she has achieved sufficient distance from her subject to enable her to reconstruct Pecola's story. She sees Pecola in her mind, or on the streets of her present-day community, "searching through the garbage—for what?" but she also sees across the dramatic distance between the blues subject and her narrative (206). Claudia does not see this traversing of distance as unequivocally positive, but she sees it as necessary. She has stood at a blues crossroads and resolved to assert her independence. She has distanced herself from Pecola and from her community in order to engage the community in a dialectic, but she looks back upon this move with a nostalgia for a time and place that no longer exist. Claudia can look back in time and see clearly because she has achieved a metaphoric distance, albeit at a price. The novel closes with a sense that Claudia has moved on while Pecola remains frozen in time—a child, trapped in the tragic first verse of her own blues, with her imagined blue eyes and the lack and self-loathing they signify, "frozen in the glare of the lover's inward eye" (206). The loving eye is Claudia's, and *The Bluest Eye* is her testifying to Pecola's pain and the community's shame.

The "Eye" of the title may refer to Pecola's disastrous longing for blue eyes, but it also refers to the *eye* that takes Pecola as its subject, and to the *I* who narrates her story. *The Bluest Eye* is Claudia's blues for Pecola and her community. The novel's central paucity is the community's lack of self-love, a lack precipitated by the imposition of a master aesthetic that privileges the light skin and blue eyes inherent in the community's internalization of this master aesthetic. Claudia is the voice for the community's blues, and Pecola is the site of the inscription of the community's blues.

Notes

1. Geneva Smitherman uses the term *songified*, which she attributes to the poet Eugene Redmond, to describe the speech patterns of Black English (3).

2. Morrison is aware of the train as a blues syntagm. In an interview with Robert Stepto, she discusses it as a gendered phenomenon. Stepto observes that most "of the major male characters in black literature are in motion." Morrison concurs and comments, "Trains—you hear those men talk about trains like they were their

first lover—the names of the trains, the times of the trains! And, boy, you know they spread their seed all over the world. They are really moving! Perhaps it's because they don't have a land, they don't have dominion" (391). On the road, on the railroad lines—in motion—black men, in Morrison's literary imagination, experience dominion. She acknowledges that "in sociological terms that is described as a major failing of black men"—that black men have been faulted for not being stable, for not always being "in place" or at home with their families, but she asserts that "that has always been to me one of the most attractive features about black male life . . . the fact that they would split in a minute just delights me." Morrison goes on to talk about how she endowed Sula with this predilection for motion, how Sula "is a masculine character in that sense" (392). I suggest that Claudia, too, is endowed with a predilection for motion, and that this is a central characteristic in her construction as a blues subject.

3. Houston Baker cites McPherson in his discussion of "Blues and Vernacular expression in America" in *Blues, Ideology, and Afro-American Literature* (11). Giles Oakley, in his history of the blues, provides an opposite, outsider's (he is British) reading of the travel theme in the blues: "Over and over again the theme of [blues] songs was travel. . . . In this respect the bluesman [sic] reflected a tendency to be found in American society at large and in black society in particular, where, especially since Emancipation, movement had symbolized freedom. Notions of 'boundlessness' have often been taken to be a part of the American Dream, but the constant migrations, over long or short distances, over all parts of the Southern states and increasingly to the North were more a reflection of the arid and sterile quality of life for most poor blacks. Trapped into a kind of economic servitude by sharecropping, with few opportunities to break out of those limitations, travel could itself be an assertion of independence" (57). In Morrison's work, travel is nearly always a form of or a means to independence. The quality of life for poor black folk in her fiction, however, is rarely "arid and sterile"; aridity and sterility tend to come with the trappings of middle- and upper-class success in her oeuvre.

4. I am assuming a heterosexual subject. The many recorded versions that I am familiar with feature a female vocalist singing about the man who has left her.

5. The third-person narrative of Cholly's journey from boyhood to manhood later in the novel provides a counterbalance to this idyllic view of the rural South. Cholly's post-funeral romp in a wild vineyard with Darlene stains her Sunday dress with purple juice, but Cholly's and Darlene's adolescent lovemaking is interrupted by the white men with the lantern. Both Cholly's and Pauline's narratives, however, construct a rural South in which black people shared what they had and lived by a value system that privileged community over the accumulation of individual wealth and consumerism.

6. The "gypsy" fortune teller of mixed race or exoticized ethnicity who dispensed advice and alternative remedies that often blended African, European, Christian, and secular knowledge systems was a significant figure in (or on the fringes of) many communities like the one Morrison depicts in *The Bluest Eye*'s Lorain, Ohio, of 1931.

7. The fortune teller/root doctor figure appears frequently in African American literature, most famously in Charles Chesnutt's *The Conjure Woman* stories (1899); in Frederick Douglass's 1845 *Narrative* in the person of Sandy, who empowers the enslaved Douglass successfully to resist the brutality of Mr. Covey; and, more recently, in Ishmael Reed's new-hoodoo fictions.

8. I refer to the Black Art Movement's foregrounding and naming of a distinct aesthetics sensibility during the 1960s and 1970s that nurtured radical African American creative and artistic production.

9. Playing the dozens, a black vernacular tradition, involves the exchange of explicit insults about one's adversary's parents, usually the mother. When Maureen shames Pecola for having seen her father naked, Claudia responds, "'Who else would she see, dog tooth?'" and suggests that all Maureen thinks about is her own naked daddy (71–72).

10. See, for example, the "fragments of talk" condemning the pregnant Pecola that Claudia and Frieda overhear and to which Claudia then responds in her narrative (188–190).

11. Claudia's narrative is intertwined with an omniscient narrative voice. I focus primarily on Claudia's voice.

12. Even blues that "end" in death typically, and comically, explore an afterlife with its own blues moments.

APPENDIX

"St. Louis Blues"

I hate to see de evenin' sun go down
I hate to see de evenin' sun go down
Cause mah baby, he done lef' dis town

Feelin' tomorrow lak I feel today
Feelin' tomorrow lak I feel today
I'll pack mah trunk, an make mah getaway

St. Louis woman wid her diamon' rings
Pulls dat man aroun' by her apron strings
'Twant for powder an' for store-bought hair
De man I love would not gone nowhere

Got de St. Louis blues, jes as blue as I can be
Dat man got a heart lak a rock cast in de sea
Or else he wouldn't have gone so far from me

Been to de gypsy, to get mah fortune tol'
To de gypsy, done got mah fortune tol'
Cause I'm most wild 'bout my jelly roll

Gypsy done tol' me, "Don't you wear no black"
Yes, she done tol' me, "Don't you wear no black
Go to St. Louis, you can win him back"

Help me to Cairo; make St. Louis by mahself
Git to Cairo, find mah ol' frien', Jeff
Gwine to pin mahself close to his side
If I flag his train, I sho can ride
I loves dat man lak a schoolboy loves his pie
Lak a Kentucky Colonel loves his mint an' rye
I'll love mah baby till de day I die

You ought to see dat stovepipe brown o' mine
Lak he owns de Dimon' Joseph line
He'd make a crosseyed 'oman go stone blind

Blacker than midnight, teeth lak flags of truce
Blackest man in de whole St. Louis
Blacker de berry, sweeter is de juice . . . (Donalson 13–14)

WORKS CITED

Atkinson, Yvonne. "Creating Community: Call/Response and Witness/Testify in Toni Morrison's *Beloved, Jazz,* and *Song of Solomon.*" Unpublished paper. Twentieth Century Literature Conference, University of Louisville, Louisville, KY, 24 Feb. 1996.

Baker, Houston A., Jr. *Blues, Ideology, and Afro-American Literature: A Vernacular Theory.* Chicago: University Chicago Press, 1984.

Bell, Bernard. *The Afro-American Novel and Its Tradition.* Amherst: University of Massachusetts Press, 1987.

Catalioffi, Robert H. *The Music in African American Fiction.* New York: Garland, 1995.

Davis, Angela Y. "Black Women and Music: A Historical Legacy of Struggle." *Wild Women in the Whirlwind: Afra-American Culture and the Contemporary Literary Renaissance.* Ed. Joanne M. Braxton and Andrée Nicola McLaughlin. New Brunswick: Rutgers University Press, 1990: pp. 3–21.

Donalson, Melvin, ed. *Cornerstones: An Anthology of African American Literature.* New York: St. Martin's Press, 1996.

Gates, Henry Louis, Jr., and K. A. Appiah, eds. *Toni Morrison: Critical Perspectives Past and Present.* New York: Amistad, 1993.

Hurston, Zora Neale. *Their Eyes Were Watching God.* 1937. New York: HarperPerennial, 1990.

Kingston, Maxine Hong. *The Woman Warrior: Memoirs of a Girlhood Among Ghosts.* 1975. New York: Vintage, 1989.

McPherson, James Alan. *Railroad: Trains and Train People in American Culture.* New York: Random, 1976.

Miner, Madonne. "Lady No Longer Sings the Blues: Rape, Madness, and Silence in *The Bluest Eye.*" *Conjuring: Black Women, Fiction, and Literary Tradition.* Ed. Marjorie Pryse and Hortense J. Spillers. Bloomington: Indiana University Press, 1985: pp. 176–191.

Morrison, Toni. "Afterword." *The Bluest Eye,* pp. 209–216.

———. *The Bluest Eye.* 1970. New York: Penguin/Plume, 1994.

———. "An Interview with Toni Morrison." With Nellie McKay. Gates and Appiah, pp. 396–411.

———. "'Intimate Things in Place': A Conversation with Toni Morrison." With Robert B. Stepto. Gates and Appiah, pp. 378–395.

———. *Jazz*. New York: Knopf, 1992.

———. *Song of Solomon*. 1977. New York: Penguin/Plume, 1987.

———. *Sula*. New York: Knopf, 1973.

———. "That Language Must Not Sweat: A Conversation with Toni Morrison." With Thomas LeClair. Gates and Appiah, pp. 369–377.

Oakley, Giles. *The Devil's Music: A History of the Blues*. New York: DaCapo, 1997.

Salaam, Kalamu ya. *What is Life?: Reclaiming the Black Blues Self*. Chicago: Third World Press, 1994.

Smitherman, Geneva. *Talkin and Testifyin: The Language of Black America*. 1977. Detroit: Wayne State University Press, 1985.

Softing, Inger-Anne. "Carnival and Black American Music as Counterculture in Toni Morrison's *The Bluest Eye*." *American Studies in Scandinavia* 27.2 (1995): pp. 81–102.

Southern, Eileen. *The Music of Black Americans: A History*. 3rd ed. New York: Norton, 1997.

Wilson, August. *August Wilson: Writing and the Blues* (videorecording). Dir. Kate Roth Knull. *World of Ideas*/The Moyers Collection Series. Princeton: Films for the Humanities, 1994.

CARL D. MALMGREN

Texts, Primers, and Voices in Toni Morrison's The Bluest Eye

*T*he *Bluest Eye* represents a remarkable undertaking, especially for a first novel. In terms of formal features, it might be described as a kind of narratological compendium. For one thing, the novel incorporates several different forms of textuality. It opens with three different versions of its epigraphic "master" text, several lines drawn from an elementary school primer. That is followed by an italicized "overture," introducing the primary narrator, Claudia MacTeer, and the dominant motifs of the work—victimization and its causes:

> *It was a long time before my sister and I admitted to ourselves that no green was going to spring from our seeds. Once we knew, our guilt was relieved only by fights and mutual accusations about who was to blame.* (5)

The body of the novel is composed of two related kinds of texts, variously interspersed: four seasonal sections, narrated in the first person by Claudia MacTeer; and seven primer sections (employing various narrational situations), so named because each section is set off by an epigraph taken from the master primer. The end is a kind of coda, beginning "So it was" (204), in which Claudia reviews the outcomes of the narrative and rehearses its

Critique: Studies in Contemporary Fiction, Vol. 41, No. 3; Spring 2000: pp. 251–262. Copyright © 2000. Published by Heldref Publications.

145

lessons. Linda Dittmar praises the architectonics of the novel as "a brilliant orchestration of a complex multi- formed narrative" (140).

Texts and Voices

The novel is not only multitextual; it is also polyphonic. The seasonal sections are in the first person, but even they are double-voiced, aware of the difference between the experiencing "I" and the narrating "I." In places Claudia speaks as the nine-year-old girl going through the experience, ignorant, for example, as to what "ministratin'" is (28). Elsewhere, she switches to an adult perspective on the incident being narrated: "We trooped in, Frieda sobbing quietly, Pecola carrying a white tail, me carrying the little-girl-gone-to-woman pants" (31). And sometimes she speaks from the moment of the enunciation itself. "But was it really like that? As painful as I remember? Only mildly" (12).

The primer sections are, if anything, even more ambitious, in that they eventually make use of the full spectrum of what Stanzel terms "narrative situations."[1] The narrator assumes authorial position and privilege when she gives the reader a lecture on the lifestyles and values of the "sugar-brown Mobile girls" (82):

> They go to land-grant colleges, normal schools, and learn to do the white man's work with refinement: home economics to prepare his food; teacher education to instruct black children in obedience; music to soothe the weary master and entertain his blunted soul. Here they learn the rest of the lesson begun in those soft houses with porch swings and pots of bleeding heart: how to behave. (83)

From the same position, she reviews the history of the Breedlove's storefront apartment (33–37); in the following primer section, she moves successively through the minds of the members of the Breedlove family during a violent morning confrontation (39–46).

The primer sections devoted to Pauline and Cholly Breedlove and to Soaphead Church are, in large part, narrated figurally, with Pauline, Cholly, and Soaphead as the centers of consciousness. Those sections focus on the *what* and *how* of their featured protagonists' experiences. But even those sections are multivocal. Those figural presentations are frequently qualified by authorial interpolations or commentary; the Pauline section, for example, begins with the following explanation of her feeling of unworthiness:

> The easiest thing to do would be to build a case out of her foot. This is what she herself did. But to find out the truth about how dreams die, one should never take the word of the dreamer. The

end of her lovely beginning was probably the cavity in one of her front teeth. She preferred, however, to think always of her foot. (110)[2]

What follows is figural narration, a recounting of Pauline's perspective on the events of her life. To make that experience even more immediate, however, the narration shifts several times to quoted and italicized first-person dramatic monologue. Pauline speaks aloud, apparently to a Lorain neighbor, deputy for the reader:

> *"That was the last time I seen real June bugs. These things up here ain't june bugs. They's something else. Folks here call them fireflies, Down home they was different. But I recollect that streak of green. I recollect it well." (112)*

In the space of a few pages, the narration shifts from authorial to figural to first person. In addition, the Soaphead Church primer section contains, in entirety, a formal and pedantic letter that Soaphead writes to God after his encounter with Pecola. And the last primer section consists of a schizoid dramatic dialogue between Pecola and her imaginary second self in which the two of them rhapsodize about the blueness of Pecola's eyes.

A number of critics have called attention to the multiple narrations (and multiple narrators) in the novel. Arguing that "the possibility of a bystander really being able to tell the whole story is implicitly obviated by the novel's shift in narrators," Demetrakopoulos stipulates at least three narrators: Claudia, "the omniscient point of view," and Pecola (35). Samuels says that Claudia "retells the story with the assistance of other, external narrators" (25). Dittmar argues that "Claudia covers a lot of ground, but she is not the novel's pivotal consciousness. She is a narrator, not the narrator" (143). The critical consensus seems to be that there are two main speakers, Claudia in the seasonal sections, and an authorial persona elsewhere. The authorial persona supplies the master primer text and uses it epigraphically and assumes the privilege of rendering the dramatic monologues of Pauline and Pecola in the primer sections (Gibson 21, 25, 30; Holloway 40; Byerman 450). In her afterword to the novel, Morrison herself refers derogatorily to her narrational doubleness, saying that it made a "shambles" of her text: "I resorted to two voices, [. . .] both of which are extremely unsatisfactory to me" (215).

I argue (*pace* Morrison) that strong evidence, textual and biographical, exists to suggest that a single narrator, Claudia MacTeer, has composed the texts and created the voices and that my reading adds an important dimension to the meaning of the text.[3] As noted above, Claudia's first person seasonal sections are double-voiced, shifting back and forth between the perspective of the nine-year-old and that of an older and wiser adult. The passage in which Claudia discusses her evolving relationship to white baby girls indicates the distance between these two perspectives:

> If I pinched them, their eyes—unlike the crazed hint of the baby doll's eyes—would fold in pain, and their cry would not be the sound of an icebox door, but a fascinating cry of pain. When I learned how repulsive this disinterested violence was, that it was repulsive because it was disinterested, my shame floundered about for refuge. The best hiding place was love. Thus the conversion from pristine sadism to fabricated hatred, to fraudulent love. It was a small step to Shirley Temple. I learned much later to worship her, just as I learned to delight in cleanliness, knowing, even as I learned, that the change was adjustment without improvement. (23)

Here is a discerning adult making nuanced discriminations. We know that she is significantly removed from the time of the events she recounts because her narration rehearses and implicitly repudiates (and therefore comes after) a love for Shirley Temple that itself came "much later" than her original hatred and sadism.

The text gives us no way to date Claudia's enunciation or to specify her adult age, but she has the mature voice and perspective of someone looking back from a distance, someone, say, in her mid-to-late thirties. *The Bluest Eye* was published in 1970, when Morrison was thirty-nine years old. Like Claudia, Morrison was born in Lorain, Ohio; like Claudia, she would have been nine years old in 1940–41, the year in which the events of the novel take place. Those similarities suggest that Claudia MacTeer is Morrison's persona in the novel, her fictional "second self." Indeed, Morrison states in the afterword that the novel had a autobiographical origin, that Pecola was based on a real-life elementary school classmate who, out of the blue as it were, confided that she wanted blue eyes (209).

That is the (suspect) argument from biography, the old mimetic shibboleth about Art and Life being intimately related. But no substantial textual evidence supports that connection. As the passage above suggests, Claudia's seasonal sections demonstrate that she has the talent and insight to make the kind of discriminations that characterize the text as a whole and that she has the stylistic resources to rise to the lyricism found in various places in the novel.[4] Most important, the Claudia sections articulate an ideological project that is carried out in great detail elsewhere in the novel: the critique of cultural stereotypes imposed by the dominant white culture. In terms of theme, then, the novel is seamless, univocal.[5] In addition, Claudia is singled out as the MacTeer sister blessed with Imagination (just as Frieda is marked as the Executive, the one who makes decisions). In the Autumn section, for example, the girls are bored, and Claudia supplies an extensive list of possible activities for them: looking at Mr. Henry's girlie magazines or Bible, threading needles for the blind lady, searching through trash cans, making fudge, or eavesdropping at the Greek hotel (26–27). When the sisters are afraid that Frieda is "ruined" after she has been molested by Henry the roomer, Claudia comes up with the solution to their problem by concocting a highly fanciful line of "reasoning" that includes fat people, the three prostitutes, whiskey, and Cholly Breedlove (101–102). Those episodes reinforce the connection between Morrison and Claudia by suggesting that Claudia has the imaginative resources to invent alternatives, to impersonate various characters, to create fictional worlds.

The novel begins with Claudia's voice: "*Quiet as it's kept, there were no marigolds in the fall of 1941. We thought, at the time, that it was because Pecola was having her father's baby that the marigolds did not grow.*" The second paragraph specifies that "we" comprises "my sister and I" (5). The novel ends with Claudia speaking for a more generalized "we": "We are wrong, of course, but it doesn't matter. It's too late. At least on the edge of my town, among the garbage and the sunflowers of my town, it's much, much, much too late" (206). Occam's razor should dictate that what comes between the beginning and end belongs to her as well.

The problem is that the primer sections, which make up about two-thirds of the novel, refuse to say "I." They contain almost no reference to the speaker's person,[6] certainly no explicit identification of that authorial speaker as the grown-up Claudia MacTeer; therefore, no *apparent* linkage is evident between the primer sections and the seasonal sections. In addition to the thematic continuity I have mentioned there are other connections. For example, the substance, rhetoric, and syntax of part of Soaphead Church's letter to God is echoed in Claudia's coda to the novel. Soaphead indites (and indicts):

> In retaining the identity of our race, we held fast to those characteristics most gratifying to sustain and least troublesome to maintain. Consequently we were not royal but snobbish, not aristocratic but class-conscious; we believed authority was cruelty to our inferiors, and education was being at school. We mistook violence for passion, indolence for leisure, and thought recklessness was freedom. (177)

Claudia reprises (and embellishes):

> And fantasy it was, for we were not strong, only aggressive; we were not free, merely licensed; we were not compassionate, we were polite; not good, but well-behaved. We courted death in

order to call ourselves brave, and hid like thieves from life. We substituted good grammar for intellect; we switched habits to simulate maturity; we rearranged lies and called it the truth. (205–206)

It is as if Claudia took the condemnation of African Americans she voiced in the persona of Soaphead Church and brought it to bear on the victimization of Pecola Breedlove.

More convincing than the rhetorical and stylistic echo is the explicit repetition of substantive commentary. In the cat primer section, Geraldine returns to her tidy home to find Pecola there and sees in the little girl only anathema:

She had seen this little girl all of her life. [. . .] Hair uncombed, dresses failing apart, shoes untied and caked with dirt. [Little girls like this] had stared at her with great uncomprehending eyes. Eyes that questioned nothing and asked everything. Unblinking and unabashed, they stared up at her. The end of the world lay in their eyes, and the beginning, and all the waste in between. (91–92)

In the coda, Claudia repeats that summary view of Pecola, but with a significant addition; she speaks elegiacly of Pecola wandering on the edge of town, "plucking her way between the tire rims and the sunflowers, between Coke bottles and milkweed, among all the waste and beauty of the world—which is what she herself was" (205).

But the most compelling evidence of linkage connects the primer section devoted to Cholly Breedlove with Claudia's coda. Having rehearsed Cholly's history, the primer section asserts that it would take a jazz musician to render the essence of Cholly's being, "its final and pervading ache of freedom. Only a musician would sense, know, without even knowing that he knew, that Cholly was free. Dangerously free. Free to feel whatever he felt—fear, guilt, shame, love, grief, pity" (159). The speaker continues for some lines detailing the contours and extent of Cholly's freedom and then links the "godlike state" of freedom Cholly enjoys to both his marriage to Pauline and his rape of his daughter. In her coda to the novel, Claudia insists that, despite what he did to her, Cholly loved his daughter, but that his touch was fatal because "love is never any better than the lover," and "the love of a free man is never safe" (206). By using that epithet for Cholly and connecting it to his crime against his daughter, Claudia rehearses the argument spelled out in Cholly's primer section and makes it her own. Because we can link Claudia directly to the cat, Soaphead, and Cholly sections, it is possible to conclude that *The Bluest Eye* is entirely her composition, her achievement. Indeed, we can say

that the eye in the title contains a multiple pun: it is at once t⌐
for by Pecola Breedlove, and the "I" that author-izes the novel ₂
"bluest I" that witnesses Pecola's fate, Claudia MacTeer.

Primers and Voices

At the very beginning of her narration, Claudia spells out why she is composing *The Bluest Eye;* she wants to figure out what happened to the marigolds she and her sister planted in the fall of 1941: "*It was a long time before my sister and I admitted to ourselves that no green was going to spring from our seeds. Once we knew, our guilt was relieved only by fights and mutual accusations, about who was to blame*" (5). The marigolds are, of course, metonymically and metaphorically connected to Pecola, so Claudia is asking "who is to blame" for what happened to Pecola, for her tragic fate. The end of the overture acknowledges that this is not an easy question to answer: "*There is really nothing more to say—except why. But since why is difficult to handle, one must take refuge in how*" (5). What follows is the first seasonal section, "Autumn."

Claudia tells us that she must begin with *how* in order to get at *why*.[7] Can we link those basic narrative questions with the shape her narrative takes? I have noted that the seasonal sections, narrated by a foregrounded first person, Claudia MacTeer, are quite different from the primer sections. She begins each section with a present tense epitomization of the season being recalled: "Nuns go by quiet as lust" (9); "My daddy's face is a study. Winter moves into it and presides there" (61); "The first twigs are thin, green, and supple" (97); "I only have to break into the tightness of a strawberry, and I see summer" (187). In each section, she then relates in detail one or two of her experiences during that season, partly from the perspective of a nine-year-old, who believes, for example, that drinking alcohol will keep her sister Frieda from being "ruined". These sections have irregular margins.[8] The entire set-up—a first-person narrator, entries keyed to a particular time of year, the present tense, the perspective of the experiencing "I," and irregular margins—suggests a particular narrative form, the diary.

The diary is a "primitive" narrative form, specifically intended to recount the *how* of experience. A diarist is someone who records events and is at the mercy of the seasons, the times, time. The seasonal sections, or diary entries, tell us what happened at that particular time. That Claudia uses seasons and not dates to identify the entries indicates, however, that the entries are retrospective, and therefore both selective and shapely. They are selective in that each of them focuses on encounters between the MacTeer sisters and Pecola Breedlove during that fateful year; shapely insofar as each encounter involves some kind of violence—verbal, emotional, physical—perpetrated against Pecola. The seasonal sections give us, in sum, an intimate, personal view of the *how* of Pecola's victimization.

The novel's epigraph consists of three versions of lines from the Dick-and-Jane primer—one regular, one without capitals or punctuation, and one without capitals, punctuation, or spacing. The standard critical reading of the three versions is that the first represents the life of white families, orderly and "readable"; the second, that of the MacTeer family, confused but still readable; and the last, that of the Breedlove family, incoherent and unintelligible.[9] The primer sections of the novel use portions of that third version as "titles," lines keyed to material presented in that section. The first primer section, for example, dealing with the history and condition of the Breedlove's seedy storefront apartment, begins

HEREISTHEHOUSEITISGREENANDWH
ITEITHASAREDDOORITISVERYPRETT
YITISVERYPRETTYPRETTYPRETTYP (33)

Subsequent sections use as epigraphs primer lines describing Dick and Jane's family, the cat, Mother, Father, the dog, and a friend of Jane's. The section following the epigraph focuses on that figure in Pecola's life but relates tales of misery that are an ironic counterpoint to the fairy-tale world depicted in the primer itself. Cumulatively the sections render in great detail the loveless "Breedlove version" of the primer text.

In terms of voice, however, the primer sections are very different from the seasonal sections. The authorial narrator here refuses to say "I," except when impersonating one of her characters. She keeps her material at a distance from herself. The Soaphead Church section, for example, begins "Once there was an old man" (164)—as if to signal her objectivity and control. From a magisterial position, she reviews and highlights the biographies of Geraldine, Pauline, Cholly, and Soaphead. Narrationally, she ranges from authorial commentary to figural presentation to dramatic monologue. She even supplies the text of Soaphead's letter to God and the script of Pecola's schizoid "dialogue" with herself. She employs a wide spectrum of novelistic techniques and practices—including justified right-hand margins—to explain what happened to the members of the Breedlove family. The conclusion would seem to be that diaries can tell us *how* or *what*, but only novels, and the narrative resources belonging to them, can tell us *why*.[10] Diaries render the experience of victimization; novels explain it. The absence of "I" in the primer sections can be taken as a sign of the unwillingness of the magisterial authorial persona to call undue attention to herself. To answer the question *why*, the novelist must go beyond the personal and diaristic. She must become im-personal if she is to rise to true impersonation. To make sense of what happened to Pecola, Claudia MacTeer has to call upon all her talents as a novelist.

The novelistic primer sections treat extensively those in Pecola's immediate family or those who come into immediate contact with her (Geraldine; Soaphead). They dwell upon the members of the African American community who act directly on her, implying that they are responsible for her fate, because they have embraced and internalized a set of values and ideas imposed upon them by the dominant white culture.[11] Accepting an essentialist view of beauty that consigns them to invisibility and condemns them to self-hatred, they become the "instruments of [their] own oppression" (Gibson 21). Claudia very clearly makes that indictment of her race at several places in her narrative. An early example is her summary remarks about the Breedlove family:

> You looked at them and wondered why they were so ugly; you looked closely and could not find the source. Then you realized that it came from conviction, their conviction. It was as though some mysterious all-knowing master had given each one a cloak of ugliness to wear, and they had each accepted it without question. The master had said, "You are ugly people." They had looked about themselves and saw nothing to contradict the statement; saw, in fact, support for it leaning at them from every billboard, every movie, every glance. "Yes," they had said. "You are right." (39)[12]

Leveling the same charge against Pecola's classmates (65), Maureen Peal (73–74), Geraldine (83–87), Pauline (122), Soaphead (168), and others, Claudia suggests that almost no one in the black community is able to resist that particular interpellation by the dominant white culture.

This near-total capitulation to white values, in combination with Pecola's awful victimization, leads many critics to see the novel as terribly bleak—in the words of Demetrakopoulos, "one of the darkest works I have ever read" (31). Commenting in the afterword on Claudia's conspiratorial opening words—"Quiet as it's kept"—Morrison herself says that the novel involves the "disclosure of secrets," that "something grim is about to be divulged " namely "a terrible story about things one would rather not know anything about" (212, 213). Dittmar worries that "the microcosm Morrison locates in her Ohio town includes few venues for anger directed beyond the black community and almost no potential for regeneration within it," and concludes that the novel "does indeed seem overwhelmingly pessimistic, given its relentless piling up of abuses and betrayals" (140). Byerman argues that the "ideological hegemony of whiteness is simply too overwhelming to be successfully resisted" and specifies that even "Claudia, the strongest character in the book, cannot defy the myth" (449, 450).[13]

But if Claudia is the single narrator and the narrative is entirely her composition, then she has indeed resisted the power of "white mythology."[14] In the first seasonal section, Claudia relates how, when she was a little girl, she dismembered white dolls to find out what made them beautiful and therefore lovable—to discover the essence of Beauty. All she found was sawdust (21). The text composed by the adult Claudia, *The Bluest Eye,* carries on the same discovery procedure on a grander scale; it undertakes the deconstruction and demystification of the ideology that makes those dolls beautiful: "And all the time we knew that Maureen Peal was not the enemy and not worthy of such intense hatred. The *Thing* to fear was the *Thing* that made *her* beautiful, and not us" (74, emphasis in original).

In that respect, Claudia's use of the Dick-and-Jane primer as master text represents a brilliant choice, for a primer is a basic tool of ideological indoctrination; it introduces readers to and inculcates the correct values.[15] As one critic notes, "the act of learning to read or write means exposure to the values of the culture from which the reading material emanates. [. . .] One cannot simply learn to read without being subjected to the values engraved in the text" (Gibson 20). The same logic adheres, of course, to reading the text that is *The Bluest Eye;* one cannot read it without being subjected to Claudia's discovery of "the unreality or emptiness behind the facade of [the white] construction of femininity" (Munafo 8). In that respect, her text constitutes a counterprimer, designed "to counteract the universal love of white baby dolls, Shirley Temples, and Maureen Peals" *(The Bluest Eye* 190); it critiques and thus dismembers the values and iconography fostering that love.

Claudia suggests in the coda that her narrative originates partly in guilt and betrayal, that she and the other members of the black community "assassinated" Pecola by scapegoating her or by turning their backs on her. Her narrative tries to make up for that betrayal. If we compare the lines from the primer mastertext to the epigraphs for the primer sections, we discover that a silencing has taken place; there is *no primer section* for the following epitext lines: "See Jane. She has a red dress. She wants to play. Who will play with Jane?" Jane (Pecola) has been effectively eliminated, erased, silenced. The eye is proverbially the window to the soul, to all that is unique, irreplaceable, essential, but Pecola's eye/I is not her own; it belongs to the dominant culture. As a result, she identifies herself with a lack, with what she has not. She is, in effect, self-less and invisible. As one critic notes, "Morrison's novel contains repeated instances of Pecola's negation as other characters refuse to see her" (Miner 187). Because she cannot speak for or defend herself, she is literally and figuratively silenced almost throughout the text, condemned to an "imitation of life." As Morrison suggests in her afterward, the novel is built on a "silence at its center: the void that is Pecola's 'unbeing'" (215).

The Bluest Eye is itself the text that counterpoints the missing primer lines. It makes "Jane" visible and gives her a kind of being; it is the attempt of Claudia/Morrison to make the silence speak, to give voice to the voiceless. As a child, Claudia herself is silenced: she notes that adults do not talk to children; they give them orders (10). Growing up means acquiring a voice, joining the world of discourse, something Pecola is prohibited from doing. In a sense, then, Claudia makes up for her betrayal by lending her voice to Pecola, by speaking her through her story. In so doing, by giving a present to the absent, Claudia makes the absent present.

That line of argument recalls a basic idea that the narrative calls into question, the idea that beauty is an essence, that it is present to itself (Walther 777). Morrison's novel not only critiques that idea, but it also transvalues it. Claudia invites readers to imagine the very beauty of Pecola's unborn baby, with "its head covered with great O's of wool, the black face holding, like nickels, two clean black eyes, the flared nose, kissing-thick lips, and the living, breathing silk of black skin" (190). As Munafo notes, "[t]his affirming vision of Pecola's unborn baby asserts black presence and reinscribes blackness as beautiful" (9). More important, Claudia insists over and over that we acknowledge Pecola's own beauty. At one point Claudia notes the pleasure that Pecola's smile gives her (106); elsewhere she frets that Pecola would never know her own beauty (46–47).[16] Claudia's narrative exists, the coda informs us, to reveal "all the waste and beauty of the world—which is what she [Pecola] herself was. All of our waste which we dumped on her and which she absorbed. And all of our beauty, which was hers first and which she gave to us" (205). *The Bluest Eye* renders both the waste and the beauty.

NOTES

1. I am referring, in traditional terms, to point of view. I use Stanzel's nomenclature because it is more exact (e.g., "authorial" is better than omniscient") and less flawed (e.g., it does not rely on oxymorons such as "limited omniscience").

2. Insofar as the implied author assumes the right to insert this kind of commentary throughout the primer sections, we can say that their narrational dominant is authorial.

3. Klotman notes in passing that Claudia is the sole narrator, but she does not develop that line of argument (123–124). Smith claims that Claudia narrates "the preschool primer with which the novel begins," but that an "ostensibly omniscienct narrator" recounts the subsequent primer sections (124). She does not explain why Claudia narrates one but not the others. Harris begins by suggesting that Claudia is the single narrator: "As storyteller, it is Claudia's job to shape the past so that it provides coherent meaning for her present audience" (16); "[a]s multivoiced narra-

tor, Claudia must make sense of what has ravaged the community" (22). Later, she retreats from that position, referring casually to the "parts of the novel Claudia narrates" (24) and saying that Claudia "occasionally gets help from some of the members of her community" (23).

4. Claudia's memory of being ill in the Autumn section: "But was it really like that? As painful as I remember? Only mildly. Or rather, it was a productive and fructifying pain. Love, thick and dark as Alaga syrup, eased up into that cracked window. I could smell it—taste it—sweet, musty, with an edge of wintergreen in its base—everywhere in the house. [. . .] And in the night, when my coughing was dry and tough, feet padded into the room, hands repinned the flannel, readjusted the quilt, and rested a moment on my forehead. So when I think of autumn, I think of somebody with hands who does not want me to die" (12).

5. Klotman says that "education by school and society is the dominant theme of *The Bluest Eye*" (123).

6. I could find only one use of first-person pronominal forms in the primer sections (other than in direct discourse). It occurs in the Pauline section: "So she became, and her process of becoming was like most of ours" (126). The speaker is also clearly present in the following passage, which serves to date her enunciation in a way similar to Claudia's: "So fluid has the population in that area been, that probably no one remembers longer, longer ago, before the time of the gypsies and the time of the teenagers when the Breedloves lived there, nestled together in the storefront" (34). Like Claudia, the speaker remembers that time very well.

7. Smith argues that both Claudia and the novel dodge the question why: "*The Bluest Eye* does not undertake to explain, for example, why black Americans aspire to an unattainable standard of beauty; why they displace their self-hatred onto a communal scapegoat; how Pecola's fate might have been avoided" (124). I argue that Claudia and her book answer all these questions.

8. Dittmar is the only critic who notes the uneven margins, connecting them with orality, but not with a specific narrative form: "While such margins may serve to suggest the text's informal, possibly spoken origins, the mere use of this unusual device is attention-getting, especially given its recurrent suspension and re-introduction" (141).

9. See Ogunyemi 112, Klotman 123, Wong 472. Wong argues that the primer lines depict each character as "maintain(ing) himself in a self-enclosed unity" and thus enact "the very conditions of alienated self-containment which underlie [white bourgeois] values" (471, 472).

10. Structurally, the number of primer sections increases in the latter half of the novel, as if, having made the how of Pecola's victimization clear, the narrative chooses to focus on the why.

11. The argument that "by acting in 'Bad Faith,' Pecola remains responsible, in the final analysis, for what happens to her" (Samuels and Hudson-Weems 15) is, therefore, flat-out wrong.

12. In her afterword, Morrison warns specifically "against the damaging internalization of assumptions of immutable inferiority originating in an outside gaze" (210). See, in this regard, Guerrero; and Miner, 184–188.

13. Cf. Dittmar: "Individual characters may not participate in [positive] change; certainly Claudia, for all her adult retrospection, provides no empowerment" (142).

14. Cf. Rosenberg: "Claudia's ability to survive intact and to consolidate an identity derives from her vigorous opposition to the colorist attitudes of her community" (440); and Munafo: "Claudia says no [to the idea of whiteness], and in so doing she retains a sense of self-affirmation" (9).

15. Powell also argues that the primer is "a highly significant beginning," but for a different reason: "it points to the fact that all Afro-American writers have, willingly or not, been forced to begin with the Master's language. The Dick-and-Jane reader comes to symbolize the institutionalized ethnocentrism of the white logos" (749).

16. In her afterword, Morrison describes her response to the classmate who wanted blue eyes as follows: "although I had certainly used the word 'beautiful,' I had never experienced its shock—the force of which was equaled by the knowledge that no one else recognized it, not even, or especially, the one who possessed it" (209).

Works Cited

Byerman, Keith E. "Intense Behaviors: The Use of the Grotesque in *The Bluest Eye* and *Eta's Man*." *College Language Association Journal* 25.4 (June 1982): pp. 447–457.

Demetrakopoulos, Stephanie A. "Bleak Beginnings: *The Bluest Eye*." Holloway and Demetrakopoulos 31–36.

Dittmar, Linda. "'Will the Circle Be Unbroken?': The Politics of Form in *The Bluest Eye*." *Novel: A Forum on Fiction* 23.2 (Winter 1990): pp. 137–155.

Gibson, Donald. "Text and Countertext in Toni Morrison's *The Bluest Eye*." *LIT: Literature, Interpretation, Theory* 1.1–2 (1989): pp. 19–32.

Guerrero, Edward. "Tracking 'The Look' in the Novels of Toni Morrison." *Black American Literature Forum* 24.4 (Winter 1990): pp. 761–773.

Harris, Trudier. *Fiction and Folklore: The Novels of Toni Morrison*. Knoxville: University of Tennessee Press, 1991.

Holloway, Karla F. C. "The Language and Music of Survival." Holloway and Demetrakopoulos, pp. 37–47.

Holloway, Karla F. C. and Stephanie A. Demetrakopoulos. *New Dimensions of Spirituality: A Biracial and Bicultural Reading of the Novels of Toni Morrison*. Contributions in Women's Studies, Number 84. New York: Greenwood, 1987.

Klotman, Phyllis. "Dick-and-Jane and the Shirley Temple Sensibility in *The Bluest Eye*." *Black American Literature Forum* 13.4 (Winter 1979): pp. 123–125.

Miner, Madonne M. "Lady No Longer Sings the Blues: Rape, Madness, and Silence in *The Bluest Eye*." *Conjuring: Black Women, Fiction, and Literary Tradition*. Ed. Marjorie Pryse and Hortense J. Spillers. Bloomington: Indiana University Press, 1985: pp. 176–191.

Morrison, Toni. *The Bluest Eye*. 1970; rpt. New York: Plume, 1994.

Munafo, Giavanna. "'No Sign of Life': Marble-Blue Eyes and Lakefront Houses in *The Bluest Eye*." *LIT: Literature, Interpretation, Theory* 6.1-2 (1995): pp. 1–19.

Ogunyemi, Chikwenye Okonjo. "Order and Disorder in Toni Morrison's *The Bluest Eye*." *Critique* 19.1 (1977): pp. 112–120.

Powell, Timothy B. "Toni Morrison: The Struggle to Depict the Black Figure on the White Page." *Black American Literature Forum* 24.4 (Winter 1990): pp. 747–760.

Rosenberg, Ruth. "Seeds in Hard Ground: Black Girlhood in *The Bluest Eye*." *Black American Literature Forum* 21.4 (Winter 1987): pp. 435–445.

Samuels, Wilfred D. and Clenora Hudson-Weems. *Toni Morrison*. Boston: Twayne, 1990.

Smith, Valerie. *Self-Discovery and Authority, in Afro-American Narrative.* Cambridge: Harvard University Press, 1987.

Stanzel, Franz. *Narrative Situations in the Novel:* Tom Jones, Moby Dick, The Ambassadors, Ulysses. Trans. James P. Pusack. Bloomington: Indiana University Press, 1971.

Walther, Malin LaVon. "Out of Sight: Toni Morrison's Revision of Beauty." *Black American Literature Forum* 24.4 (Winter 1990): pp. 775–789.

Wong, Shelley. "Transgression as Poesis in *The Bluest Eye*." *Callaloo* 13 (1990): pp. 471–481.

JENNIFER GILLAN

Focusing on the Wrong Front:
Historical Displacement, the Maginot Line, and
The Bluest Eye

Recent theoretical work has examined the ways that the abstract idea of the bodiless citizen has marked women and non-white Americans as outside the boundaries of full citizenship, because the attention paid to the various markings of gender or race on their bodies precludes them from being categorized as the unmarked, representative norm. Peggy Phelan most clearly explains rhetorical and imagistic gender marking, in the process making a distinction between the invisible marking of abstract value and the visible bodily marking of difference: "The male is marked with value; the female is unmarked, lacking measured value and meaning. . . . He is the norm and therefore unremarkable; as the Other, it is she whom he marks" (5). As Deborah Tannen says, corporeally "there is no unmarked woman" because women's bodies and the choices they make in terms of appearance and self-identification in the public sphere always mark them in specific, gendered ways. Examining marking in light of political theory, Carole Pateman analyzes how the language of the Constitution, premised as it is on the idea of the social contract, accords the white male citizen the privilege of abstracting himself into the concept of the disembodied citizen, whereas women, in contrast, can never achieve this state of disembodiment because the sexual contract precedes the social contract. Drawing on such political theories, Lauren Berlant considers the corporeal implications of the theory

African American Review, 2002 Summer; 36 (2): pp. 283–98. © 2002 Jennifer Gillan.

of disembodied citizenship for racial and gendered subjects. When the abstract, disembodied citizen is figured as white and male, all others cannot embody such citizenship because they are hyperembodied by the racial and/or gendered markings visible on their bodies. Thus, women and African Americans, in particular, Berlant contends, have never had the "sign of real authority"; that is, "the power to suppress that body [i.e., the facts of one's historical situation], to cover its tracks and its traces" (113).

Considered in light of this division between the unmarked and the marked, the disembodied and the hyperembodied, Toni Morrison's *The Bluest Eye* can be read as a commentary on the artificial boundaries of citizenship, gender, race, and history. While the theories of Berlant, Pateman, and Phelan enable us to understand the marking of the boundaries of citizenship, race, and gender, the difference between marked and unmarked history needs some explanation. Unmarked history refers to historical narrative that features as its prime actor the deeds of the abstract, disembodied citizen. Once this history is marked as having cultural value, its centrality is soon seen as unremarkable; that is, as representative. In order to centralize this one story, however, others need to be shifted to the periphery and soon become remarkable only in their relation to the center. According to Priscilla Wald, what unmarked history leaves out "resurfaces when the experiences of individuals conspicuously fail to conform to the definition of personhood offered in the narrative," and Morrison's Breedloves are certainly conspicuous for their "ill-fitting selfhood." By carefully outlining the history of their exclusion from the "terms of full and equal personhood," Morrison demonstrates that this family's unequal position is a product not of their intrinsic inadequacy, but rather of the systematic reinforcement of a racial and gendered criteria for full citizenship (10). This critique, in turn, disrupts the official stories that feature the United States as a brave defender of democracy and staunch critic of racialized nationalism abroad.

In setting her story of the quest for and repercussions of Pecola Breedlove's desire for blue eyes and the unmarked whiteness they represent against the backdrop of World War II, Morrison recounts the history of this significant year from the vantage point of those who have been marked *as* peripheral in accounts of this era of American history.[1] More particularly, it is significant that Morrison sets her story during 1940–41, because this year, during which the United States decided to intervene in World War II, is an important watershed date for the initial positioning of the United States as the crusader against racialized forms of nationalism abroad. The marked foregrounding of anti-racialist U.S. foreign policy during this year permits the backgrounding of racialist national history. More specifically, as Hitler's crimes against humanity came into sharp focus, the United States' own conflicts over race purity were displaced, and receded into the background.

Throughout her novel, Morrison explores several such historical displacements by which something of lesser significance comes to occupy a central position and, thereby, effaces a more disturbing issue: The domestic support for racialized nationalism is overshadowed on the international front by the United States' intervention in the war against racialized nationalism in Europe; the economic threat of black male labor to white male ascendancy is transformed by lynching rhetoric into a sexual threat of black males to white womanhood; black exclusion from the national family, especially the thwarting of the black male appropriation of the breadwinner role, is superceded by the inclusion of the ideal black female servant into the white family; black economic inequality is refigured as the retardation of black male progress by the presence of a matriarchal kinship network. In each case, the original exclusionary practice is rewritten through a counternarrative of reversal or justification. Morrison skillfully and subtly inserts each of these peripheral histories into her novel through a particular metaphoric description: naming the prostitute Marie "Maginot Line," describing Maureen Peal's "long brown hair" as "braided into two lynch ropes," depicting Pecola as a scapegoat, and characterizing the public sphere as a hemmed garment.

Through these metaphoric allusions to larger historical issues, Morrison constructs her novel as a subtle interplay between its foreground history of the Breedlove family and its background history of the racial determination of American citizenship. In other words, Morrison eschews the dramatic foreground of national history for the undramatized background.

Much excellent critical attention has been paid to the foreground story of the Breedloves,[2] but few commentators have considered the background stories in the novel. Understanding the implications of Morrison's subtle historical references can aid the reader in interpreting Morrison's text, and is the key to discerning the range of the cultural critique Morrison is making in *The Bluest Eye*. On one level, the novel is the personal story of a little girl's identity crisis, symbolized by her cataclysmic desire for blue eyes, but, on another level, it is a story about a national identity crisis. More particularly, it comments on the crisis produced by the post-war revelation of the gap between the United States' self-image as crusader against racialized nationalism and its well-known support of a racial basis of full American citizenship.

Although the details of political and military history of the era are largely absent from the main stage of Morrison's novel, she encodes subtle references to this history in her naming of the three prostitutes—China, Poland, and Maginot Line. That these three women function as the only positive domestic influences in the life of Pecola Breedlove is ironic, because as prostitutes they represent the unsettling of domestic respectability. Through these characters who blur the line between the reputable and disreputable on the domestic front, Morrison then establishes a reference to the blurring of the line between the reputable and the disreputable on the international front. In national terms, the United States' involvement in the fronts of World War II establishes the nation's respectability abroad. In turn, the fallout from the war and the international scrutiny of racialized nationalism unsettle this respectability.

By focusing attention on its intervention on the international front in other nations' racial and ethnic conflicts, the United States can repress its own domestic racial problems and histories of oppression. This tendency to concentrate attention on the wrong front is signified through Morrison's bestowing the name Maginot Line on the prostitute on whom most of the town's respectable black women focus their anger. While the names China and Poland[3] signify the European and Asian fronts of World War II, Maginot Line[4] refers literally to the failed French border fortifications and metaphorically to the tendency to focus on the wrong front that historian Sidney Lens calls "the Maginot Line syndrome." There is much focusing on the wrong front in the novel: The townswomen concentrate on vilifying the prostitutes for denigrating black womanhood, but do not acknowledge the economic inequalities that foster prostitution in the first place; the prostitutes focus on hating the townswomen, but exempt from their scorn the churchwomen who seem most to embody the ideology of true womanhood that, in actuality, excludes black women[5]; and the Breedloves focus on attaining the material goods that will enable them to maintain an aura of citizenship, instead of recognizing that the system of commodity compensation not only excludes black people, but also distracts attention from the growing economic inequalities between the rich and the poor of all races.

By focusing on the wrong front the characters participate in what Berlant calls "the will-to-not-know, to misrecognize, and to flee [their bodies]"; that is, in forgetting their own painful histories (113). Finding it easier, perhaps, to forget what they feel they cannot change, the black characters do not critique the culture that systematically excludes them; instead they reprimand each other for their personal failures and shortcomings.

One of the few characters who escapes reprimand is Maureen Peal, a green-eyed, middle-class mulatto. Because she already has the light eyes coded as unmarked by American culture, Maureen is the only character who is seemingly successful in achieving the status of disembodied citizen. Of course, on her person is marked the history of her embodiment and, more especially, that of the exploitation of black women's bodies by their white masters. When the townspeople look at Maureen, however, they focus on her presence and forget the history she represents. They see her ahistorically as a dream child instead of willing themselves to acknowledge that she is born out of the nightmare of the sexual exploitation of black women justified by a slave-owning culture's hierarchy of racialized personhood. Only Claudia MacTeer, the novel's narrator, is willing to recognize Maureen's whiteness for the painful history that it emblematizes, for its power to confer on her white acceptance and black homage. Only Claudia realizes that the "Thing" that makes Maureen the representative of beauty and her dark counterparts of ugliness is a racialized conception of full citizenship (62).

Significantly, Morrison uses the description of Maureen to introduce the submerged history of lynching in America. By characterizing green-eyed Maureen as "a high-yellow dream child with long brown hair braided into two lynch ropes that hung down her back" (52), Morrison encourages the reader to look more closely at the interwoven history of sexual and racial discrimination encoded in that braided hair. This metaphor establishes a link to the intertwined history of ante-bellum miscegenation and its displacement in post-bellum lynching campaigns, a history well documented in the anti-lynching pamphlets written by Ida B. Wells,[6] who argued that Southern whites used lynching to undermine the political, social, and economic power of newly freed slaves. To offset this threat, whites terrorized blacks into submission by hanging, burning, and/or tarring and feathering them, with the primary intent, according to Wells, of keeping them from voting. Such terrorism was a response, W. E. B. Du Bois claims, to the fear that freed slaves "might accumulate wealth, achieve education, and finally, they might even aspire to marry white women and mingle their blood with the blood of their masters" (167). Citing a correlation between increased economic tensions and lynching, Jacqueline Dowd Hall theorizes that lynching was always more about economic than sexual fears (130–133). To focus on the sexual front, of course, enabled attention to be distracted from the economic front.

Economics is also the primary reason that inroads were made in the battle against lynching. As Ida B. Wells put it, "Cognizance of the prevalence of this crime . . . has not been because there was any latent spirit of justice voluntarily asserting itself, especially in those who do the lynching, but because the entire American people now feel, both North and South, that they are objects in the gaze of the civilized world and that for every lynching humanity asks that America render its account to civilization and itself" (72). Well-aware of this concern for reputation, Wells took her lynching campaign to England in order to draw international attention to the widespread and systematic use of lynching as a way to control newly freed Black Americans. Simply put, it took public scrutiny on the international front to effect domestic change.

After World War II, international scrutiny also brought reluctant acknowledgment of racial problems on the homefront. When in the years after

World War II the United States tried to call Germany to account for its racial crimes, that nation launched a counteroffensive and censured the United States for its own history of racialized nationalism. As with the aftermath of Wells's anti-lynching campaign, these accusations presented in the international arena served to magnify the problem of racialized nationalism at home. Still concerned with the nation's reputation, policymakers, in the aftermath of this public scrutiny, had to balance an acknowledgment of the nation's well-documented and publicized racialized past with an assurance that the current administration was doing everything it could to tackle the heinous problem of racial inequality. Striking this balance, the Moynihan Report, the popular name for Daniel Patrick Moynihan's 1965 Department of Labor report *The Negro Family: The Case for National Action,* acknowledges America's slave-owning past, but it overlooks the lingering impact of this history, most especially, of the slavemaster's sexual exploitation of his slaves. Its inattention to the sexual aspects of slavery is particularly ironic since its effects are so indisputably visible in the physical features of those whom Morrison calls "high-yellow dream" children (52). Ignoring this sexual dimension of slavery as well as the subsequent post-bellum displacement of economic exploitation and sexual guilt onto the cultural fiction of the black rapist, the Moynihan Report attributes current black economic "impotence" to the inherited matriarchal family structure that places black men outside the norm of American society. By redirecting attention from the convoluted familial and sexual relations inherited from the patriarchal American plantation slavery system to the matrilineal kinship ties associated with African ancestry, the Moynihan Report uses the specter of the emasculating black matriarch to shield from blame the American patriarchal system and its policies of social and economic exclusion.

In this way, the Moynihan Report claimed to address African American inequality, but did not confront the United States' own implication in racist nationalist policies based on assumptions about race purity; instead, it took as its focus the assumption that the black community needed to overcome its inadequate preparation for taking on the "rights and responsibilities" of full citizenship. Focusing on these inadequacies allowed the Moynihan Report to strike the needed balance between discussing obvious inequality and distracting attention from it. The report achieved this balance by transforming a supposedly tangential discussion of national reputation into its central focus. Its admission of the heinousness of the slave system, for instance, is overshadowed by the subtle assertion that slavery was really only a temporary divergence from the nation's destined role as the world exemplar of liberty: "It is clear that what happens in America is being taken as a sign of what can, or must, happen in the world at large." Such phrasing transforms the United States' stance on Civil Rights from antagonism to sponsorship. The report goes even further, recuperating the struggle for Civil Rights as evidence of the persistence of the American spirit of democracy: "The course of world events will be profoundly affected by the success or failure of the Negro American revolution in seeking the peaceful assimilation of the races in the United States" (1). This reference to "assimilation" subtly introduces the one condition that the report later claims is necessary for overcoming the problem of inequality: the willingness of African Americans to embrace the nuclear family structure as a means of placing them on an equal footing with whites. The report asserts that the matriarchal structure of the black family is "so out of line with the rest of American society" that it "seriously retards the progress of the group as a whole" (29). With this redirection of attention from the documented pathology of plantation patriarchy to the supposed pathology of African matriarchy, the Moynihan Report, one might argue, exemplifies the "Maginot Line syndrome."

Morrison indirectly comments on this process of acknowledging the existence of a national racial division followed by a subtle denial of responsibility for it when she characterizes Pecola Breedlove, a child who is the product of what Moynihan would certainly term a pathological family, as a scapegoat. It is clear from her description that Morrison intends the scapegoating of this one young girl as a microcosm of the larger scapegoating process[7] necessary for the bolstering of a narrative of national innocence. Significantly, Claudia's commentary on scapegoating ends the novel:

> All of us—all who knew her—felt so wholesome after we cleaned ourselves on her. We were so beautiful when we stood astride her ugliness. Her simplicity decorated us, her guilt sanctified us, her pain made us glow with health, her awkwardness made us think we had a sense of humor. Her inarticulateness made us believe we were eloquent. Her poverty kept us generous. . . . We honed our egos on her, padded our characters with her frailty, and yawned in the fantasy of our strength. (159)

With these remarks, Claudia links the transference of the town's self-hatred onto a hyperembodied Pecola to the widespread scapegoating of Blacks in America, concluding, "The land of the entire country was hostile" (160). In a nation obsessed with purity, whether it be racial, sexual, or ideological, there need to be scapegoats. As Sander Gilman theorizes about the pathologizing of the Other, when "self-integration is threatened" stereotypes arise because they are "part of our way of dealing with the instabilities of our perception of the world" (18). Because the history of slavery and miscegenation threatens the American iconic identity as champion of liberty and equality, it needs to be redescribed so as to deflect attention from national culpability. With this scapegoating reference, Morrison seems to be commenting on the displacement of blame for black inequality from a racially structured economic and social system in the larger culture onto the matriarchal structures of the black community.

In shifting blame from systematic inequality to the structural inequality of the black social structure, the Moynthan Report ignored several obstacles in postwar America to the black community's adoption of the gendered divisions of the nuclear family model: the exclusion of black males from breadwinner roles and the corresponding re-channeling of black females into domestic servant roles, the de facto exclusion of black families from the commodity culture through which families publicly display their success at achieving economic power through consumerism, and the need for black families to pool resources in order to consolidate their economic weakness and maintain some semblance of economic and social stability. Morrison refers to these issues in her description of the public sphere as a garment. As Claudia explains, "Being a minority in both caste and class, we moved about anyway on the hem of life, struggling to consolidate our weaknesses and hang on, or to creep singly up into the major folds of the garment" (18). To compare the public sphere to a garment has several ramifications. The first is that citizenship is measured by one's ability to purchase the commodities that identify one as looking American. Neither the MacTeers nor the Breedloves have this ability because they are black and poor; in contrast, the Peals can "creep singly up into" the folds of the garment because their near-white skin and their penchant for winning bias lawsuits enable them to move up from the hem to the skirt. Through their generations of marrying lighter, they are slowly peeling away the layers of blackness that prevent them from seamlessly integrating themselves into mainstream culture. To do so in a celebratory manner is to will themselves not to remember the sexualized economy of slavery, of which their whiteness is a sign, and to fail to recognize that legally their blackness still marks them. Above the Peals would be the Villanuccis, the Italian American neighbors of the MacTeers who, while not in the main class of citizens because of their own foreignness and darker skin, can intermarry and "creep" more inconspicuously into the "folds of the garment."[8]

Morrison's references to a garment with a hem and folds is intriguing because it conveys an image of a woman's full-skirted, calf-length dress, the emblem of the mid-twentieth-century domestic ease and the division of separate spheres that still characterized the pre-war period.[9] That Morrison chooses a particular feminized image of the public sphere is important because the ability to maintain this division of separate spheres was thought to be central to one's ability to embody American citizenship fully. The MacTeers are able to maintain this separation between breadwinner and homemaker, but it produces a strain within their family. They barely survive, and the mother takes in boarders and foster children such as Pecola. The state's intervention in the affairs of the Breedloves signals the extent to which they are totally cut off from kinship networks that at least to some extent help families like the MacTeers pool their resources. Of course, that Mrs. MacTeer complains that, if she keeps helping others, she'll never have anything for her own family indicates how vulnerable that kinship system is to social and consumer pressure to adopt the nuclear family model. Succumbing to this pressure, Pauline and Cholly Breedlove, Pecola's parents, embrace the nuclear family model, but are not able to maintain this gendered division; consequently, they are forced by economic circumstance into a role reversal in which the wife is the primary breadwinner.

When Pauline Breedlove realizes that she cannot achieve full citizenship in her own domestic space, she contents herself with occupying the space of her employers. Morrison's hemming metaphor takes on added significance here because, as the Fishers' servant responsible for domestic tasks such as hemming and cooking, Polly is able to hang on to the hem of their lives. In her role as the Fishers' cherished servant Polly, Pauline feels what it's like "to wear their white skin" and, as Berlant phrases it, to assume the "privileges" of citizenship that such whiteness affords her (111–113). At their house, "she could arrange things, clean things, line things up in neat rows. . . . Here she found beauty, order, cleanliness, and praise" (Morrison 101). Living in this house vicariously fulfills her consumer desire, just "knowing there were soap bars by the dozen, bacon by the rasher, and reveling in her shiny pots and pans and polished floors." Pauline is the perfect advertisement for these domestic products, and as the Fishers say, "'Really, she is the ideal servant'" (101). If to name is to "arrest, and fix, the image of that other," then the Fisher's renaming of Pauline as Polly[10] is an act of containment (Phelan 2). As a representative ideal servant, Polly becomes safely part of the everpresent but overlooked background of their household. The Fishers turn Polly into a fetish; she is the signifier of happy servitude, of benevolent rescue from her own culture's inherent debasement. When they look at her, what is reflected are the "constituent forces of their desire" to reconceptualize an exploitative relationship as a mutually beneficial one (Phelan 26).

For Claudia, the novel's narrator, Polly is the signifier of the intimate forms of exploitation inherent in the relationship between black and white families; in other words, she realizes that it is the black-white interfamial relationship that is inherently flawed and not the black family itself (as policymakers like Moynihan would later argue). When Claudia witnesses Pauline's mothering of the Fisher girl, she recalls, "The familiar violence rose in me. Her calling Mrs. Breedlove Polly, when even Pecola called her mother Mrs. Breedlove" (86). That her role as Polly detracts from the quality of mothering Pauline gives her own daughter is not surprising given the historical precedent set in the plantation household. The mistress-mammy relationship allowed the white woman to maintain the idealized status of mother, while freeing her from the actualities of mothering.[11] In turn, this transference of mothering established a burden of superhuman mothering on the black woman.[12] Thus, Mrs. Fisher, like a plantation mistress, remains associated with the "universal qualities of nurturance and self sacrifice" despite the fact that she leaves the mothering to Pauline (Bridenthal 232; Fox-Genovese 113). Because the mammy is represented in Hollywood films as "satisfied, even pleased, with this inequitable arrangement," Jeremy G. Butler argues, the mammy "does not just represent nurturing; she also promotes black women's exploitation as nurturers of white characters who hire and use her" (292). Thus, the viewer is led to believe that this seemingly familial relationship cannot be exploitative.

Only by glossing over the continuing discrimination against freed Blacks could one claim that black people naturally gravitate toward such roles, since they still performed and seemed content with them after slavery. What is overlooked in such an argument is that black men had little opportunity to become breadwinners[13] while black women who became family wage-earners did so by taking jobs that imitated the service positions they would have held during slavery.[14] Gloria Wade-Gayles writes about how women often slipped back into their pre-Emancipation roles as mammies, caretakers, and cooks—jobs as plentiful in the North as in the South. Black men had a harder time finding a niche as white immigrants crowded the low-level industrial sector. It is this economic reality and not a flaw in their "natures" or abilities that denied black men breadwinner status and sometimes, consequently, a secure place in the home. In order to find work they often had to travel.

Despite these systematic obstacles to the Breedloves' achieving this gendered model, Pauline sees her failures as individual and familial ones. She learns to measure herself against a cinematic scale of style[15] that measures the difference between white and black, beautiful and ugly: "She was never able, after her education at the movies, to look at a face and not assign it some category in the scale of absolute beauty, and the scale was one she absorbed in full from the silver screen." The movies have also revealed to her the idea of the perfect family, of which she desired to be a part: *"I'd move right on in them pictures. White men taking such good care of they women, and they all dressed up in big clean houses"* (97). After she loses her front tooth eating candy at the movies, she concludes that she is destined never to be so beautiful or cared for as those women on the screen.[16] She does not understand that her rotten tooth is the physical embodiment of her inability to be an unmarked citizen who has the economic power to erase the unwanted traces of her body by purchasing a new artificial tooth. Instead, she directs blame inward and loses interest in her physical appearance and her home: "Soon she stopped trying to keep her own house. The things she could afford to buy did not last, had no beauty or style, and were absorbed by the dingy storefront" (101). Not understanding this systematic aspect of her situation, Pauline imagines that her inability to be beautiful or stylish stems from some inherent fault; in so doing, she fails to account for the economic barriers to her attainment of the privileged homemaker position in one of those white houses.

With white houses as the standard of beauty, Pauline finds everything in her home decor wanting. She compares her zinc tub to her employer's porcelain one, her "stiff, grayish towels" to their "fluffy white" ones, her daughter's "tangled black puffs of rough wool" with the Fisher girl's silky, yellow hair (101). Measuring her own success by a consumer yardstick, Pauline employs what Joan Kron terms a "semiotics of home decor," in which one's home furnishings are read as part of a "system of symbols" indicating one's social status and self-perception (80). The fuller description of the Breedloves' decor makes apparent that they feel demoralized by their inability to use their possessions to convey a positive self-image. Morrison uses a description of this decor to signify their disenfranchisement and the histories of their furnishings to tell of their systemic oppression, not individual shiftlessness. Their sofa "had been purchased new," the narrator explains, "but the fabric had split straight across the back by the time it was delivered. The store would not take the responsibility" (32). The Breedloves are held responsible for the sofa and the debasement it represents, but Morrison makes it clear that the accountability should be directed elsewhere. The sofa functions as a sign of the Breedloves' inability to compete in American consumer culture. The literal humiliation of the ripped sofa and the metaphorical shame of consumer impotence also affect other parts of the family's life: "If you had to pay $4.80 a month for a sofa that started off split, no good, and humiliating— you couldn't take any joy in owning it. And the joylessness stank, pervading everything" (32). The ripped sofa is just the outward manifestation of the Breedloves' all-pervasive alienation from themselves, from any political or personal constituency, and from industrial and consumer culture.

When the narrator details the history of Pauline's life, her apparent preference for the white family over her own is revealed to be much more complicated and at least partially connected to her overcompensation for the unhappy reality of her own family life, especially as it contrasts to Mrs. Fisher's. It is apparent from the description of the Breedloves' home,[17] where they remain "festering together in the debris of a realtor's whim," that systematic obstacles stand in the way of their successful adoption of the breadwinner/homemaker model (31). Considered in this light, Pauline can be understood to embrace her role as the Fishers' servant in order to trade in her own troubling body and history. As their servant she can "move unconsciously and unobstructed through the public sphere" (Berlant 111) in a way that she cannot as Mrs. Cholly Breedlove: "The creditors and service people who humiliated her when she went to them on her own behalf respected her, even were intimated by her, when she spoke for the Fishers" (Morrison 101). As Polly she gets as close as she can as a black woman to experience the privileges of disembodied citizenship. Embodying the role of Polly becomes a substitute for what Pauline wants: a satisfying and substantial self. When she cannot access that self on her own, through her family or the black community, she accepts the self imposed upon her by the Fishers. Pauline wills herself not to know her own history because it is too painful. She seems to forget her own role in creating the seeming naturalness of Hollywood's image of "*white men taking such good care of they women, and they all dressed up in big clean houses*" (97). This comment makes apparent Pauline's acceptance of the equation that home decor equals identity: Because she believes that she is squalid and dark like her apartment and the Fishers are stately and clean like their house, Pauline can only maintain a positive self-perception by affiliating herself with the Fishers. Yet houses such as theirs are clean because she and others like her labor in them; they are big because white employers can still find black labor to exploit. Moreover, the white men are viewed as good caretakers because they protect white women not only from economic vicissitudes but also from the supposed threat of the rapacious black male predator.

White men maintained their status as chivalric protectors, in other words, by contrasting themselves to the dishonorable defilers embodied in the figure of the black rapist. Yet, when "chivalrous white men" of the South cried rape, Ida B. Wells argues, they did so to "shield themselves by their cowardly and infamously false excuse" in order to "escape the deserved execration of the civilized world" for their own institutionalized practice of the rape of slave women (12–13). In other words, this chivalric pose is a false front:

> To justify their own barbarism they assume a chivalry which they do not possess. True chivalry respects all womanhood, and no one who reads the record, as it *is* written in the faces of the million mulattoes in the South, will for a minute conceive that the southern white man had a very chivalrous regard for the honor due to the women of his own race or respect for the womanhood which circumstances placed in his power.

They can only reassert their chivalric reputations by once more recreating the figure of the black rapist, thereby justifying the need for a corresponding chivalric, white avenger. Focusing on this chivalric front distracts attention from the real issue that during and even after slavery white men could sexually exploit black women without any fear of retaliation. Moreover, focusing on the figure of the black male sexual predator coupled with that of the emasculating black matriarch distracts attention from the entrenchment of racialized conceptions of citizenship that justified economic inequality.

The history of Cholly Breedlove suggests that his demoralization over his exclusion from full citizenship is the emasculating force in his life. Contrary to the Moynihan Report's claim that it is the matriarchal structure of the black family that imposes a "crushing burden on the black male," Morrison demonstrates that it is the attempt to embrace patriarchy that crushes Cholly's spirit. Although Morrison begins Cholly's section with the line "SEEFATHERHEISBIGANDSTRONG," the experiences detailed therein reveal the negative impact of the patriarchal assumptions inherent in the artificial social demarcations intrinsic to the nuclear family (105). Within the kinship network of his Aunt Jimmy, Cholly's manhood is nurtured, even though he is surrounded by females. One night as he sleeps by his aunt's bedside the women's "lullaby of grief envelops him" and he dreams that "his penis changed into a long hickory stick, and the hands caressing it were the hands of M'Dear," the root doctor who treats Aunt Jimmy (110). Along with this healthy model of sexuality, the kinship network encourages an understanding of manhood that involves nurturing as well as strength. Exemplifying this nurturing masculinity, Cholly's relationship with a local man named Blue Jack is based on sharing: "Together the old man and the boy sat on the grass and shared the heart of the watermelon. The nasty-sweet guts of the earth" (107). From Blue Cholly learns that any man in the community can father a child. This conception of masculinity as something that is nourished in harmony with the community of women and with nature is opposed to a more hierarchical conception of manhood which is determined by the work a man does, the authority he has, or the mastery he achieves. Significantly, Cholly also learns about the history of lynching from Blue, a man who had "talked his way out of getting lynched once" and who tells stories of others who hadn't (106). With this second reference to lynching in the novel, Morrison demonstrates again what a false front lynching is because the almost-lynched Blue, Cholly's father-figure, is the antithesis of the stereotype of black brute/buck upon which the justification for lynching relied.

Morrison further undercuts the chivalric justification of lynching not only by having a member of the black community offering a counternarrative to standard lynching history, but also through depicting Cholly's encounter with two white hunters while he is engaged in sexual experimentation with a neighbor. Before the hunters arrive, Cholly's sexual awakening is described in organic terms—"His mouth full of the taste of muscadine . . . The smell of promised rain, pine, and muscadine made him giddy" (115)— but, after the hunters leave, all of this becomes rotten. For these white men, black male sexuality is simply an entertaining spectacle, reinforcing their own inherent manliness and superiority. That Cholly accepts their superiority and adopts their perspective is evident by his reaction. He blames his partner Darlene, "the one who bore witness to his failure, his impotence. The one whom he had not been able to protect, to spare, to cover from the round moon glow of the flashlight. The hee-hee-hee's" (119). These two hunters bear little resemblance to the white men who are depicted in chivalric lynching scenarios as "patriarchs, avengers, righteous protectors" (Hall 218). Instead, they more closely resemble Wells's characterization of white men in a lynch mob that "did not embody white manliness *restraining* black lust—it embodied white men's lust running amok, *destroying* true black manliness" (220). They destroy Cholly's idea of mutually nurturing natural relations between people learned at Aunt Jimmy's bedside, and replace it with the artificial hierarchical power relations revealed by flashlight. After his encounter with them, fourteen-year-old Cholly flees his kinship network and feels the need to find his own father and his own place within the patriarchal hierarchy. But when he locates his father in Macon after an arduous search, and his father abandons him for the second time, Cholly forsakes his connection to all of his kin. The brutishness Cholly has developed is a product of his experiences trying to assimilate into the consumer culture of the North and has nothing to do with any sense of impotence caused by his family's matriarchal structure. In short, an innocent black boy's feelings of impotence, to borrow from Wells's anti-lynching rhetoric, can be attributed to his encounter with two "unmanly" and "unrestrained" white men who revel in their own lustiness.

This lustiness recalls the fact that historically it was the white masters and not the black servants who were the sexual aggressors. Elizabeth Fox Genovese claims that the slaveholder's often-used metaphor "'my family, white and black,'" effaced the economic heart of slavery by representing the plantation household as an "organic community" (100). This metaphor conjures an image of mutual devotion, of responsibility, but leaves out the mitigating factor of bondage. As Catherine Clinton and Hazel Carby (*Reconstructing*) have argued, black and white intra- and inter-family relationships in such a sexualized plantation economy were pathologically entangled, especially when white masters sold their own black offspring and white children played with and later owned their black half-brothers and sisters. Moreover, relations in the plantation household were quite pathological because, as Fox-Genovese argues, "the beneficent paternalism of the father was ever shadowed by the power of the master, just as the power of the master was tempered by the beneficent paternalism of the father" (101). The slaves were children, in a sense, but not the legitimate children worthy of comfort and care. This reality caused contradictory feelings: "Intimacy and distance, companionship and impatience, affection and hostility, all wove through their relations" (144).

African Americans have the same fraught relationship with the United States itself: All children of the nation are supposed to be equal citizens, but it is clear that some are more worthy of comfort and care than others. As Morrison phrases it, the American "soil is bad for certain kinds of flowers"

(160). Many Black Americans, like the Breedloves, seemed during this era to will themselves not to know this history and optimistically tried to embrace consumer culture and its promises. Without their kinship networks, however, many found that they had no reliable social and economic support. Their loss of any connection to a kinship group is precisely what, according to Claudia, puts the Breedlove family "outdoors," a condition which does not merely entail the loss of a roof over one's head, but signifies more precisely the state of being completely outside the community and its help. Claudia explains the irrevocable nature of this condition, "If you are put out, you go somewhere else; if you are outdoors there is no place to go." She recognizes that economic fluctuations are inevitable for those on the bottom of the socioeconomic ladder, for those who "moved about anyway on the hem of life," but the Breedloves forsake kinship networks that function as a safety net for the back community, enabling them to "consolidate [their] weaknesses and hang on" (18). Other black people in Lorrain, even if they are on the periphery—like Della Jones, whose sister from North Carolina comes to take care of her when she has a stroke—still have "people"; that is, a community of kin who can pool their resources (15). Thus, while the Breedloves' poverty is not unique, their lack of "people" is. The hemming metaphor is significant here because it can refer to the hemming of clothes and, thereby, signify a non-consumer network of sharing and recycling items through which the black families in the South remained afloat even when their needs were not met by consumer culture.

Viewing kinship networks as failed nuclear families, U.S. society in general and the Moynihan Report in particular fail to consider the importance of these kinship networks that share household spaces, services, and goods among non-blood as well as blood relations. In addition, they take no account of the elaborate system of male and female responsibility among these extended networks that guarantee financial support and child care as long as obligations and connections are maintained within the networks.[18] As Carol B. Stack concludes,[19] "A pattern of cooperation and mutual aid among kin during the migration north . . . and the domestic cooperation of close adult females and the exchange of goods and services between male and female kin" were strategies these communities used for coping with poverty (9). Ann Zollar qualifies Stack's argument, claiming that these networks were not just reactions to conditions, but rather that they are inherent features of African American family units.[20]

Such a network was certainly part of Cholly Breedlove's life until he came north. While his life in Georgia wasn't easy, it was marked by the care of people like Blue and Aunt Jimmy. Jimmy's network of women is described as truly free, a liberation which arises from the strength of their mutual bonds. The extended network of care that these women provide for each other is distinct from their other lives as maids and housekeepers for white women. Their experiences outside of this protective realm are harsh; everyone orders them around, drawing from their strength as if it were inexhaustible. But because of their circle, they transform these indignities into something usable: "They took all of that and re-created it in their own image" (Morrison 109). Moreover, as the reader learns later in the book when Pecola is crushed by her inability to create an image of herself outside of the images of full personhood and citizenship that a white consumer society has manufactured, their having these images of themselves makes all the difference in the world:

> The hands that felled trees also cut umbilical cords; the hands that wrung the necks of chickens and butchered hogs also nudged African violets into bloom . . . They plowed all day and came home to nestle like plums under the limbs of their men. The legs that straddled a mule's back were the same ones that straddled their men's hips. And the difference was all the difference there was. (110)

Their internal perimeter of strength enables Aunt Jimmy and her community of women to be free in their minds and hearts. While this network cannot change the harshness of their lives, it can mediate it.

Morrison describes the importance of this network even more clearly in an interview in which she discusses techniques that have enabled African American survival: "Taking that which is peripheral, or violent or doomed or something that nobody else can see any value in and making value out of it or having a psychological attitude about duress is what made us stay alive and fairly coherent" (Jones and Vinson 175). Morrison uses embedded metaphors throughout *The Bluest Eye* in order to take that which seems peripheral in American history and foreground it. By demonstrating how destructive it is for her characters not to know their history, she suggests how damaging such an amnesiac approach also is for the nation. Writing about this amnesiac approach to national history, Ann Douglas contends that by the 1920s a few American writers attempted to re-centralize the "sin [of slavery] in modern consciousness," but those who took an "amnesiac approach" to that history dominated. Douglas laments that the latter thereby consigned slavery—the "tragic nexus of black and white—with all other signs of cultural miscegenation to a death sentence of oblivion and denial" (272). While Michael Rogin[21] describes such an approach as a form of public "inattention to what continues to be seen" (*Ronald* 234), Morrison uses her metaphoric references to draw attention to the histories of those marked by their conspicuously ill-fitting personhood. In short, by telling the story of her characters' will-not-to know their painful history, Morrison is also able to relate the parallel story of the national misrecognition of its history.

NOTES

1. For historical background, see Gregory; Langer and Gleason; Blum; Kennan.

2. See Awkward; Christian; Harris, "Reconnecting"; Hedin; Towner; Weinstein.

3. If China and Poland are nations that during World War II could metaphorically be considered damsels in distress who need to be protected from violation by aggressors, the use of those names for two black prostitutes is ironic. As Ida B. Wells argues, the chivalric rhetoric of lynching positioned some women as worthy of rescue while leaving others unprotected. The second irony here is that, as Cynthia Enloe points out, American chivalric rescuers were often "serviced" by the women channeled into prostitution precisely because of the presence of these foreign servicemen in their countries. For an insightful discussion of the role prostitutes have played in maintaining masculinity, especially in times of war, see Enloe, *Bananas* 145–156; Enloe, *Morning*.

4. The "Maginot Line" refers to France's fixation in World War II on a series of strategic points from which artillery could be fired. While France was assuming that World War II would mirror World War I and be a war of positions in which soldiers could defend the country in trenches one hundred miles from the enemy, this war was completely different. In 1939, German troops invaded Poland, unleashed a blitzkrieg, and destroyed all resistance. In 1940, Nazi armies invaded northern France by going through neutral Holland and Belgium, bypassing the Maginot Line and its defensive fortifications. See Chelminski; Lens.

5. Useful here is Gail Bederman's discussion of how black women were depicted as "unwomanly harlots" and contrasted to "high-minded and sexually pure" white women (230).

6. For a discussion that contextualizes Wells's anti-lynching campaigns in terms of ideologies of manhood and womanhood, see Carby, "On the Threshold."

7. For more on scapegoating see Mary Douglas 9.

8. Even though American culture of the 1940s may have marked Italian Americans as darker and akin to black, they were not labeled legally "other," as were those with black ancestry, such as the Peals. The Villanuccis are representative of the minorities who are able to make their presence in the public sphere less noticeable.

9. The stability of this division was briefly threatened by the entrance of women into the workforce during World War II, but recontained by the post-war emphasis on the attractive and efficient homemaker. See May; Coontz.

10. See Trudier Harris's argument ("Reconnecting" 72–73) that the nicknaming of Pauline is a perversion of the communal claiming function of African American nicknames.

11. See Anderson; Harris, *From Mammies;* Parkhurst 353; Jones 233–36.

12. For more on how the idealization of "mother*hood*" is separated from actual "mother*ing*," see Bridenthal 232.

13. May discusses how many advertisements of the era focused on the way the male breadwinner could be the cornerstone of a stable family structure. They played on "men's guilt at a time when many men felt responsible for placing the security of

their families in jeopardy" (49). Of course, black men were excluded from the fundamental idea of American manhood. Roland Marchand claims that advertisements of the 1920s and '30s portrayed blacks as contented porters, janitors, and maids and never portrayed them as "consumers, or as fellow workers with whites, or as skilled workers. Primarily, they functioned as symbols of the capacity of the leading lady and leading man to command a variety of personal services" (193). Several other chapters in Marchand's book also examine these issues. See esp. 248–254.

14. See Ottley and Weatherby for a discussion of the channeling of black women into domestic work and the exclusion of black men from public utilities and trade unions, leaving them either unemployed or working as messengers, porters, and cleaners. Especially interesting is their discussion of maid auctions in New York City (260). With continued discrimination and second-class status in the North, conditions for Blacks in New York became a refiguration of slave conditions and Jim Crow laws of the South (270).

15. For a discussion of the record attendance at movies in the 1930s, see May. Significantly, the motion picture industry was one of the few economic enterprises that did not suffer serious losses during the Depression (41).

16. Hollywood film has its roots in racialized entertainment spectacles such as Buffalo Bill's Wild West show and the scientific racism of the World Columbian Exposition's anthropological exhibits. For an analysis of how the fair's grammar positioned black and white as antonyms, see Bederman. For treatments of the cinema in the novel, see Gerster; Fick.

17. The Breedloves' storefront shares a similarity to Elizabeth Fox-Genovese's description of a typical slave cabin: "Even with improvements slave cabins hardly offered a solid foundation for an independent domestic sphere over which the mother of the family could preside. Primarily places to sleep, take shelter, eat the last meal of the day, they did not harbor the real life of slave families, much less of the slave community" (15).

18. For the way black slave women responded to this loss of family ties by developing networks with each other, see Hine.

19. For more on Stack's analysis of a community in a Midwestern city on the rail line between the South and Chicago, see *All Our Kin*.

20. For a similar claim, see McAdoo.

21. Rogin also discusses political amnesia in "'Make My Day.'"

WORKS CITED

Anderson, Lisa. *Mammies No More: The Changing Image of Black Women on the Stage and Screen*. Lanham: Rowman and Littlefield, 1997.

Awkward, Michael. "Roadblocks and Relatives: Critical Revision in Toni Morrison's *The Bluest Eye*." McKay, pp. 57–68.

Bederman, Gail. "Civilization, The Decline of Middle-Class Manliness, and Ida B. Wells' Anti-Lynching Campaign (1892–94)." *Gander and American History Since 1890*. Ed. Barbara Melosh. New York: Routledge, 1993: pp. 207–239.

Berlant, Lauren. "National Brands/National Body: *Imitation of Life*." *Comparative American Identities: Race, Sex, and Nationality in the Modem Text*. Ed. Hortense J. Spillers. New York: Routledge, 1991: pp. 10–40.

Blum, John Morton. *From the Morgenthau Diaries: Years of Urgency, 1938–1941*. Boston: Houghton, 1965.

Bridenthal, Renate. "The Family: The View From a Room of Her Own." *Rethinking the Family: Some Feminist Questions.* Ed. Barris Thorne with Marilyn Yalom. New York: Longman, 1982: pp. 225–239.

Butler, Jeremy G. *"Imitation of Life* (1934 and 1959): Style and Domestic Melodrama." Imitation of Life, *Douglas Sirk, Director.* Films in Print Ser. 16. Ed. Lucy Fischer. New Brunswick: Rutgers University Press, 1991: pp. 289–301.

Carby, Hazel V. "On the Threshold of Woman's Era': Lynching, Empire, and Sexuality in Black Feminist Theory." *Race, Writing, and Difference.* Ed. Henry Louis Gates, Jr. Chicago: University of Chicago Press, 1985: pp. 301–316.

———. *Reconstructing Womanhood., The Emergence of the Afro-American Novelist.* New York: Oxford University Press, 1987.

Cheiminski, Rudolph. "The Maginot Line." *Smithsonian.* June 1997: pp. 91–97.

Christian, Barbara. "The Contemporary Fables of Toni Morrison." *Black Women Novelists: The Development of a Tradition, 1892–1976.* Westport: Greenwood Press, 1980: pp. 137–179.

Clinton, Catherine. *The Plantation Mistress: Woman's World in the Old South.* New York: Pantheon, 1982.

Coontz, Stephanie. *The Way We Never Were: American Families and the Nostalgia Trap.* New York: Basic Books, 1992.

Douglas, Ann. *Terrible Honesty: Mongrel Manhattan in the 1920s.* New York: Farrar, 1995.

Douglas, Mary. *Risk and Blame: Essays in Cultural Theory.* London: Routledge, 1994.

Du Bois, W. E. B. *The Souls of Black Folk.* 1903. New York: Vintage, 1990.

Enloe, Cynthia. *Bananas, Beaches, and Bases: Making Feminist Sense of International Politics.* Berkeley: University of California Press, 1990.

———. *The Morning After: Sexual Politics at the End of the Cold War.* Berkeley: University of California Press, 1993.

Fick, Thomas H. "Toni Morrison's 'Allegory of the Cave': Movies, Consumption, and Platonic Realism in *The Bluest Eye.*" *Journal of the Midwest Modem Language Association* 22 (1989): pp. 10–22.

Fox-Genovese, Elizabeth. *Within the Plantation Household: Black and White Women of the Old South.* Chapel Hill: University of North Carolina Press, 1988.

Gerster, Carole. "From Film Margin to Novel Center: Toni Morrison's *The Bluest Eye.*" *West Virginia University Philological Papers* 38 (1992): pp. 191–99.

Gilman, Sander L. *Difference and Pathology: Stereotypes of Sexuality, Race, and Madness.* Ithaca: Cornell University Press, 1985.

Gregory, Ross. *America 1941: A Nation at the Crossroads .* New York: Free Press, 1989.

Hall, Jacquelyn Dowd. *Revolt Against Chivalry: Jesse Daniel Ames and the Women's Campaign Against Lynching.* New York: Columbia University Press, 1979.

Harris, Trudier. *From Mammies to Militants: Domestics in Black American Literature.* Philadelphia: Temple University Press, 1982.

———. "Reconnecting Fragments: Afro-American Folk Tradition in *The Bluest Eye.*" McKay , pp. 68–76.

Hedin, Raymond. "The Structuring of Emotion in Black American Fiction." *Novel* 16.1 (1982): pp. 35–54.

Hine, Darlene Clark. "Female Slave Resistance: The Economics of Sex." *Western Journal of Black Studies* 3 (Summer 1979): pp. 123–127.

Jones, Bessie, and Audrey Vinson. "An Interview with Toni Morrison." *Conversations with Toni Morrison.* Ed. Danille Taylor-Guthrie. Jackson: University Press of Mississippi, 1994: pp. 171–187.

Jones, Jacqueline. *Labor of Love, Labor of Sorrow: Black Women, Work, and the Family from Slavery to the Present.* New York: Basic Books, 1985.

Kennan, George F. *Memoirs, 1925–1950.* Boston: Little Brown, 1967.

Kolmerten, Carol A., Stephen M. Ross, and Judith Bryant Wittenberg, eds. *Unflinching Gaze: Morrison and Faulkner Re-Envisioned.* Jackson: University Press of Mississippi, 1997.

Kron, Joan. "The Semiotics of Home Decor." *Home-Psych: The Social Psychology of Home and Decoration.* New York: Crown, 1983: pp. 72–82.

Langer, William L., and S. Everett Gleason. *The Undeclared War, 1940–41.* New York: Harper, 1953.

Lens, Sidney. *The Maginot Line Syndrome: America's Hopeless Foreign Policy.* Cambridge: Ballinger, 1982.

Marchand, Roland. *Advertising and the American Dream: Making Way for Modernity, 1920–1940.* Berkeley: University of California Press, 1985.

May, Elaine Tyler. *Homeward Bound: American Families in the Cold War Era.* New York: Basic Books, 1988.

McAdoo, Harriette. "Black Kinship." *Psychology Today* May 1979: pp. 67+.

McKay, Nellie, ed. *Critical Essays on Toni Morrison.* Boston: Hall, 1988.

Morrison, Toni. *The Bluest Eye.* 1970. New York: Washington Square Press, 1972.

Moynihan, Daniel Patrick. *The Negro Family: The Case for National Action.* Office of Policy Planning and Research, United States Department of Labor. Mar. 1965. Rainwater and Yancey, pp. 38–124.

Ottley, Roi, and William Weatherby. "The Depression." *Justice Denied: The Black Man in White America.* Ed. William M. Chace and Peter Collier. New York: Harcourt, 1970: pp. 256–270.

Parkhurst, Jessie W. "The Black Mammy in the Plantation Household." *Journal of Negro History* 23 (July 1938): pp. 349–369.

Pateman, Carole. *The Sexual Contract.* Stanford: Stanford University Press, 1988.

Phelan, Peggy. *Unmarked: The Politics of Performance.* New York: Routledge, 1993.

Rainwater, Lee, and William L. Yancey. *The Moynihan Report and the Politics of Controversy.* Cambridge: MIT Press, 1967.

Rogin, Michael. "'Make My Day': Spectacle as Amnesia in Imperial Politics." *Cultures of United States Imperialism.* Ed. Amy Kaplan and Donald Pease. Durham: Duke University Press, 1993: pp. 499–534.

———. *Ronald Reagan: The Movie and Other Episodes in Political Demonology.* Berkeley: University of California Press, 1987.

Stack, Carol B. *All Our Kin: Strategies for Survival in a Black Community.* New York: Harper, 1974.

Tannen, Deborah. "Marked Women, Unmarked Men." *New York Times Magazine* 20 June 1993: pp. 18+.

Towner, Theresa M. "Black Matters on the Dixie Limited: *As I Lay Dying* and *The Bluest Eye.*" Kolmerten et al., pp. 115–127.

Wald, Priscilla. *Constituting Americans: Cultural Anxiety and Narrative Form.* Durham: Duke University Press, 1995.

Weinstein, Philip M. "David and Solomon: Fathering in Faulkner and Morrison." Kolmerten et al., pp. 48–74.

Wells-Barnett, Ida B. *Southern Horrors: Lynch Law in All its Phases.* 1892. Rpt. as *On Lynchings: Southern Horrors, A Red Record, Mob Rule in New Orleans.* Salem: Ayer, 1991.

Zollar, Ann. *A Member of the Family: Strategies for Black Community Continuity.* Chicago: Nelson-Hall, 1985.

JEFFREY M. BUCHANAN

"A Productive and Fructifying Pain": Storytelling as Teaching in The Bluest Eye

It is the urgency of a simple childhood desire—the desire for a bicycle—that prompts Claudia and Frieda, two of the main characters in Toni Morrison's *The Bluest Eye,* to await impatiently the arrival of marigold seeds packets. At the moment of the seeds' arrival, Claudia's and Frieda's desire takes outlet in routine, compelled as they are now to spend "a major part of every day trooping about the town selling" in hopes of raising money for the bicycle (146). In service to this everyday routine, Claudia and Frieda quickly come to understand that to possess a highly desirable object they must sacrifice—walk from door to door, knock and make a sales pitch. By naming the girls' behavior "trooping about," Morrison highlights both the everydayness of the girls' performance and its potential burdensomeness. But, Morrison's name, "trooping about," also normalizes the behavior, suggesting that burdensome routine is an expected part of everyday adult life. And to draw her readers' attentions to the taken-for-granted routines enacted throughout everyday life, Morrison spines her story with extraordinary tragedy. Claudia's and Frieda's "trooping about" literally carries their bodies around town, exposing them to the secrets they cobble together into an awful story of incest and rape.

"Trooping about" itself becomes a trope, in Morrison's novel, highlighting a kind of routinized bodily performance cut off from its initial impetus and carried out simply through a kind of reproductive inertia.

Reader: Essays in Reader-Oriented Theory, Criticism, and Pedagogy, 2004 Spring; 50: pp. 59–75. © 2004 University of Pittsburgh.

Claudia and Frieda can imagine no other way to sell the seeds, for their mother, by restricting them to sell only to her friends and acquaintances, limits the possible ways they might respond to the marigolds' arrival. "Trooping about," then, becomes the everyday activity through which Claudia and Frieda simultaneously put off and live out their desire for the bicycle—until they piece together the story of Pecola's rape and subsequent pregnancy. Pecola's circumstance, however, dictates no directive, provides Claudia and Frieda with no protocol for response; it asks, simply, that they feel sorrow for Pecola. Unwilling to accept that as all they are to receive in exchange for the work[1] they have put in for the bicycle, Claudia and Frieda "become headstrong, devious and arrogant" and decide "to change the course of events and alter a human life" (149).[2] The impetus for their decision is born of feelings of "fondness for Pecola" (148) and the lack of fondness they hear expressed in the circulating stories about her. But, even more than that, Claudia says, "I felt a need for someone to want the black baby to live" (148).

For *The Bluest Eye* is a striking condemnation of a social system that produces in the African-American characters in the novel self-loathing, a disciplinary, self-hatred that is internalized, and projected onto others.[3] Pecola is viciously scapegoated, judged especially lacking when compared to pervasive standards of beauty, white standards of beauty, standards that actually mark all characters in *The Bluest Eye* inadequate. Pecola's peers, the children in the novel, including at times Claudia and Frieda, place Pecola on the lowest rung of the social order through the routines that make up their everyday lives, most notably schoolyard teasing, as a way to feel better about themselves, as a way to cover over their own deficiencies. But, alive, Pecola's baby might fulfill a desire Claudia and Frieda take up at the end of the novel, a desire to redeem Pecola herself and to strike back at "the universal love of white baby dolls and Shirley Temples," the dominant discourse of physical value in the novel, the impetus for the leveling of judgment against Pecola, the judgment exercised by others solely for the improvement of their own social positioning (148).

As a sign of their change of heart, of their awareness of the gravity of Pecola's situation, and of their desire for Pecola to be all right,[4] Claudia and Frieda take up a new routine. They trade, in effect, the everyday activity associated with selling marigold seeds for activity that shows them putting another's needs ahead of their own. In this way, Morrison communicates to her readers that Claudia and Frieda have learned from Pecola's story and lays a path for her readers to follow. Claudia and Frieda give away their desire for the bicycle by burying the money gained from the seed packets already sold and take up a desire for Pecola to be all right by planting the seeds that remain; one sister sings and one says "magic words" as the seeds are planted, and they agree that "when they come up, we'll know every-thing is all right" (149).

Of course the marigolds never do sprout or grow or bloom, and every-thing would not have been all right even if they had. And the girls, after blaming each other for burying them too deeply or for not executing the right magic, come to set responsibility for the death of Pecola's baby and Pecola's subsequent insanity at the feet "of the earth, the land, of [their] town," noting that "the land of the entire country was hostile to marigolds that year" (160). There are certain seeds, Claudia suggests, that the earth just won't bear, and there's nothing we can do for them. "We are wrong, of course," she then goes on to say, and "It's much, much, much too late" (160). Too late for Pecola and too late even to insure that the lives of Claudia and Frieda will also always be alright.

But it's not too late to think further about the way one desire is trad-ed for another in the novel, to develop, through a reading of *The Bluest Eye,* an economics of desire, a characterization of the exchanging of one desire for another and the relationship within such an economy of desire to everyday routine. And it's not too late to learn to read the painful ab-sence of marigolds as representative of some-thing other than loss, lack, or failure; in learning to do so, we also learn to make routine intellectual practices, like reading and revision, critically meaningful whenever we exercise them. To begin such an project; I wish to turn to the opening of an essay by Jacques Derrida, "The Time of the King," where Derrida draws out the systematicity inherent in relations of exchange, the struc-tures, mechanizations, and functionings that bound, limit, and mark such relations, and the place desire occupies within those relations. In other words, in "The Time of the King," Derrida articulates an economics of ex-change, a means of giving advantage to and taking advantage of in pursuit of fulfilling one's desire. Derrida's characterization of such an economy of relations provides, then, a way to comprehend the relationship Morrison constructs with her reader, a relationship similar to that drawn between Claudia and Frieda and Pecola in the novel, a relationship that, for the reader, leads to understanding.

Giving, Taking, and the Desire for Desire

In just the first few pages of "The Time of the King," Derrida makes clear that relationships of exchange are governed by systems of rules, expecta-tions, behaviors, and mechanizations. As Derrida reads his essay's own epigraph, a sentence from a letter written by Madame de Maintenon, a woman who became the morganatic wife of King Louis XIV,[5] he illus-trates an economy of exchange at work. Madame de Maintenon's sen-tence—"The King takes all my time; I give the rest to Saint-Cyr, to whom

I would like to give all"—raises the problematic of the gift, the impossible desire to give without entering into a cycle of exchange, turning gift to debt.

Madame de Maintenon's sentence expresses her (unfulfilled) desire to give all to charity and her seeming regret at not being able to do so—because the King takes what she wishes to give. Derrida begins reading this sentence by re-characterizing time, arguing that it is not some thing to be possessed and cannot, therefore, be given by Madame de Maintenon or taken by the King. Rather time marks "the things one does *in the meantime* or the things one has at one's disposal *during* this time" (3, Derrida's emphasis). Derrida writes, time "designates metonymically less time itself than the things with which one fills it" (3). In this way, time functions as an organizing structure, defined by the activity encircled within it. By defining performed activity, and not the passing of hours and minutes, as a marker of everyday life, Derrida articulates the theoretical underpinnings of a practice like Morrison's. The trope of "trooping about" in *The Bluest Eye*, for instance, works similarly, designating time as activity, as well.

To understand Madame de Maintenon's sentence, one must think time as activity, must see Madame de Maintenon wanting to give not time itself but the activity with which she fills time, the activity the King takes. Thus, Derrida shows that the exchanging of time among Madame de Maintenon, the King, and Saint Cyr is only possible via metonymy, via another form of exchange, that is, the exchanging of time for activity. In addition, Derrida illustrates that time is only visible through such a symbolic exchange, one that allows what is in or organized by time and not time itself to be seen. As a result, to give, Madame de Maintenon must immediately activate and enter into relationships—multiple relationships—of exchange; she cannot not do so. But by doing so she closes off the possibility for true giving, the kind of giving that is offered without expectations of return, the kind that may be received without feelings of debt, without worry of repayment.

Giving and taking, as presented in Derrida's essay, then, are always part of an economics of exchange and can never be seen as complete activities in themselves, for they fail to return what they seem to promise. Yet what remains withheld within those activities functions to prolong the relationships of those involved and further the cycle, a lesson also crafted by Morrison through the absent presence of marigolds in *The Bluest Eye*. For Claudia and Frieda to understand that they must strive to always place others' needs ahead of their own, that they must always care for individuals like Pecola and the injustices created by a racist social order, Morrison must make their seed-planting ritual fail. Further, by keeping the girls from understanding the reasons for its failure to protect Pecola, Morrison keeps them looking and working to support other girls in similar need. In this way, Claudia and Frieda, like Madame de Maintenon, can be said to wish to give all even when all is taken by another. Derrida illustrates the presence of this possibility in Madame de Maintenon's sentence; he notes that her sentence leaves "some left, a remainder that is nothing but that *there is* since she *gives it*. . . . The King takes all, she gives the rest" (3, Derrida's emphasis). To this seeming impossibility, Derrida quips, "She never gets enough of giving this rest that she does not have" (4). This impossibility, which Derrida illustrates as being the only possibility, makes us understand the seemingly irrational reason Claudia and Frieda believe that blooming marigold seeds might affect Pecola's circumstance. It explains why Claudia and Frieda believe in the necessity of their seed-planting ritual even if they have doubts about its efficacy.

Claudia's and Frieda's behavior comes to represent a way to act even in the face of sure failure. Claudia and Frieda cannot affect Pecola's material circumstances, yet they perform their ritual anyway and, in effect, make visible their desire for Pecola to be all right. Similarly, Madame de Maintenon cannot really give all her time, for it is taken by the King. Yet she expresses her desire to do so and, as Derrida makes clear, gives what cannot be given. I wish to underline this notion of giving what one doesn't have to give and argue that it is a practice also available to writers, readers, teachers, and students. It is a practice Derrida exercises, as a reader, when he reminds us that Madame de Maintenon is writing a letter and to "pay attention to the *literal* writing of her *letter*" (4, Derrida's emphasis). In its original French, Madame de Maintenon's sentence is ambiguous; her sentence says, Derrida points out, both "I would like to give it all, that is, all of it" and "I would like to give all, that is, everything" (4). This ambiguity is caused by the French word for all, which can be either tout or le tout—and which Madame de Maintenon intends is not clear. This uncertainty represents to Derrida the sounding of "the infinite sigh of unsatisfied desire" (4); summarizing her sentence, Derrida writes, "Madame de Maintenon says to her correspondent that everything leaves her something to be desired" (4), yet as long as one still has the desire to desire, one can take advantage and give.

Time, that which structures the relationship among the King, Madame de Maintenon, and Saint Cyr in Derrida's essay, is satiated with desire; desire, in fact, is abundant within all such relationships. Madame de Maintenon's desire to give all remains, Derrida notes, "in the conditional," in the "would like" of her sentence (4). Yet, even if all is taken, there is some left to give, a remainder that cannot be given or taken yet can be desired to be given or taken, something always withheld while wished to be given away. This Derrida characterizes as "the whole of her desire" (4). Madame de Maintenon wants what she cannot give that is, to give, and that is the whole of her desire. Desire, thus, can never be wholly fulfilled, so it is vented, channeled into activity, most often routine activity, activity that serves to put desire off, to pacify and recycle it.

This is a process that simultaneously gives and takes, a process both productive and costly, one that relieves one's wanting and causes one to want more, one that brings fulfillment and longing, gain and loss. It is a process, I want to suggest, like the educative process, an economy that induces intellectual development and the acquisition of knowledge but at a price; it is an economy based on the exchanging of one('s) self for (an)other('s). Profit is realized in the new self, achieved through violation and loss of the old. But I don't wish to characterize this process solely as a negative one; education gives and takes, is pleasurable and painful often at the same time. Morrison's storytelling, in *The Bluest Eye*, exemplifies the equivocation inherent in such a process. Claudia and Frieda perform, take part in the seed-planting ritual, and feel better while at the same time feel poignantly the loss of Pecola's companionship and the sting of their failed attempt to redeem her. Their seed-planting activity provides outlet for their desire for Pecola to be all right, yet doesn't fulfill it; through the seed-planting their desire is also deferred and extended, prolonged within relationships among such subjects as beauty standards, race, childhood teasing, and subjectivities like parents and school children.

In the rest of this essay, I intend to revisit occasions in Morrison's novel where desire is mobilized and acted upon within such relationships, occasions that show Morrison no longer just teaching fictional characters. Morrison aligns her reader with Claudia, the novel's "primary narrator,"[6] in order to tell a didactic story, ultimately to teach her readers how to read. In this way, Claudia's (Morrison's) storytelling functions as a mode of teaching in *The Bluest Eye*. The other side of the analogue is also suggested by the novel, that is, that teaching functions as a mode of storytelling. But analysis of the latter remains beyond the scope of this present essay.

Narrating, Revising, and the Desire to Teach

Carl D. Malmgren writes that the "bluest I" in Morrison's novel belongs to Claudia. As primary witness to Pecola's tragedy, Claudia is, according to Malmgren, "the 'I' that author-izes the novel" (256). To make this case, Malmgren refers to both biographical and textual evidence. He notes that Morrison would have been the same age as Claudia in the year the novel takes place, that she grew up in the Ohio town in which the novel is set, and that the novel is inspired by an actual experience of Morrison's while a school girl (254). More important to Malmgren, though, is the textual evidence that links Morrison's voice to Claudia's. He argues that Claudia is given the intellectual tools that characterize authors. He writes, "she has the talent and insight to make the kind of discriminations that characterize the text as a whole and that she has the stylistic resources to rise to the lyricism found in various places in the novel" (254); he notes that she is represented as imaginative, creative, and inventive. Further, the sections of the novel in which it is clear Claudia is narrating articulate the ideological project of the novel. Malmgren also notes that the novel begins and ends in Claudia's voice, and that early themes are repeated and extended with a "rhetorical and stylistic echo," suggesting the presence of one narrator (253). Yet even as told by one narrator, *The Bluest Eye* is a story made up of different kinds of narrations; it is framed, for instance, by the Dick and Jane primer, includes long flashback sections that trace the histories of Cholly and Pauline, tells Pecola's tragic story, and provides reflection on the events related in the novel As Linda Dittmar argues, the novel exercises "disrupted chronology, splintered plots, decentered accountability, and disparate modes of narration, "and it does so in order to foreground 'reconstitution'" (143). "All of these devices," she writes, "insist on the reader's self-conscious participation in the reconstitution of the text" (143). And, in these moments of reconstitution—or moments of what I would call revision—moments when both a character and a reader are engaged in seeing again, Morrison intercedes to teach her readers how to read.

The most explicit moment of revision in the novel occurs as Claudia remembers being sick. She is, when she characterizes herself while telling the story of Pecola's tragedy, a young girl, taught by the adults in her life to listen for directions, not for ways to participate in conversation, and, like the other young school children in the novel, she is weak, lacking the maturity and knowledge to intercede on Pecola's or her own behalf. Her illness seems a physical manifestation of that weakness. When she falls ill, her mother can only complain of the extra work this causes her, of how Claudia's illness alters her daily routine, for now it will also have to include stuffing the window to keep the draught out, covering Claudia's head and neck, rubbing salve on her chest, and cleaning up her vomit. Claudia notes that once she falls ill, "no one speaks to [her] or *asks how [she] feel[s]*" (13 my emphasis); rather, her family members become caught up in the routines prescribed by the fact that sickness is present. Even she is expected to perform: she is to sleep.

And, then, as soon as Claudia inscribes a world where her individuality is given over to the routines prescribed within her family, she begins revising, dreaming as she sleeps, infusing her storytelling with memory. As she continues to narrate, Claudia notes that falling ill wasn't simply like she describes it, that the pain her sickness brought with it was also "a productive and fructifying pain," for somewhere in the habits of dealing with illness, Claudia's mother not only re-covered her head and neck, she also rested her hand on Claudia's forehead (14). Claudia recognizes this, while she tells the story now, as a habit of love and affirms that when she thinks of autumn, of the time of oncoming illness, she thinks "of somebody with hands who does not want [her] to die" (14). Here, Claudia explicitly revises the seemingly impersonal habits of caring for the sick by reading her own memory for what appears absent: love. And she presents that to her reader, for it is there in her story, an absent presence.

The Bluest Eye is a critique of the hierarchal relationship that is presented as normative in the novel between feeling and doing. Feeling is consistently switched into patterned activity. The message related by the social order represented in *The Bluest Eye* is that one gains little by responding emotively to others, but Claudia's revision of that message is that the price of that exchange is too high to pay. Yet one comes to that message only by learning to read the "failure" of Claudia's and Frieda's seed-planting differently. The privileging of doing and the consequent cost of giving away one's feelings become clearer, though, when Claudia and Frieda opt out of this system.

When Claudia and Frieda plant the marigold seeds they exchange their feelings for Pecola for ritualized activity as they have been taught to do. But this is a revised exchange. They choose this ritual to take the place of a former one, their "trooping about." They bury the money received from the work of selling seeds, as if burying the profit gained from sacrificing feeling to doing, so that they might foreground instead their desire for Pecola to be all right. In other words, this seems a ritual designed to reverse the doing/feeling hierarchy. The other school children throughout the novel respond to Pecola by teasing and taunting her; they act to mark themselves as better than her, and they do so through the routine of school-yard teasing. This activity becomes the means of soothing their anxiety and nervousness about questions of identity and beauty, activity engaged by exchanging emotional for logical response, by subordinating feeling to doing. Claudia's and Frieda's seed-planting acts instead as an outlet for sorrow and as an expression of hope. Because Pecola fits a shorthand formula for prejudging unattractiveness, she is despised; because she disappears when one looks at cultural standards of value and worth, she is judged, logically, value- and worthless. As a result, she is taunted. She is acted upon rather than felt for. And every time children yell "Black e mo. Black e mo. Ya-daddsleepsnekked" (53) and grown ups recoil from her "jerking" head and flailing arms, this hierarchy is reconstituted. This everyday activity directed against Pecola is simply seized and repeated by the community in *The Bluest Eye* without reflection on the impetus for doing so. Hence, Pecola comes to wear her ugliness and worthlessness, for she fails to exist without it, and takes on the role of scapegoat, bearing the blame for all the mistakes and crimes of others who escape responsibility through her. But we come to understand this as Claudia does; Claudia says,

> all of us—all who knew her—felt so wholesome after we cleaned ourselves on her. We were so beautiful when we stood astride her ugliness. Her simplicity decorated us, her guilt sanctified us, her pain made us glow with health, her awkwardness made us think we had a sense of humor. Her inarticulateness made us believe we were eloquent. Her poverty kept us generous. Even her waking dreams we used—to silence our own nightmares (159).

Pecola then serves a purpose in the world of Morrison's novel, illustrating the destructive power of exchanging feelings of lack, of anxiety, for activities that superficially mark one as all right, as strong, free, and good.

To come to this conclusion, however, takes time; and this lesson is conveyed in Claudia's older, experienced voice. It is a product of revision. Feeling better was produced, during Claudia's girlhood, out of activity that put Pecola down; one felt good about oneself because one separated oneself through routine from Pecola. But the feelings were artificial, falsely produced by an exchange made in a context devoid of critical reflection. With their desire remobilized, Claudia and Frieda act through a routine that gives all they have to offer: feelings of sympathy and sorrow, a desire to desire.

And so, as Claudia reflects further on her girlhood, she makes additional revisions:

> we were not strong, only aggressive: we were not free, merely licensed; we were not compassionate, we were polite: not good, but well behaved. We courted death in order to call ourselves brave, and hid like thieves from life. We substituted good grammar for intellect; we switched habits to simulate maturity; we rearranged lies and called it truth (159).

Here, Claudia and her readers come to understand that self-acceptance, in the world of Morrison's novel, was premised on the destruction of others, taking place in habitual moments like childhood teasing (and institutions like polity and "good" grammar). But one can also see this same mechanism at work in one's own everyday habits, like crossing the street to avoid the homeless beggar or crazy woman, in daily routines like locking the car doors just as one crosses into the black neighborhood. As Morrison makes clear in *The Bluest Eye*, when an emotive response to Pecola and others like her, one that embraces her humanity, one that requires that one see her as beautiful in order to see oneself that way, is exchanged, switched, into "licensed" behavior, one chooses habits and routines that only simulate reality, that produce a dreamlike world premised on nightmare. It's a sacrifice many of us make too willingly.

And, while Morrison's novel shows the costs of such a sacrifice, she acknowledges the social pressure to make it. *The Bluest Eye* causes us to wonder why one is not licensed to feel one's own weaknesses, is not allowed to admit one's faults. Morrison challenges us to recognize that a condition of our being alive is to see others as close to death, to see our world as structured by competition and to notice the costs of that competition. Yet she also makes us feel for Pecola, acknowledge her life as one deserving to be lived rather than as one prejudicially marked as needing to be killed. And she ultimately asks us how we let this happen to children like Pecola again and again, every day.

And then, Morrison says, there is really no more to say—"except why" (9), why marigolds come to symbolize such a complex of relations between people, culture, and ideas, why social relations seem competitively formed and remain to display the outcomes of that competition, and why to create awareness of the destructive power of constructions like beauty, one resorts to a story about failure, loss, and lack. But, "since why is difficult to handle," Morrison notes, "one must take refuge in how" (9). And there, in that directive to take refuge in how" (9). And there, in that directive to take refuge in how, Morrison instructs us how to read, Morrison makes possible a kind of reading, a kind of reading that might see failure as productive, might allow for the presence of absences, and might make intellectual reflection a part of routine performance.

Morrison's novel, then offers itself as, what Michel de Certeau calls, a *"possibility,"* for it makes "explicit the relation of theory to the procedures from which it results and to those which are its objects" (78 Certeau's emphasis). Morrison inscribes a way of thinking through her storytelling that is both narratable and readable; she writes stories that are responseable. Morrison posits a way of knowing and thinking by way of her telling; through story, she suggests a counterlogic, an alternative economy, by "manipulat[ing], dispos[ing], and 'plac[ing]'" (Certeau 79). Moreover, she points to herself undertaking this in process, especially at the novel's beginning, where she alters the discourse of "normalized" childhood as represented by the Dick and Jane primer and provides an alternative frame in the italicized section about the marigold seeds. Morrison's novelistic discourse is, then, "characterized more by a way of *exercising itself* than by the thing it indicates," as Certeau notes; consequently, it should be read for the effects it produces (79 Certeau's emphasis). As a result, the theory Morrison practices takes "the form of a way of narrating" (Certeau 80); that is, *The Bluest Eye* works to dissolve conventional gaps between theory and practice, feeling and doing, and mindless routine and reflective action.

Telling, Teaching, and the Desire to Conclude

Before beginning work on my doctorate, I taught high school English in the Detroit Public Schools. As a student teacher, I had an unforgettable class of ninth graders; we had a semester of remarkable occasions for frustration, joy, creativity, struggle. One particularly restless and imaginative young man sat in the row of desks right next to the second floor windows and would often pester the young woman who sat right in front of him. One warm fall afternoon, he had taken her book—a small paperback novel—and was teasing her by telling her he was going to toss the book out the open window. Initially unaware, I learned of his teasing when he came up to me to ask if he could go down and get the book he had just tossed out the window. I remember my own lack of comprehension; I just couldn't seem to understand why he would do such a thing and was only articulate enough to agree with him that he needed to get the book to return to the student who would need it. So he did.

When he returned just a minute later, he did so with more than one book; he brought back the novel he had tossed out the window, a novel from another English class, and an English textbook. Why did so many other students seemingly experience the same temptation from the open window?

To ask the question I have just asked of my story is to read it, I think, exemplifying an application of the theory Morrison practices and is, thus, a teacherly move that reconstitutes the relationship between theory and practice, feeling and doing, and mindless routine and reflective action. Responding in this way treats my student's book tossing as stemming from something other than a lack of respect for or understanding of classroom decorum; rather it acknowledges the presence of an extended invitation from an open window (an invitation accepted by more than this one student) and, perhaps, a curriculum disconnected from his experience or a lesson that ignores his intelligence or creativity. To ask why any student might toss a book out an open window is to begin to read differently, to exercise a desire to understand the position that students present to us; it is not to act to place them. It is to foreground an emotive response. In responding this way, we take advantage of what our students give, returning to them a gift that they cannot help but want to exchange.

Notes

1. I purposely choose the word "work," believing that this kind of routine, performed habitually in response primarily to itself and not to a stimulus source, makes up a large part of what we do everyday while we are at work." In other words, our working lives require us to participate in routine, often burdensome, performance; this is a normal, expected part of our lives. But, as I will argue later, this work doesn't have to be solely defined by its burdensomeness. As Morrison will make clear through Claudia and Frieda, there are ways to alter behavior so that it is no longer a mindless repetition of what has come before.

2. Michael Awkward argues that *The Bluest Eye* privileges "feelings and experience over ownership of objects," that the "false security" of the primer is rejected in favor of experience (179). Awkward's words suggest that Morrison is privileging the idea of learning by doing, as well. Claudia and Frieda feel for Pecola, but their feelings have no power until they perform the seed-planting ritual; and it is through this ritual that they learn hard lessons about beauty standards, popularity, and social stratification. The primer that frames Morrison's novel suggests, too, that when one learns through experience in formal situations like school, one better have the "right" experience to bring to the table.

3. Carl D. Malmgren, in "Texts, Primers, and Voices in Toni Morrison's *The Bluest Eye*," argues that the ideological project of the novel is to critique "cultural stereotypes imposed by the dominant white culture" (254).

4. I use this phrase, the desire for Pecola to be all right, because it is Morrison's. She does not define more specifically what Claudia and Frieda mean when they wish for Pecola to be all right, and I resist doing so, as well.

5. Morganatic, according to Webster's, is a term "designating or pertaining to a marriage in which a person of high rank, as a member of the nobility, marries someone of a lower station with the stipulation that neither the low ranking spouse nor their children will have any claim to the titles or entailed property of the high-ranking partner."

6. I am persuaded by Carl D. Malmgren that *The Bluest Eye* may very well be "entirely [Claudia's] composition" (256). The term, "primary narrator," is quoted from the beginning of Malmgren's "Texts, Primers, and Voices in Toni Morrison's *The Bluest Eye*" where he discusses the questions regarding "the multiple narrations (and multiple narrators) in the novel" (253). Ultimately, it is Malmgren's purpose to suggest that *The Bluest Eye* is Claudia's "achievement" (256).

Works Cited

Awkward, Michael. "'The Evil of Fulfillment': Scapegoating and Narration in *The Bluest Eye*." *Toni Morrison: Critical Perspectives Past and Present*. Henry Louis Gates Jr. and K. A. Appiah, eds. New York: Amistad, 1993: pp. 175–209.

Certeau, Michel. *The Practice of Everyday Life*. trans. Steven Rendall. Berkeley: University of California Press, 1984.

Derrida, Jacques. "The Time of the King," *Given Time: I. Conterfeit Money*. trans. Peggy Kamuf. Chicago: University of Chicago Press, 1992: pp. 1–33.

Dittmar, Linda. "'Will the Circle Be Unbroken?': The Politics of Form in *The Bluest Eye*." *Novel: A Forum on Fiction*. 23:2; (Winter 1990): pp. 137–155.

Malmgren, Carl D. "Texts, Primers, and Voices in Toni Morrison's *The Bluest Eye*." *Critique.* 41:3; (Spring 2000): pp. 251–262.

Morrison, Toni. *The Bluest Eye*. New York: Washington Square Press, 1970.

DEBRA T. WERRLEIN

Not So Fast, Dick and Jane: Reimagining Childhood and Nation in The Bluest Eye

In *The Bluest Eye*, Toni Morrison challenges America's complacent belief in its benevolent self-image through representations of children who experience race, class, and gender oppressions. She is not the first African American author to use images of childhood to undermine cherished conceptions of national identity. In his 1845 slave narrative, Frederick Douglass condemns American democracy and Christianity through detailed accounts of his own childhood as a slave. Similarly, Pauline Hopkins confronts the ideal of an all-white American nation by placing the image of a black baby next to an American flag on the cover of her October 1900 issue of *The Colored American Magazine*. Morrison, however, centralizes childhood more deeply than her predecessors. Anticipating the currently emerging field in childhood studies, Morrison puts the concept of childhood itself under scrutiny. In *The Bluest Eye*, a child provides the primary voice through which the reader hears, the primary lens through which the reader sees, and the object of the reader's gaze.

My interest in the novel's children centers on Morrison's treatment of their supposed innocence. In her critical work, *Playing in the Dark. Whiteness and the Literary Imagination*, Morrison comments on "thematics of innocence" that typically define Americanness in literature. She asks, "What are Americans always so insistently innocent of?" (44-45). I contend that, in

MELUS, 30:(4); 2005 Winter: pp. 53–72. © 2005 *MELUS: The Journal of the Society for the Study of the Multi-Ethnic Literature of the United States.*

The Bluest Eye, Morrison first explored this question, and the implications of its answer, long before she explicitly asked it. This article first emphasizes the connection between thematics of *childhood* innocence in American culture and an ideology of *national* innocence. Next, I argue that Morrison's allusions to the Dick and Jane Basic Readers highlight images of childhood that promote superficial and ahistorical conceptions of the United States. I show how Morrison contrasts these images with child-characters painted as intimate extensions of long familial, socio-economic, and national histories that contradict the innocent ideal. From public education I turn to popular culture. Through Morrison's references to Shirley Temple, I examine images of children as both producers and consumers of commodities that are themselves ironically charged with the ideology of childhood innocence. Finally, I analyze Morrison's allusion to John M. Stahl's film, *Imitation of Life* (1934), to better understand the symbolic significance of both Pecola's body and Claudia's consciousness. Throughout these analyses, I argue that Morrison shows us the counterhegemonic potential of reimagining childhood in the context of history. She portrays children as victims, activists, recorders, and even oppressors—all as a way of demythologizing the "innocent" past.

Almost a century after Pauline Hopkins's child-image challenged the southern opposition to Reconstruction, Morrison confronts another tense political climate, publishing her first novel during the transition between a waning Civil Rights Movement and the backlash that emerged against it. Morrison faced the repercussions of civil rights legislation in their infancy, but the nation's anxiety about questions of race, class, and gender equity continued to evolve, creating the neo-conservative paranoia regarding "reverse discrimination" and immigration that continues today. By the 1990s, the growth of such conservatism ushers in what Henry Giroux calls "organized forgetting," a phenomenon where Americans look nostalgically back to a "mythic" pre-Civil Rights Era (*Channel* 77). Claiming that children often serve as "signposts" for America's self-image, Giroux finds evidence of such nostalgia in 1970s Hollywood. He explains that 1970s films such as *The Last Picture Show* and *American Graffiti* "resurrected white, suburban, middle-class youth in the nostalgic image of Andy Hardy and Frankie Avalon" (*Channel* 35, 42). In this mythically innocent past, domestic unrest evaporates while post-war prosperity thrives, despite such tragic realities as the lynching of fourteen-year-old Emmett Till in 1955.

Popular representations of American youth have grown increasingly dark since the days of Frankie Avalon, however. According to Giroux, this phenomenon reflects an ongoing crisis in American society and democracy, yet he explains that Hollywood's images of troubled youth also blame the victim, silencing child-figures by ignoring the socio-economic contexts that produce suffering (*Channel* 35, 42–44, 86). While acknowledging the loss of childhood innocence, such representations preserve its ideal by suggesting that children themselves have ruined childhood. In contrast, Morrison lets her child-characters speak while critically invoking their socio-economic contexts. Instead of blaming the children for their own suffering, she blames their families, their community, and, ultimately, their nation.

Morrison situates her narrator, Claudia, and her protagonist, Pecola, on the cusp of the "mythical" post-war period. The novel begins in 1940, a time when Michael Rogin contends that Americans had begun to look beyond the domestic worries of the Depression to define America's role in a growing international conflict. According to Rogin, domestic concerns about ethnicity and class dominated American politics from 1870 to the New Deal, but World War II "provided the occasion for the emergence of the national-security apparatus." Rogin locates the residue of emerging national fears in film, explaining that Hollywood immediately tuned in to the anxieties that came with war. As early as 1940, therefore, films such as *Murder in the Air* had traded in their mobsters for the spies and fake identities that encompass the fresher material of international intrigue (237, 246, 2).

Conversely, in a war-time setting that barely acknowledges the looming threat of military conflict, *The Bluest Eye* clearly subordinates national and international matters to local interests. In the small towns of Morrison's midwestern United States, concerns about how to keep children warm, fed, and healthy supersede questions about the nation's role in an escalating conflict abroad. Furthermore, while 1940 marks the eve of both war and economic recovery in American history books, it also marks the year Richard Wright's *Native Son* kicked off an angry protest movement against racism. Morrison captures this underrepresented aspect of American history. Thus, when 1970s America had already begun to assemble nostalgic myths about suburban life during and after World War II, Morrison focuses on family, education, and popular culture to expose childhood innocence as a pervasive ideology that simultaneously perpetuates and mystifies the harsher realities of white nationalist hegemony. In a wrenching narrative of childhood without innocence, she evokes the forgotten domestic tensions that simmered in the 1940s and boiled over in the 1950s.

The Bluest Eye explores the contrast between oppressed local culture and innocent national ideal through the friction that erupts between Pecola's life and 1940s models of childhood. Morrison first locates such models in pedagogy by subversively appropriating William Elson and William Gray's nationally recognized Dick and Jane stories. Many of Morrison's critics have commented on her reference to the Elson-Gray primers. Mark Ledbetter explains their importance in literary terms, arguing that they establish a victimless "masterplot" for the novel (28). Nancy Backes points out that the primers offer an ideal that does not exist for anyone (even white middle-class children) (47), while Andrea O'Reilly argues that the books instruct pupils in the ideology of the family (87). According to Gurleen Grewal, primers prime, or make ready, and Morrison shows how they prime black subjects (125). The thread that connects these observations: they all point to ways that the primers contribute to a national ideology of innocence. According to some educators, schools teach more than math, science, and literacy. They reproduce existing class structures, reinforce dominant ideologies, and bolster the political power of the state in capitalism (Aronowitz and Giroux 65). Similarly, Dick and Jane primers not only posit the literary "masterplot" in *The Bluest Eye;* as textbooks in America's public schools, Morrison suggests they posit a *national* masterplot that defines Americanness within the parameters of innocent white middle-class childhood.

Dick and Jane's popularity grew immensely in the 1940s, but the characters originate in the 1930s. In books such as the pre-primer, *Dick and Jane* (1930), the authors characterize safe American childhoods that thrive in families that defy depression-era hardships with economic and social stability. After World War II, Cold War politicians assigned such families both a practical and a symbolic role in combating the threat of communist takeover in the United States. Elaine Tyler May argues that creating and caring for healthy families became the patriotic responsibility of women who were expected to leave their wartime jobs to raise children and bolster the world's capitalist population. In the uncertainty of the nuclear age, she adds, women were expected to make domestic spaces into safe havens, figurative (and sometimes literal) bomb shelters for frightened Americans. The era's popular culture reflects such expectations. As early as 1941, according to May, Hollywood films such as *Penny Serenade* emphasized motherhood, associating beauty with maternity and positioning children as "moralizing" and "harmonizing" agents in families (125). Similarly, Rogin argues that Hollywood films of the 1940s, '50s and '60s associated Communism with public and private instability, portraying seductive women as Communist spies and family patriarchs as loyal patriots. He argues that in films such as *I Was a Communist* (1951), *My Son John* (1952), and *The Manchurian Candidate* (1962), the loving family is equated with the nation (247–251). Consequently, as the cornerstone of postwar prosperity and security, nuclear families like Dick and Jane's signaled the triumph of American democracy and capitalism (May xviii, 121).

The Elson-Gray curriculum surrounding Dick and Jane reflects these attitudes, placing responsibility for the nation's future prosperity and security squarely on the shoulders of middle-class children. From the outset in 1930, the *Basic Readers* invite young students to "come with me, your book-comrade, I can carry you into the homes of some brave and true American boys and girls. They will tell you how you, too, may become a helpful American citizen" (9). In the stories of units such as "Little American Citizens," young white children serve their country through self-sufficiency, self-sacrifice, and bravery. Similarly, the unit "Busy Workers and their Work" underscores the inherent morality and practical necessity of hard work while connecting it to the technological and territorial expansion of the deserving nation. Proponents of Cold War politics burdened only white children and their families with such patriotic sentiments, however. Since the government housing subsidies that prompted whites to free crowded cities excluded African Americans, few black families occupied the suburbs that demonstrated America's successes to the world (May xx). Thus, by associating white suburban families with prosperity, morality, and patriotism, Americans painted black urban working-class families as un-American. Eventually, the Moynihan Report of 1965 outwardly dissociated black families, and especially black women, from the national ideal by characterizing black family life and its matriarchal aspects as "a tangle of pathology" -that deviated sharply from the American standard (qtd. in Stacey 5).

Likewise, despite their emphasis on historical figures and events, the primers in general never allude to events such as conquest, slavery, immigration, or exclusion. In fact, beyond the occasional appearance of a "savage" Indian, they never feature nonwhite Americans. The Dick and Jane books in particular exist almost entirely outside of history—as if no thing and no time exists beyond the suburban present. They therefore treat American childhood as an abstraction that excludes all but white middle-class children. Given the emphasis on citizenship and Americanness, Dick and Jane inhabit what Lauren Berlant would call the national bodies of "abstract citizenship." Through the abstraction of citizenship, she argues, Americans assume all citizens have access to the Rights of Man, regardless of race, class, and gender differences. In reality, only white male citizens possess these Rights; thus, she explains, the white male body *is* the abstract body (113). Since Jane never complains about her forced domesticity or her subordination to Dick, she lets the privileges of Dick's innocent world stand for the experience of *all* American childhoods. Reinforcing the abstraction, primers before 1965 deport color, gender, and poverty to "other lands," implicitly defining such variations as culturally un-American or politically irrelevant. Significantly, Morrison's allusion to actual pedagogical texts artistically engages the real, concretely marking the centrality of such disavowal in the lives of America's children while also asking us to consider the ways in which images of "innocent" children are themselves hardly innocuous.

Some public schools still used the Elson-Gray readers in 1970, despite growing concerns over their treatment of race and gender. While Morrison's publication of *The Bluest Eye* responded to the controversy three decades ago, her appropriation remains urgent today. The primers, long out of use, have acquired new appeal in a nostalgia-driven collectors' market that demonstrates how many Americans yearn for the fantasy of a mythically homogenous pre-Civil Rights era. In *Growing Up with Dick and Jane: Learning and Living the American Dream* (1996), the authors capitalize on collector desires. Their book jacket advertises, "They're back!" while entreating readers to "step back into the innocent watercolor world of Dick and Jane." Collector websites also feature nostalgia as their most salient selling point. On the Scott Foresman and Co. website, the seller remarks: "To many Americans, the simple phrase, *"See Spot Run"* brings a warm and nostalgic smile. . . . Check out the books and reflect on your childhood and feel warm and cozy with the memories. Ahhh, when life was simple . . . " (sic). The implications of childhood's "simpl[icity]" come clear when Dave Schultz, another collector, makes unapologetic references to the changes of the Civil Rights Movement. He registers irritation over the way many Americans now think about race, class, sexuality, gender, and family. He says:

> It was an innocent time. . . . Cars had style, and toys such as wagons, trikes, and pedal cars were made out of metal. Father worked and Mother (with a freshly pressed dress on and dinner on the table) waited at the door for him to come home.

> There were no microwaves. . . bus drivers were nice, schoolteachers cared, and the corner store had penny candy. . . . It was a different era where second graders could read Dick's use of the word queer and third graders could read a story called "Tar Baby."

The Bluest Eye unravels profiteering reveries at every turn. While offering a sharply different version of 1940s family and childhood, Morrison suggests that familial "pathologies" do not simply spring from individual shortcomings. Just as the Dick and Jane stories equate white privilege with a historyless version of Americanness, the poverty and suffering of Morrison's Breedlove family symbolizes America's brutal history of racial persecution in the United States. The Breedloves emerge from a history of what Grewal calls a "race-based class structure of American society that generates its own pathologies" (118).

Through an innovative literary form that both fragments and compresses her primer-imitation, Morrison emphasizes the historical gloss by which Elson and Gray sanitize American family life. Pin-chia Feng argues that, in the fragments, the narrator acts out Claudia's rage, dismembering the white narrative as Claudia dismembers her white baby dolls (53). Similar to Claudia's pile of plastic body parts, Morrison creates a jumble of words that together symbolize the incoherence of America's mythic homogeneity. While compressing words and sentences, however, she also dissects the stories, separating their standardized elements into isolated and unintelligible phrases such as "SEEFATHERHEISBIGANDSTRONG" and "SEEMOTHERISVERYNICE" (105, 88). While highlighting the meaninglessness of the Dick and Jane formula, Morrison uses the string of letters as chapter headings that in part determine the shape of her narrative. In the contrast between such unnaturally elongated phrases and the depth and density of the lengthy paragraphs that follow on the page, Morrison visually illustrates the shallow ahistoricism of the white text. In addition, she complements form with content, filling the "SEEFATHER" and "SEEMOTHER" chapters with complex histories that articulate Cholly's sense of powerlessness and Pauline's sense of worthlessness. By including narratives that would not otherwise fit into the simplified space of a Dick and Jane primer, Morrison shows how national narratives of the white middle-class family obscure the way unjust histories can shape a family's struggling present.

In "SEEFATHER," Cholly endures a life marked by powerlessness from his birth. After suffering familial abandonment and sexual humiliation, Cholly says he feels "small, black, helpless" (119). Vanessa Dickerson argues that Cholly is a "naked father," an emasculated figure who is incapable of accumulating wealth or playing the patriarch (111, 116–117). Morrison emphasizes such powerlessness when Cholly accepts a new couch that arrives broken in half, but she seals his fate in a scathing critique of American meritocracy when he literally dies "in the workhouse," forever trapped in a cycle of working poverty (159). Similarly, the "SEEMOTHER" section articulates Pauline's feelings of worthlessness. The ninth of eleven children, Pauline grows up in a "cocoon" where she develops a "general feeling of separateness and unworthiness" (88). When she loses her tooth while emulating Jean Harlowe at the movie theater, Pauline gives in to the intraracial prejudice of Lorraine, Ohio's Northern black women and "settle[s] down to just being ugly" (98). At a time when Americans associate fatherhood with upward mobility and motherhood with beauty, Cholly and Pauline fall far short of America's patriotic ideal for parents.

Through Cholly and Pauline, Morrison suggests that parents who emerge from histories of oppression might reproduce that degradation within the family unit. Instead of providing for and protecting his family, Cholly bums down the insular domestic space that should have symbolized not only his family's, but the nation's affluence and security. Similarly, Pauline feels no patriotic obligation to nurture the offspring that, to her, reflect her own ugliness. Instead, having learned that a white family's servant wields far more power than a black family's mother, she spends all of her time working as a domestic for the Fishers, where "Power, praise, and luxury were hers" (101).

Unlike Dick and Jane, whose innocent lives spring spontaneously into the present, Morrison connects the lives of children to the joy, suffering, and

coping of their parents. She offers a gendered response to Pauline's abandonment when she pairs Pecola with her brother Sammy. In the post-slavery
tradition of his wandering father and grandfather, Sammy runs away at least
twenty-seven times by the age of fourteen. Conversely, "Restricted by youth
and sex," Pecola stays home and "experiment[s] with methods of endurance"
(38). Furthermore, Sammy's escape leaves her alone to emulate the Dick and
Jane standard that according to Deborah Cadman, creates the Breedloves'
feelings of worthlessness (76). When Cholly recognizes his own failures in
Pecola's unhappiness, he feels an "accusation" that fills him with guilt. He elicits the Dick-and-Jane ideal when he looks at Pecola as "a child, unburdened,"
and wonders, "why wasn't she happy?" (127).

Instead of serving as a "moralizing" force, Pecola's abject presence pro-
vokes Cholly to rape her in what Lothar Bredella argues is "the pain of a love
which can only be expressed destructively" (372). Through Cholly's inability
to express love constructively, Morrison paints a picture of black fatherhood
so incapacitated that it sacrifices its children to save itself. Likewise, when
the sight of Pecola's abused body on the kitchen floor incites Pauline to beat
instead of comfort her daughter, Morrison portrays a similarly affected motherhood, suggesting that histories of suffering not only debilitate parents, but
turn them from nurturers into oppressors. By juxtaposing the Breedloves with
Dick and Jane, Morrison attributes their "pathologies" in part to the pathology of a nation that defines its own virtue through an ideology of childhood
innocence that ironically allows for the expendability of children like Pecola.

Morrison's distortion of her primer look-a-like accentuates her ideological critique of Dick and Jane, but she also infuses the muddle with a more
literal meaning. Elson and Gray produced the Basic Readers to promote literacy, not specifically to propagate destructive ideologies. Through the ideological content, however, Elson and Gray point to *who* they expected to educate—who they envisioned as the nation's future citizens. While Morrison's
ideological critique suggests that the primers alienate students who do not fit
the white middle-class standard, her garbled imitation makes the very tools
designed to teach literacy into a symbol of forced illiteracy—as if the alienated reader could never decipher them.

While discounting the books' racism, Kismaric and Heiferman celebrate
the Dick and Jane stories for teaching eighty-five million children to read. In
contrast, Morrison suggests that, from their inception, Elson-Gray primers
participated in a national *il*literacy campaign that systematically disenfranchised young black Americans, especially young black girls. Significantly, Elson and Gray published Dick and Jane amid intense national resistance to the
idea that the nation was obligated to educate black youths. Institutionalized
efforts to sabotage black literacy began during Reconstruction and extended
through the Jim Crow era, disenfranchising black parents and their children

throughout most of the twentieth century (Anderson 33-35). Since illiterate parents must rely on schools to educate their offspring, Morrison's critique suggests yet another way that histories of discrimination might interfere with a family's ability to protect or empower its children.

Morrison joins a tradition of similarly concerned African American writers that ranges from ex-slaves such as Frederick Douglass and Harriet Jacobs to twentieth-century intellectuals such as Malcolm X, bell hooks, Patricia Hill Collins, and Angela Davis. Like many of her contemporaries, Morrison looks beyond the reading curriculum; she presents teachers who explicitly thwart the education of their black students. Aronowitz explains that, in elementary schools, teachers serve as "surrogate parents," figures who regularly remind students of how the school system perceives them. He adds that teachers' evaluations of students often reflect the expectations of the students' economic class rather than the quality of their intellect (81, 76–79). Although he omits racial factors from his discussion, race is an implicit consideration in the 1940s when Jim Crow laws confined many black Americans to the unskilled labor pool that Aronowitz studies. Morrison highlights the racial aspect of his argument with representations of teachers who reinforce existing hierarchies by consistently favoring lighter students. In Lorraine, Ohio, schoolteachers favor Maureen Peal, "a high-yellow dream child" who "enchanted the entire school." Stewing over how teachers "smiled encouragingly" when they called on Maureen, Claudia complains that such favoritism makes her and Frieda feel "lesser" (52-53). Similarly, Pecola notes that her teachers "tried to never glance at her, and called on her only when everyone was required to respond" (40).

While Claudia wonders what made Maureen different, what was the "*Thing* that made *her* beautiful and not us?" she and Frieda try to resist their feelings of inadequacy by dubbing Maureen "six-finger-dog-tooth-meringue-pie" (61, 53). Significantly, Morrison attributes Maureen's power not just to lightness, but to its beauty. Likewise, Kismaric and Heiferman point to this power when they claim that, despite settling for "second banana in a famous brother-sister act," readers can find "a lot to envy about Jane." They admire her because "Her perky dresses never wrinkle or get dirty. . . . Her blond, wavy hair is not too curly . . . not too frizzy," and she is "not too fat or too thin" (23). The teachers in *The Bluest Eye* exhibit similar values, leaving Claudia to desperately wonder, "What was the secret? What did we lack? Why was it important?" (61). Through Claudia's anxiety, Morrison points to the particular predicament of black *girls* in a white nation. For power they need beauty, and for beauty they need whiteness. Without the familial support that strengthens Claudia and Frieda, and unlike her brother who transforms "ugliness" into "a weapon to cause others pain," Pecola succumbs to the "*Thing*" (35). She accepts that it "made her ignored or despised at school, by teachers and classmates alike" (39). At school, therefore, Pecola learns her place outside an abstracted standard of citizenship.

In *The Bluest Eye,* multiple narratives of childhood encompass a broad spectrum of school systems and families that cooperatively perpetuate racial hierarchies. In addition to Pecola's family and school, Morrison offers Geraldine, an upper-class, light-skinned girl whose wealthy family and private education teach her to value lightness over darkness. Furthermore, in Soaphead Church, a "cinnamon-eyed West Indian" who learned young that his family's white supremacy earned them consistent recommendations for study abroad, Morrison evokes a colonial geography that posits global implications for racist education systems. In *The Bluest Eye,* such families and schools produce ideologies of innocence, not innocent children. Surrounded by them, Pecola learns the paradoxical necessity of erasing herself if she hopes to mature into a politically visible subject.

Morrison buttresses the ideological work of compulsory school with images of popular culture. Giroux emphasizes the explosion of kid-specific media and advertising that erupted in the 1990s, asking, "what non-commodified public sphere exists to safeguard children?" (*Mouse* 20). *The Bluest Eye* suggests, however, that the media already bombarded black communities and their children with commercial messages in the 1940s. Susan Willis agrees, arguing that such messages equate American culture with white culture in the novel (173). Pauline only encounters the image of Greta Garbo when she discovers the cinema as an adult. When Henry moves into the McTeer house, however, he flatters young Claudia and Frieda with an already familiar reference to "Garbo and Rogers." In addition, Maureen admits that she learned from her mother to emulate the almost white Peola over her "black and ugly" mother, Delilah, in Stahl's film, *Imitation of Life* (57).

Like Maureen, Pecola looks to Hollywood for standards of female beauty and, thus, power. Having never seen *Imitation of Life,* she idolizes Shirley Temple, a depression-era icon whose childhood frivolity conveyed hope to the struggling nation. Despite the common theme of orphanhood in Temple's films, titles such as *Curly Top* (1935) and *Little Miss Broadway* (1938) preserve childhood innocence by reducing adversity to a plot device. Presaging the moralizing and harmonizing role that children supposedly played for their families during the Cold War, Temple's characters, Elizabeth and Betsy respectively, pull themselves up by their bootstraps. They both charm wayward (and wealthy) bachelors into marrying financially bereft women so that the happy couple can adopt their orphaned matchmaker. These child-characters understand that their power resides in the childish sex appeal of blonde hair and blue eyes. In *Curly Top* especially, Elizabeth flirts with her eventual benefactor, Mr. Morgan, while on their "first date." Through the childish naivete of Temple's characters, however, the films easily attribute powers of seduction to willful determination, not white beauty. In the song "Be Optimistic" from *Little Miss Broadway,* Temple advises her fellow orphans that if they "just smile," someone will love them.

Like Dick and Jane, Temple's characters exist in a state of innocence, only brushing with larger socio-economic and historical contexts. They operate, therefore, like Pecola's racist schoolteachers, implicitly blaming darker victims who must endure rather than transcend their own suffering. Morrison highlights the power of such blame when Pecola begins to menstruate shortly after drinking three quarts of milk from a Shirley Temple cup. While nursing herself to maturity on Temple's standard of female beauty, Pecola cultivates a self-loathing that prompts her to ask Claudia and Frieda, "how do you get somebody to love you?" (29). Since edicts like Temple's "just smile" occlude the oppressive histories that might otherwise explain Pecola's loveless family, Temple offers Pecola no one to blame but herself.

As a national icon, Temple illustrates the connection between the ideology of childhood innocence and the ideology of national innocence. Kimberly B. Hébert argues that images such as Temple's organize Western culture around whiteness, creating "destructive images of African-descended and other black peoples who share the same space of neighborhood and nation" (193). By comparing Temple's coquettish performances to Harriet Beecher Stowe's Topsy from *Uncle Tom's Cabin,* Hébert argues that Temple's style originates not in whiteness, but in the white appropriations of blackness seen in minstrelsy. If, as Hébert argues, Temple offers a "white-faced performance of blackness" (190, 193), then her national acceptance suggests that American whiteness is itself a performance of blackness. Furthermore, her popularity also illustrates how the guise of childhood innocence so easily mystifies the irony. Despite her age, Claudia lacks the naiveté that supposedly characterizes childhood. Instead, she views Temple's performance as a trespass into black culture. She says, "I hated Shirley. Not because she was cute, but because she danced with Bojangles, who was *my* friend, *my* uncle, *my* daddy, and who ought to have been soft-shoeing it and chuckling with me" (19). In contrast, a captivated Pecola embraces the example of how her own blackness should look in the abstract.

Pecola outwardly emulates Temple in the novel, but Morrison directly connects Pecola to Stahl's Peola when she signifies on the name. By inserting the letter "c" into "Pecola," Morrison creates a name that is the same, yet different from Peola's. She highlights the distinction when Maureen mistakenly asks, "Pecola? Wasn't that the name of the girl in *Imitation of Life?*" (57). With the allusion, Morrison suggests that each narrative complements the other. Interestingly, Berlant bases her theory of abstract citizenship on the same story, using it to discuss the difference between having a visible body and being a visible subject in a capitalist public sphere. Berlant explains that Peola relinquishes her black body and passes for white because she understands that to "choose to be visible in a culture of abstraction . . . would be to choose a form of slavery" (127). Faced with political and economic dispossession, Peola rejects her black mother, Delilah, so she can adopt the invisible, but juridically defined, politically and economically empowered white subject position that she associates with the abstracted qualities of white beauty.

Pecola shares Peola's desires, but she occupies a different body, a variation Morrison captures through their similar, but different names. When Claudia compares Maureen's long beautiful braids to lynch ropes, Morrison offers a chilling metaphor that portends the stakes raised by the corporeal differences between Peola and Pecola. Unlike the light Peola, Pecola inhabits a dark, unabstracted body. Berlant calls the body's visible qualities, the parts that resist abstraction, "surplus corporeality" (112-14). Burdened with such "surplus," society can "see" and thus, reject Pecola. Morrison articulates Pecola's struggle between visible body and visible subject when the immigrant grocer, Mr. Yacobowski, registers a "total absence of human recognition" while looking at her. The scene also emphasizes the connection between American consumerism and subjectivity by showing how Pecola's corporeality, like her father's, interferes with her role as a consumer. Finding nothing "desirable or necessary" about trying to "*see*" Pecola, Yacobowski intimidates her into silence, asking, "Christ. Kantcha talk?" (emphasis in original 42). As Yacobowski proves his own whiteness through exclusion, Morrison suggests that Americans stir the nation's melting pot over flames fed by silenced black bodies.

Pecola rejects her place as a non-consumer, praying every night to rid herself of her surplus corporeality. When she lies in the darkness of her parents' store-front home and whispers, "Please God. . . . Please make me disappear," she tries to force her body into the Dick and Jane abstraction. Although "Little parts of her body faded away," she ultimately fails because her eyes remain. Pecola says, "They were everything. Everything was there, in them" (39). More than the physical evidence of her surpluses, Pecola's eyes represent her consciousness, her ability to see the "ugliness" she associates with blackness. Without the ability to "see"—or without the "c"—Pecola believes she can be Peola; she hopes to enact her own blue-eyed, white-faced version of blackness. Paradoxically, for successful abstraction, Pecola must endure self-erasure *and* blindness, a self-lynching that Furman calls, the "awful safety of oblivion" (19)—what I call childhood innocence.

Contrary to Pecola's self-annihilating fantasies, Peola's dark mother, Delilah, outwardly accepts her lot as an invisible subject in a visible body as she labors for Bea's pancake business. Berlant reads Delilah as an allusion to Aunt Jemima. While Jemima's black-faced trademark represents a site of collective American identity rooted in historical amnesia, however, Berlant argues that Delilah's character is more complex (122–125). Revealing a suppressed subjectivity in brief asides to the film's audience, she tells her employer, Bea, "Yesm. We all starts out [intelligent]. We don't gets dumb till later on." Berlant asks, "What is 'dumbness' here, if not Delilah's name for the mental blockages to rage and pain—what I earlier called 'the-will-to-not-know'—that distinguishes the colonized subject?" (126). While Berlant refers to Peola's willful denial, Delilah's use of "dumb" also alludes to the silence of muted black bodies like Aunt Jemima's. In contrast to these "dumb" bodies, Stahl lets Delilah's body speak in life and in death. Berlant argues that, in her funeral scene, Delilah emerges as a site of collective identity in a black public sphere that demythologizes the homogenous nation. Instead of representing amnesia (like Jemima), Delilah's corpse represents "pain, memory, history, and ritual" (124–125).

Through the intertexuality between *The Bluest Eye* and *Imitation of Life*, Morrison illuminates Pecola's relationship to Shirley Temple. In *Imitation of Life*, Bea puts a white face on Delilah's labor and body, exploiting them for her own benefit. Similarly, in *The Bluest Eye*, Shirley Temple and her creators profit by putting her white face on the black music and culture embodied by Bojangles. Delilah advises Peola to "submit," and suppress her rage over such injustices, but Pecola refuses. Similarly, Pecola cannot endure invisibility and "dumbness." Instead, she wants to embody the Shirley Temple trademark—to consume and be consumed like the quintessential American child. While Pecola behaves like Pecola, however, she operates in the narrative like Delilah. When Claudia invokes Pecola's pregnant body, she inscribes it, like Delilah's, with the "pain, memory, history, and ritual" of their community. Claudia, therefore, substitutes Pecola's body for the Temple trademark that would otherwise offer little more than nostalgic banalities about 1940s America.

In *The Bluest Eye*, Pecola's pregnancy and psychosis represent extreme consequences of racism. By weaving Pecola's story into a web of very different but interconnected narratives, however, Morrison suggests that the erasures of abstraction occur in layers, rather than as an absolute. Claudia, who despises Shirley Temple, minimally resists the self-effacing impetuses that seduce Pecola. In contrast, with lighter skin, greater economic stability, and long familial and pedagogical histories that promote assimilation, Maureen, Geraldine, and Soaphead all suppress their "surpluses." To complicate matters, however, Morrison dissociates their abstraction from the hoped-for empowerment of citizenship. Instead, all of these characters endure varying degrees of powerlessness while also suffering a devastating lack of familial or communal intimacy. Through their social and political bankruptcy, Morrison suggests that self-abstraction offers nothing more than a false promise to black Americans.

Furthermore, since Morrison arranges these peripheral characters in separate but inextricable stories that defy linear narration, she simultaneously culminates multiple and contemporaneous histories in the specter of Pecola's demise. The protagonist of each subplot participates in Pecola's oppression. To defend herself against Claudia and Frieda, Maureen denies her own blackness in a taunt that crushes Pecola. She calls all three girls "Black and ugly black e mos" (61). Similarly, when Geraldine finds Pecola in her home, she suppresses the eruption of surplus corporeality that Pecola symbolizes by ordering the "nasty little black bitch" out of the house (75). Finally, to preserve the illusion of his own power, Soaphead persuades Pecola that he has given her the blue eyes she desires. As these characters variously label, degrade, and define Pecola's body so as to disavow the realities of racism in their own lives, Morrison suggests that they mirror the work of a nation that ironically invests in the ideology of childhood innocence at the expense of its children.

With these overlapping narrative circles, Morrison's literary form shows how seemingly isolated experiences of oppression can interconnect and compound each other to corrupt individuals as well as their families, communities, or nations over time. As adults like Geraldine and Soaphead Church unwittingly cooperate to create a Dick-and-Jane-style innocence within their individual and communal lives, Morrison puts insight into the eyes of a child who already recognizes the perils of such aspirations. Claudia holds the entire town responsible for Pecola's tragic end when she says, "All of us—all who knew her—felt so wholesome after we cleaned ourselves on her. We were so beautiful when we stood astride her ugliness." Since love, according to Claudia, "is never any better than the lover," even those who loved Pecola, especially Cholly and his legacy of powerlessness, could not save her (159).

While Morrison clearly indicts African American communities for their acceptance of oppressive ideologies, Claudia goes further, implicating the nation in Pecola's demise when she explains, "I even think now that the land of the entire country was hostile to marigolds that year. This soil is bad for certain kinds of flowers" (160). Furthermore, Claudia explains her unwillingness to let Temple's version of innocent American childhood go unchallenged. Through the mouth of a child Morrison tells us that no good can come from innocence or nostalgia. Claudia aligns the former with the devastation of rape when she says, *"Our innocence and faith were no more productive than [Cholly's] lust or despair"* (emphasis in original 9). She criminalizes the latter when she shows that America's nostalgia for past wartime patriotism or postwar bliss masks a desire for a time when community and nation refused to "see" the destruction of little black girls like Pecola.

In the early 1970s, when Giroux suggests nostalgia for wartime America first emerges, Morrison critic Sara Blackburn defensively complains that "Toni Morrison is far too talented to remain only a marvelous recorder of the black side of provincial American life." She advises Morrison to "address a riskier contemporary American reality . . . and take her place among the most serious, important, and talented American novelists" (qtd. in McKay 5). In Blackbum's narrow view, Morrison should write about white people and their prosperous nation, not black people and their struggling town. By bringing nationally recognized child-figures to a small Ohio town, however, Morrison connects local and national. Additionally, in the contrast between Pecola's demise and Claudia's survival, Morrison suggests that childhood experiences might encompass anything from blind and silent victimization to insightful narration and resistance. With such a revelation, Morrison leaves the ideologies of innocent childhood and benevolent nation standing with Pecola at the local garbage heap. She suggests that childhood innocence is neither a reality nor an ideal. Instead, she asks us to consider it apart from children, to explore what other, seemingly unrelated investments we might have in preserving it.

WORKS CITED

Anderson, James. "Literacy and Education in the African-American Experience." *Literacy Among African-American Youth: Issues in Learning, Teaching, and Schooling.* Cresskill: Hampton Press, 1995.

Aronowitz, Stanley. *False Promises: The Shaping of American Working Class Consciousness.* Durham NC: Duke University Press, 1992.

Aronowitz, Stanley and Henry A. Giroux. *Education Still Under Siege.* 2nd ed. Westport CT: Bergin and Garvey, 1993.

Backes, Nancy. "Growing Up Desperately: The Adolescent 'Other' in the Novels of Paule Marshall, Toni Morrison, and Michelle Cliff." *Women of Color: Defining the Issues, Hearing the Voices.* Ed. Diane Long Hoeveler and Janet K. Boles. Westport CT: Greenwood, 2001: pp. 147–157.

Berlant, Lauren. "National Brands/National Body: *Imitation of Life.*" *Comparative American Identities: Race, Sex and Nationality in the Modern Text.* Ed. • Hortense Spillers. New York: Routledge, 1991: pp. 110–140.

Bredella, Lothar. "Decolonizing the Mind: Toni Morrison's *The Bluest Eye* and *Tar Baby.*" *Intercultural Encounters—Studies in English Literatures.* Ed. Heinz Antor and Kevin L. Cope. Heidelberg, Germany: Carl Winter Universitätsverlag, 1999: pp. 363–84

Bruer, Julie. "'Dick and Jane' books and readers." *Julia's Collectibles and Antiques.* 16 July 2005 <http://www.pan-tex.net/usr/j/Julie/>.

Cadman, Deborah. "When the Back Door is Closed and the Front Yard is Dangerous: The Space of Girlhood in Toni Morrison's Fiction." *The Girl: Constructions of the Girl in Contemporary Fiction by Women.* Ed. Roth O. Saxton. New York: St. Martin's Press, 1998: pp. 57–78.

Dickerson, Vanessa. "The Naked Father in Toni Morrison's *The Bluest Eye.*" *Refiguring the Father: New Feminist Readings of Patriarchy.* ed. Patricia Yaeger and Beth Kowaleski-Wallace. Carbondale: Southern Illinois University Press, 1989: pp. 108–127.

Elson, William H. and William S. Gray, "Busy Workers and Their Work." *The Elson Basic Readers: Book Four.* Chicago: Scott, Foresman and Company, 1930.215-56.

———. *The Elson Basic Readers: Book Four.* Chicago: Scott, Foresman and Company, 1930.

Feng, Pin-chia. *The Female Bildungsroman by Toni Morrison and Maxine Hong Kingston: A Postmodern Reading.* New York: Peter Lang, 1998.

Furman, Jan. *Toni Morrison's Fiction.* Columbia: University of South Carolina Press, 1996.

Giroux, Henry. *Channel Surfing: Racism, The Media, and the Destruction of Today's Youth*. New York: St. Martin's Press, 1997.

———. *The Mouse that Roared: Disney and the End of Innocence*. New York: Rowman and Littlefield, 1999.

Grewal, Gurleen. "'Laundering the Head of Whitewash': Mimicry and Resistance in *The Bluest Eye*." *Approaches to Teaching the Novels of Toni Morrison*. Ed. Nellie McKay and Kathryn Earle. New York: MLA, 1997: pp. 118–128.

Hébert, Kimberly B. "Acting the Nigger: Topsy, Shirley Temple, and Toni Morrison's Pecola." *Approaches to Teaching Stowe's Uncle Tom's Cabin*. Ed. Elizabeth Ammons and Susan Belasco. New York: MLA, 2000: pp. 184–198.

Kismaric, Carole and Marvin Heiferman. *Growing up with Dick and Jane: Learning and Living the American Dream*. New York: Collins, 1996.

Ledbetter, Mark. *Victims and the Postmodern Narrative or Doing Violence to the Body: An Ethic of Reading and Writing*. New York: St. Martin's Press, 1996.

May, Elaine Tyler. *Homeward Bound: American Families in the Cold War Era*. 1988. New York: Basic Books, 1999.

McKay, Nellie. Introduction. *Critical Essays on Toni Morrison*. Ed. Nellie McKay. Boston: G.K. Hall, 1988: pp. 1–15.

Morrison, Toni. *The Bluest Eye*. New York: Washington Square Press, 1970.

———. *Playing in the Dark: Whiteness and the Literary Imagination*. New York: Vintage, 1993.

O'Reilly, Andrea. "Maternal Conceptions in Toni Morrison's *The Bluest Eye* and *Tar Baby*: 'A Woman has to be a Daughter Before She Can Be Any Kind of Woman.'" *This Giving Birth: Pregnancy and Childbirth in American Women's Writing*. Ed. Julie Tharp and Susan MacColium-Whitcomb. Bowling Green: Bowling Green State University Popular Press, 2000: pp. 83–102.

Rogin, Michael Paul. *Ronald Reagan, the Movie and Other Episodes in Political Demonology*. Berkeley: University of California Press, 1987.

Schultz, Dave. Home page. 6 December 2002 <http://www.daveschultz.com/dickandjane/>.

Stacey, Judith. *In the Name of the Family: Rethinking Family Values in the Postmodern Age*. Boston: Beacon Press, 1996.

Willis, Susan. "'I Shop Therefore I am': Is There a Place for Afro-American Culture in Commodity Culture?" *Changing Our Own Words: Essays on Criticism, Theory, and Writing by Black Women*. ed. Cheryl A. Wall. New Brunswick NJ: Rutgers University Press, 1989: pp. 173–195.

CHRISTOPHER D

What The Bluest Eye *Kn*
Culture, Race, 1

Forays into family history are Toni Morrison's standard strategy for establishing character motivation in *The Bluest Eye*. But midway through the narrative, her strategy changes. Just before Junior sadistically hurls his mother's
cat "right in [Pecola's] face," Morrison provides a rather startling description
of a group of people to which Junior's mother, Geraldine, belongs, and to
which, therefore, Junior's actions can be traced. Geraldine's genealogy is
typological, not familial. She is one of a type of people who are losing a
cultural identity that is rightfully theirs because of their racial ancestry.[1]

"They," as Morrison terms the type, "come from Mobile," or perhaps
from "Aiken. From Newport News. From Marietta. From Meridian" (81).
What distinguishes "[t]hese particular brown girls" is that they are learning "how to get rid of the funkiness. The dreadful funkiness of passion, the
funkiness of nature, the funkiness of the wide range of human emotions"
(82, 83). Setting up a fundamental ambivalence, *The Bluest Eye* on the one
hand locates funk as a species-wide quality; we all have, or once had, funk.
On the other hand, this quality is understood to have been already lost by
white people in a process that was either racial or cultural (perhaps this loss
is what makes someone white); accordingly, funk is the heritage of the "particular brown girls," who are threatened with its loss. The funk is embodied
and racialized through the various phenotypic differences that mark the so-

American Literature, Volume 78, Number 1, March 2006. Copyright © 2006 by Duke
University Press.

of race and that threaten to overwhelm the whitening pro-
old their behind in for fear of a sway too free; when they wear
ey never cover the entire mouth for fear of lips too thick, and they
worry, worry about the edges of their hair," which has been straight-
with "Dixie Peach" (83, 82). In this struggle, it seems as if culture as
arned behavior might combat an inherited, biology-derived identity.

Or at least that is the possibility that *The Bluest Eye* takes up: whether,
following desegregation and the Civil Rights Movement, black Americans
could or should adopt dominant white cultural practices and values. In what
we might call a generative moment in the history of literary multiculturalism,
the novel tells the story of a black girl in 1941 who is all but destroyed by her
desire for white beauty and by other African Americans acting in response
to the oppression of white cultural normativity. *The Bluest Eye* thus staked a
claim in the national debate about minority citizenship that took place during its composition (1962–1970), a debate shaped not only by literature but
also by social science and law. In fact, a cornerstone of our current paradigm
of literary multiculturalism is this novel's rejection of integrationist law and
assimilationist social science, although the novel's discomfort with fixed notions of identity formation is not characteristic of the multiculturalism it
helped inaugurate.

An uneasiness with identity characterizes *The Bluest Eye* as a whole,
but that uneasiness is not on display in Morrison's vigorous and extended
typology of the "brown girls," who learn in school "the rest of the lesson begun in those soft houses with porch swings and pots of bleeding
heart: how to behave" (83). Because their bodies continually threaten to
undermine the pursuit of whiteness, it is the focus of their attention: "They
wash themselves with orange-colored Lifebuoy soap, dust themselves with
Cashmere Bouquet talc, clean their teeth with salt on a piece of rag, soften
their skin with Jergens Lotion" (82). Their future husbands do not yet know
about the sexual reticence produced by their carefully ordered worlds: "Nor
do they know that she will give him her body sparingly and partially. He
must enter her surreptitiously, lifting the hem of her nightgown only to her
navel" (84).

Not surprisingly, perhaps we are to understand, the product of this
surreptitious acknowledgement of the body is a boy whose identity as "colored" (as his mother calls "them") is continually threatened by the body's
intrusion into the cultural order. Even though Geraldine has her son's hair
cut "as close to his scalp as possible to avoid any suggestion of wool" with a
part "etched into his hair by the barber," and even though she puts more Jergens onto his "light-skinned" face "to keep the skin from becoming ashen,"
Junior's body resists these attempts to erase or mitigate racial difference
(87). "The line between colored and nigger," Geraldine knows, "was not

always clear; subtle and telltale signs threatened to erode it, and the watch had to be constant" (87). But Junior has what appears to be an almost innate desire for blackness:

> Junior used to long to play with the black boys. More than anything in the world he wanted to play King of the Mountain and have them push him down the mound of dirt and roll over him. He wanted to feel their hardness pressing on him, smell their wild blackness, and say "Fuck you" with that lovely casualness. He wanted to sit with them on curbstones and compare the sharpness of jackknives, the distance and arcs of spitting. In the toilet he wanted to share with them the laurels of being able to pee far and long. (87)

Junior's desire for blackness is strongly signaled in sensual and sexual terms. The boys will "roll over him," their "hardness" will press on him, they will say "fuck" together, and they will, wielding their penises, "pee" together. All of these activities can be described as cultural practices. Although they don't appear, separately or together, to be particular to a certain culture, the passage associates them specifically with "black boys." Furthermore, the novel draws our attention to the ways in which these actions seem to be true to Junior's body, in a way that actions associated with an equally performative white culture, exemplified by Geraldine's efforts, are inauthentic, at least to the bodies of Geraldine and her son. That is, in both the typology of the "brown girls" and the description of Geraldine and Junior that follows it, the novel does not present culture as performative. While doing certain things and holding certain values might abstractly define membership in a culture, the text devalues such membership in favor of an identitarian, body-based, essentialist "culture" which has its origin and true value in race. That these girls are "brown" is the condition for but also the cause of the slippage between race and culture; being racially mixed permits and necessitates a cultural answer. As Walter Benn Michaels argues about Oliver La Farge's *Laughing Boy,* "Biology is an essential but not a sufficient condition of an identity that here requires a relatively autonomous set of practices to complete its constitution . . . ."[2]

The narrative purpose of Morrison's extended typology in *The Bluest Eye* seems to be to introduce Geraldine, who accounts for the internalized rage and sadism of her son. When Junior throws his mother's cat into Pecola's face, Geraldine's subsequent epithet for Pecola—"black bitch"—completes the sequence of events, conditioned by the U.S. racial order in 1941, that leads to Pecola's deep psychic damage. But Morrison's exuberant typological set-up for Geraldine is about four times as long as Geraldine's own history and her relation to her child. Indeed, the narrative signals its nonchalance toward Geraldine at the very moment it pretends to be turning from typology to focus on a single character: "One such girl from Mobile, or Meridian, or Aiken . . ." (86). The text is supposedly narrowing the typology to a specific "One," but it clearly doesn't care about getting the facts of this "One" straight, since such facts are understood not to really count, or perhaps to threaten the very representativeness of the typological account that has been offered in the first place. In this feint from "They" to "One," then, we are not witnessing the cultural practices that give rise or meaning to the individual; rather, Morrison is describing a typology of cultural loss. Geraldine can't change her race, but she can try to change her culture, and this process is described as loss rather than a gain or transformation.

This typology is part of the novel's larger project of examining the grounds for group identity in the midst of a crisis of minority citizenship in the United States. Geraldine's typology and its conflation of race and culture must be understood not only within the novel's 1941 timeframe but also within the intellectual context of the novel's composition: the philosophical struggle between the Black Arts movement and the Civil Rights movement. That Geraldine, like Pecola, does not believe that "black is beautiful" is the thematic center of the novel. "The reclamation of racial beauty in the sixties stirred these thoughts, made me think about the necessity for the claim," Morrison wrote in her 1993 Afterword to the 1970 novel (210). Conceiving of this reclamation as one tactic in a larger decolonization, Black Aesthetician Hoyt Fuller wrote in 1968: "Across this country young black men and women have been infected with a fever of affirmation. They are saying, 'We are black and beautiful,' and the ghetto is reacting with a liberating shock of realization which transcends mere chauvinism. They are rediscovering their heritage and their history. . . ."[3] This passage is from "Towards a Black Aesthetic," which was reprinted in Addison Gayle's *The Black Aesthetic* the year after *The Bluest Eye* was published, where it joined other key documents that outlined the development of the Black Arts movement. In that collection, Gayle argued that the central project of the Black Arts movement was the "de-Americanization" of black communities.[4] Gayle's collection also reprinted Larry Neal's 1968 article, "The Black Arts Movement," where Neal argued that "Black Art is the Aesthetic and spiritual sister of the Black Power concept," both of which were to define and substantiate African American self-determination and nationhood. Neal noted that there are "two Americas—one black, one white."[5]

Black nationalism was contesting what we might call the newly official national narrative of minority citizenship enshrined by *Brown v. Board of Education* in its overturning of *Plessy v. Ferguson's* "separate but equal" segregationist logic, the ramifications of which were being worked out in the Civil Rights movement. Morrison repeatedly invokes *Brown* to critique its model of minority citizenship, which was made possible by a new paradigm in the social sciences based on ethnicity and assimilation. Against this newly official model, black nationalism and the Black Aesthetic posed an alternative, separatist, racially essentialist model that imagined African American double consciousness as a problem to be solved not through unification (as DuBois had hoped) but through a reclamation of racial pride. As Neal put it, "Implicit in the Black Arts Movement is the idea that Black people, however dispersed, constitute a *nation* within the belly of white America." [6] Insofar as *The Bluest Eye* understands Geraldine's cultural behavior and values as inappropriate, given her race, it is a Black Arts novel; in concurrence with Neal, it imagines a different kind of national belonging for African Americans than the model set forth by *Brown*.

Along with the passages from the Dick-and-Jane reader that begin each chapter and the Hollywood images that attract Pauline, Pecola's mother, Geraldine constitutes the white norm of 1940s cultural citizenship that the novel critiques. She has largely assimilated into white society, assuming its waspy, middle-class trappings: lace doilies, "a large Bible in the front room," the making of "soufflés in the Home Economics Department"—a hygiene-cum-sterility of both house and person (84, 83, 86). Her values, habits, and possessions signal a cultural membership that her race undercuts. She is, in other words, the incomplete solution to "the Negro problem" imagined by the University of Chicago's School of Sociology in the 1920s and 1930s; this sociology helped to promulgate the new citizenship model in *Brown* that Geraldine represents.[7] Although Michael Omi and Howard Winant attribute the changing conception of race in the social sciences from biological hierarchy to biological equality to Robert Park's sociology in the 1920s, Dorothy Ross has shown that this change was initiated by Franz Boas in anthropology, and later taken up by William Thomas and, through him, eventually Park (*OASS*, 350–359).[8]

Thomas met Park at a conference at the Tuskegee Institute in 1912, where Park had been an aide, publicity agent, and ghostwriter for Booker T. Washington for seven years, becoming, as Park put it, "for all intents and purposes, for the time, a Negro, myself."[9] Park joined Thomas and the sociology faculty at the University of Chicago the next year, where he contributed to the growing orientation of this sociology toward realism, empiricism, and hard facts. Park built on the work of Thomas and Boas, embracing their assumption of racial equality and using their empirical research methods, such as gathering data by interviewing urban and ethnic subjects. When his and Ernest W. Burgess's *Introduction to the Science of Sociology* was published in 1921, it became "the dominant text in the field for the next twenty years"; according to Ross, it "disseminated Park's conception of sociology" (*OASS*, 359). "The heart of the text," Ross notes, "was a group of chapters on competition, conflict, accommodation, and assimilation" (*OASS*, 359). Park grappled for years with what would become a central problem in this vision of Americanization: could racialized minorities marked by skin-color difference be assimilated? Of Park's career, Ross notes: "The one area of social life Park had not been able to subdue to his vision of liberal history was race relations. . . . Until the mid-1920s, Park remained uncertain about racial assimilation" (*OASS*, 438). But then, according to Ross, a new research interest in American-Japanese relations helped him settle the question: "Listening to a young Japanese-American woman, he felt that he was listening to 'an American woman in a Japanese disguise.'" Returning from a conference in Hawaii, where he had been impressed with "the mixing of races," Park began to argue for the potential cultural assimilation of racialized minorities, an idea he extended to African Americans and that became academically influential in the 1930s and 1940s (*OASS*, 438).

Indeed, Park's formulation of assimilationist sociology became the dominant paradigm for the new discipline in the 1930s, influencing heavily the theory and method behind Gunnar Myrdal's *An American Dilemma: The Negro Problem and Modern Democracy* (1944) and Kenneth Clark's work on racial preferences among school children in the late 1940s, both of which were cited by the Supreme Court in the *Brown* decision. When the NAACP's Legal Defense and Education Fund began considering the grounds for a challenge to segregation laws, the organization turned to the newly reputable social sciences, which were becoming authoritative in the courts. The NAACP's legal team, emerging from Howard University Law School, some of whom had been "trained in sociological jurisprudence," selectively chose evidence from the disciplines of anthropology, sociology, and social psychology.[10] The NAACP (for the purposes of *Brown*) accepted Boas's anthropological concept of racial equality but not his concept of slow cultural-historical change, opting instead to combine the first strand of Boasian anthropology's racial equality with Park's more flexible model of social transformation involving the stages of competition, conflict, accommodation, and assimilation (*FSN*, 179). As Lee Baker points out, this strategic combination of social-science theory differed markedly from the New Negro movement that had come before, which had remained closer to Boasian ideas of slow cultural change over time, an idea that preserved the possibility of identifying retained African cultural traditions.[11]

Discerning the differences among these ideas in social science helps to highlight how their political implications were viewed at the time, as in Zora Neale Hurston's resistance to forced desegregation after *Brown* was decided.[12] While the NAACP accepted only the first tenet of Boasian anthropology—racial equality—Hurston as an anthropologist in her own right (indeed, trained by Boas) saw African American folklore and cultural practices as maintaining a certain continuity with West African cultures

(*FSN*, 161–63). Unlike the NAACP, she accepted the second tenet of Boasian anthropology, that cultures were "long-standing, slow to change," and historically specific (*FSN*, 179). This instinct toward cultural conservation in Hurston's conservative politics reflects her Boasian belief in the value of studying distinct cultural formations and her rejection of the assimilation model of Park's sociology—which emphasized the absence of African traditions (*FSN*, 177) and encouraged what she saw as the "pathological" reading of African American culture implied by the sociology of *Brown*.[13] Other Park-influenced sociologists, for instance, had argued in the 1920s that Negro culture had "progressed" but that noncosmopolitan, middle-class Negroes "deviated from American cultural and behavioral standards" in response to "deleterious environmental conditions, racial discrimination, and the heritage of slavery" (*FSN*, 178). Thus reconsidered, the famous antipathy between Hurston and Richard Wright (who was informally trained in Chicago sociology) comes into focus as a disciplinary argument between Boasian anthropology and Parkian sociology. It was these discourses of "deviation" and "pathology" that angered Hurston throughout her career, and that Morrison later received suspiciously.

• • •

Two competing paradigms of group identity during the 1940s produced antagonistic models of minority citizenship. One model was cultural, energized by the Boasian notion of racial equality and extended to assimilable racialized minorities by Park in the 1930s. By the 1950s, this model was codified with "the force-feeding of *An American Dilemma* to the American public by the press and the federal government" (*FSN*, 198). The model was the grounds for the NAACP argument that segregation was unconstitutional. This model of the cultural assimilation of racial minorities became the impetus for the Civil Rights movement in the next decade (*FSN*, 207–8). The other paradigm, though sometimes cultural in its declarations as well, found race to be the real origin of and authorization for cultural identity; it is perhaps best illustrated by Hurston's own field work, her resistance to the discourse of black pathology and the pressures of assimilation (which she found in the sociology behind *Brown*), and her insistence on the vitality of African American culture and art, all of which would find strong, new, nationalist articulators in the Black Aesthetic and Black Power movements.

The debate between these two positions in the 1960s formed the intertextual ground for *The Bluest Eye*, which took up many of the issues articulated in *Brown*. Most obvious, perhaps, is the pathology of self-loathing that a racialized society can produce. Morrison dramatizes that pathology in Pecola, but in such a way that its formation becomes not more comprehensible but more complicated. (We bear the weight of knowing that both the narrator and the author believe that the novel's task has in some important way failed.) Pecola and Claudia go to an integrated school, and Claudia, at least, lives in an integrated neighborhood in Lorain, Ohio. But in what might be an ironic commentary on the premise of *Brown*—that black self-esteem is irreparably harmed when law sanctions social segregation, especially during elementary education—the pathology of self-loathing emerges forcefully in the character of Pecola despite her partially integrated environment.

The most interesting allusion in *The Bluest Eye* to *Brown* is the dolls test developed by Kenneth Clark and Mamie Clark. In May of 1951, Kenneth Clark accompanied Thurgood Marshall and his lieutenant Robert Carter to Charleston, where, while Marshall and Carter prepared a legal argument, Clark interviewed sixteen black children in Clarendon County's segregated schools. Using his dolls test, in which children were asked to compare otherwise identical brown- and white-colored dolls, he discovered that "[t]en of the sixteen children said they preferred the white doll. Eleven of the children referred to the black doll as 'bad,' while nine said the white doll was 'nice.' Seven of the children pointed to the white doll when they were asked to choose the doll most like themselves."[14] In the case that would become *Briggs v. Elliott* (1951), Clark testified, based on these tests, "that school segregation was distorting the minds of black youngsters to the point of making them self-hating" (*TM*, 202). Although the majority opinion rejected the introduction of Clark's sociology into legal interpretation, it found the material conditions of the segregated schools unequal and gave the county six months to equalize the black and white schools.

Briggs v. Elliott was one of the four cases on appeal before the Supreme Court in 1952 and 1953, all of which ended together in *Brown v. Board of Education*. In the renowned footnote 11 to this decision, the Court referenced Clark's work as one of the seven social-science studies substantiating the psychological damage that attended school segregation.[15] A decade after *Brown*, toward the end of the Civil Rights movement that it had enabled, and as the Black Arts movement commenced, Morrison turned to this figure of the black child's desire for the white beauty and subjectivity embodied in a doll. Unlike the black children in the Clarks' studies in the 1940s, who tended statistically to prefer white dolls, *The Bluest Eye*'s narrator, Claudia, thinks back to what she realizes is her atypical reaction, as a black child in the 1940s, to the "blue-eyed" dolls received at Christmas.[16] "From the clucking sounds of adults I knew that the doll represented what they thought was my fondest wish," Claudia recalls (20). This was the Clarks' conclusion as well: "It is clear . . . that the majority of these Negro children prefer the *white* doll and reject the colored doll" ("RI," 175). For Claudia, however, the white dolls, "which were supposed to bring me great pleasure, succeeded in doing quite the opposite" (20). She can read the racial code, at least retroactively, understanding the white doll to be "beautiful" (21), but she lacks the spontaneity of many of the Clarks' students who chose a white doll "'cause he's pretty" ("RI," 178). Instead of pleasure and desire, the doll elicits only revulsion from this atypical pupil:

> I had only one desire: to dismember it. To see of what it was made, to discover the dearness, to find the beauty, the desirability that had escaped me, but apparently only me. Adults, older girls, shops, magazines, newspapers, window signs—all the world had agreed that a blue-eyed, yellow-haired, pink-skinned doll was what every girl child treasured. (20)

Indeed, Claudia seems unfazed by the move from preference to identification that, for the Clarks' students, appeared to initiate a crisis of "racial mental hygiene" ("RI," 169, 175).[17] As the Clarks note, "[S]ome of the children who were free and relaxed in the beginning of the experiment [the phase of racial preference] broke down and cried or became somewhat negativistic during the latter part when they were required to make self-identifications. Indeed, two children ran out of the testing room, unconsolable, convulsed in tears" ("RI," 178). Claudia, however, "could not love [the white doll]. But I could examine it to see what it was that all the world said was lovable. Break off the tiny fingers, bend the flat feet, loosen the hair, twist the head around. . ." (21).

Claudia somehow escapes the pathology that the Clarks identify, which was at the center of *Brown,* and which eventually engulfs Pecola, who shares with one of the Clarks' students the desire for a white doll "'cause it's got blue eyes—cause it's got pretty eyes."[18] Pecola imagines, in fact, that she has achieved the dolls' blue eyes by the end of the novel. Pecola's problem mirrors the conclusion that the Clarks came to in a 1950 study:

> The negation of the color, brown, exists in the same complexity of attitudes in which there also exists knowledge of the fact that the child himself must be identified with that which he rejects. This apparently introduces a fundamental conflict at the very foundations of the ego structure. Many of these children attempt to resolve this profound conflict either through wishful thinking or phantasy. . . .[19]

Such fantasies of racial identity and preference—the grounds of the Clarks' studies used in *Brown*—are at the center of *The Bluest Eye.* Claudia not only rejects the white dolls that she understands the world deems lovable, but she also hates Shirley Temple, whom Pecola and Frieda adore: "I couldn't join them in their adoration because I hated Shirley. Not because she was cute, but because she danced with Bojangles, who was *my* friend, *my* uncle, *my* daddy . . ." (19). Claudia rejects what Clark would see as a pathological racial preference, choosing instead a healthy racial identity, imagining racial belonging progressively as friendship, kinship, and then paternity. But this is only because Claudia, younger than her sister and Pecola, "had not yet arrived at the turning point in my development of my psyche which would allow me to love her" (19). Morrison's point is thus not that the social construction of white beauty uncovered by the Clarks' study doesn't exist, and that it doesn't exert an overwhelming pressure on girls of any race but, rather, that the application of this phenomenon is bumpy, incomplete, complicated, and resisted. *Brown's* answer of integration is also rendered strangely problematic by the novel, whose semi-integrated setting seems not to have eradicated the pathologies of the past but, perhaps, to have created others. The assimilation that Park and Myrdal imagined as being a panacea is represented by the sadistic Junior, who is only allowed to play with white boys, not the black boys he desires (87). Claudia, in an integrated school and an integrated neighborhood, transfers her violent impulses from the white dolls to her white neighbor Rosemary, whose face she scratches, and whose "fascinated eyes in a dough-white face" remind us of the dolls that Claudia detests (30). In these instances, being at school with or living next to white people is not imagined as the answer that *Brown's* social science seemed to promise.

When *The Bluest Eye* describes both the psychological violence of white norms of beauty and cultural citizenship and a black resistance to that violence in the form of Claudia's angry response,[20] it reveals its affinity to the Black Arts movement that formed the novel's intellectual context. But beyond their common exploration and critique of "racial self-loathing," as Morrison puts it in her afterword (210), *The Bluest Eye* and the Black Arts movement also shared suspicion, even hostility, toward the social-science discourse that underlay *Brown*, and toward the minority-citizenship model that *Brown* helped inaugurate. In short, they rejected the assimilationist trajectory of Park and Myrdal, and the portrayal of Negro pathology—that black people need to be near or around white people in order to be spiritually, psychologically, and culturally healthy—implied in Clark.[21] In this sense, the Black Aesthetic would seek a return to the concept of culture formed by Boas, embraced by Hurston, but denied by Park—one that saw African American culture as cohesive, slow to change, and potentially continuous with African traditions.

While Morrison was writing *The Bluest Eye*, Thurgood Marshall, then Associate Justice of the Supreme Court, was harassed by the Black Panthers as "an establishment voice" when he spoke at the University of Wisconsin in September 1968 (*TM*, 342–343), and Ralph Ellison was verbally confronted and called an "Uncle Tom" by black students at Oberlin College, where he came to speak in April 1969.[22] Marshall rejected the militancy of the younger black generation and their "separatism" in a confrontation that received widespread press (*TM*, 343–344). As Fuller argued that same year in "Towards a Black Aesthetic," "black intellectuals have rejected the NAACP" just as they were rejecting "the Literary Establishment."[23] Morrison, having graduated in 1953 from Howard University—which had trained Marshall in its law school and Clark in its psychology department—likewise questioned the wisdom of *Brown*, not understanding why "black children were going to learn better if they were in the company of white children." As she recalled, in a 1983 interview, "I was not in favor of integration. But I couldn't officially say that, because I knew the terror and the abuses of segregation. But integration also meant that we would not have a fine black college or fine black education."[24] Morrison's statements directly echo Hurston's 1955 letter to the *Orlando Sentinel* (widely reprinted in Southern papers), in which she questioned both the premise that black children learn better while sitting next to white children and the possibility that the "very good" black schools in existence might be diminished.[25]

It is revealing to compare the fates of Wright and Ellison as the Black Arts movement grew in the 1960s. Ellison's novel was being called "the most distinguished single work published in the last twenty years" by an almost exclusively white "Book Week" poll in the *New York Herald Tribune* in 1965, while Wright was found to be "the most important black American writer of all time" in a 1968 *Negro Digest* poll.[26] The ascendance of Wright's reputation in the Black Aesthetic was due to *Native Son*'s portrayal of white liberal hypocrisy and to its promise of violence; in this sense, the Black Aesthetic was not embracing realism or its status as protest literature. Like *The Bluest Eye*, the Black Aesthetic eschewed both protest and the realism that enabled it, opting instead, as Neal put it in 1968, for writing authentically and "directly to Black people."[27] As Arthur Davis argued in response to *Brown*, protest literature, in view of the integration to come, was an outdated form: "When the enemy capitulated, he shattered our most fruitful literary tradition. The possibility of imminent integration has tended to destroy the protest element in Negro writing."[28]

The Black Arts movement's rejection of the NAACP and "the Literary Establishment"—embodied, respectively, in Marshall (co-opted by the Supreme Court) and Ralph Ellison (co-opted by the 1965 White House Arts Festival)—came from a cultural politics of racial authenticity. In its rejection of protest, realism, and the premises of *Brown*, *The Bluest Eye* is a Black Arts novel, and its themes of racial beauty and cultural oppression were received in the current terms of the Black Aesthetic. This is probably why the mostly male, Black Aesthetic critics did not criticize Morrison's novel as they did the novels of some other African American women at the time.[29] Reviewers Liz Gant in *Black World* and Sharyn Skeeter in *Essence* recognized the themes of racial beauty and ugliness in *The Bluest Eye*, noting Pecola's ultimate inability to see "the beauty deep within herself."[30] The novel's engagement with African American psychology was thus acknowledged through Black Aesthetic concepts. As Ruby Dee puts it in her review: "The author digs up for viewing deep secret thoughts, terrible yearnings and little-understood frustrations common to many of us. She says these are the gnawings we keep pushed back into the subconscious, unadmitted; but they must be worked on, ferreted up and out so we can breathe deeply, say loud and truly believe 'Black is beautiful.'"[31]

• • •

In reviewing how the Black Arts movement situated itself in relation to realism and protest literature in the 1960s while Morrison was composing *The Bluest Eye*, my aim is to indicate how such complications were aligned with contemporaneous moves in citizenship law and the social sciences. To put that alignment most simply, the realist methodology that both the Black Arts movement and *The Bluest Eye* rejected was associated, directly and in spirit, with the empirical strain of current social science, and with the so-called legal realism or sociological jurisprudence whose era *Brown* was said to inaugurate.

It was Park and his mentor Thomas who helped establish, borrowing from anthropology, a "field work" model for sociology, in which details were to be gathered by visiting the actual sites of ethnic urban difference. But the parallel between literary realism and sociology is not just an affinity of method—whereby an accurate picture of the real is established through patient observation of detail and accumulation of fact. Nor is it only a political trajectory that both shared in the 1930s and 1940s—with realist protest literature and sociological models of assimilation and psychopathology both leading toward *Brown*'s official model of integrated citizenship. There is also strong evidence that literary realism and the newly established social sciences recognized in one another a similar attentiveness to the facts of ethnic life, and that these discourses borrowed concepts and evidence from one another during this time. William Thomas and Florian Znaniecki's *The Polish Peasant in Europe and America,* for example, an important 1918 work on immigration and nonpluralist assimilation, "quickly became a paradigmatic work for the new empirical social science" (*OASS,* 352), pioneering "the use of personal documents, such as letters, diaries, and especially life histories or autobiographies written at the request of an inquirer."[32] As Carla Cappetti has shown, the major figures of the Chicago school were sometimes trained in literature or made heavy use of literature in order to inspire or illuminate their work on the city.[33] Michael Elliott has more recently pushed back the beginning of this collaboration, arguing that the classical age of U.S. realism shared many of the methods and goals of late-nineteenth and early-twentieth-century ethnography, producing texts he calls "cultural realism."[34]

By the 1940s and 1950s, the sociological use of literary writing became an accepted method of verifying empirical findings. Only a page after a reference to the Clarks' dolls study, the Truman Administration's *Personality in the Making: The Fact-Finding Report of the Mid-Century White House Conference on Children and Youth* (1950) referred to Wright's *Native Son* as a "fictional case history" when making a point about the hostility that racial prejudice creates.[35] Both "studies" are about the psychological effects of prejudice, but the problem here, of course, is that *Native Son* is being used as evidence in support of sociological findings that Wright was quite aware of—which, in fact, had greatly influenced his thinking and the composition of *Native Son*.[36] Werner Sollors makes a similar warning in *Beyond Ethnicity*, after noting that Park misread a Jewish autobiography in his important "Human Migration and the Marginal Man":

> Even when the literary evidence is not so overtly misread, there are some problems with the way in which literature is viewed by the more theoretical analysts. Richard Wright's fiction, for example, is frequently invoked in sociological accounts of the ghetto. Yet it is—precisely in its depiction of psychological alienation and cultural deprivation—the partial product of Wright's immersion into Chicago school of sociology readings (Fabre 232). Such uses of literature as social evidence may be circular.[37]

We confront a conceptual circuit here, in which social-science findings—on "culture," the pathology of the Negro family, the effects of race prejudice—in turn influenced the composition of literary texts, which were then read as evidence of the original theory. Nor is this circuit finished. In 1996, Midge Wilson and Kathy Russell used *The Bluest Eye* to answer the research question "How is girls' cross-race play affected by dolls that are White instead of Black?" They do not appear, however, to notice that Morrison's novel has as its intertextual source and inspiration the initial social-science evidence about dolls and "cross-race play" (the Clarks' studies) that their book mentions only a few pages earlier.[38] Such intersections of literature and social science raise important questions about discipline and method that I will address at the end of my essay.

This alliance between realism and social science was joined by a third constituent at this key historical moment, announced by *Brown*: "legal realism," or "sociological jurisprudence," which was the self-conscious turn to "extralegal facts" and fact-finding as substantiated in particular by the newly authoritative social sciences.[39] What we might call an alliance of the real, then, was formed in the conjunction of protest fiction, the sociology of racial pathology, and legal realism—summarized neatly when *Brown* cited the *Mid-Century White House Report,* which substantiated the effects of prejudice by referring to both Wright's *Native Son* and the Clarks' dolls study. This alliance helped bring forth a new model of citizenship for racialized minorities in the United States.

Morrison's *The Bluest Eye* and the Black Arts movement were, together, refutations of this mid-century alliance. Against the ethnic, culturalist paradigm of citizenship in *Brown*—where integrated, assimilative childhood education was considered the "foundation of good citizenship"—*The Bluest Eye* posed a racial understanding of culture that concurred with the Black Aesthetic's call for separatism and racial authenticity. This is what it means for Morrison, in the extended typology of Geraldine, to peel back the layer of cultural assimilation in order to reveal the racial truth that remains. ("Brown girls" are learning "how to get rid of the funkiness.") And though funk here seems to be a species-wide quality, its etymology suggests a more specific set of associations. Indeed, to explain funk's roots in slavery, Neal had to footnote LeRoi Jones's *Blues People,* where Jones explains that in the 1950s "[e]ven the adjective *funky,* which once meant to many Negroes merely a stink (usually associated with sex), was used to qualify the music as meaningful (the word became fashionable and is now almost useless). The social implication, then, was that even the old stereotype of a distinctive Negro smell that white America subscribed to could be turned against white America."[40] According to the *Oxford English Dictionary,* the seventeenth-century meaning of *funk* as a bad smell associated with tobacco became racialized in the early twentieth century as it was applied to African Americans; it was then applied to jazz in the 1950s and then contemporary music later (the *OED* offers Mick Jagger as an example). In other words, the word has a racial history. It was adapted for use as a racial concept, and then, Jones notes, the stereotype was redeemed (perhaps after social psychologists went after it).[41] In one sense, Morrison invites us to consider funk as human in general, in a way that might have us see (in accordance with her collection of essays *Playing in the Dark* [1992]) that whiteness produces itself as non-funk, thus allowing Mick Jagger to then rediscover something natural he has lost.[42] But funk's history involves fascination with the bodies of black people, and it's this fascination that Morrison's typology restores, both with its discussion of Geraldine's sexual repression and the subversive body of her son Junior.

My argument here, then, is that Morrison's *The Bluest Eye* shares with the Black Arts movement a rejection of the culturalist explanation of identity that grounded *Brown*'s citizenship model; or, more accurately, the text understands, along with the Black Arts movement, that the question of who has or should have African American culture can only be answered by one's racial identity. And yet as the novel uncovers the racial logic on which this culturalist model of group identity depends, it betrays the problematic thinness of the energetic literary type through which its racial-essence model of group identity is achieved. This lovingly developed typology of Geraldine resonates with the history of the type in both the social sciences and in realism—but when that resonance is heard, this method of racial knowledge undercuts any adequate ground for group identity. *The Bluest Eye*'s collapsing paradigms of group identity—cultural and racial—call into question the epistemological and ontological grounds for the concept of the group itself. We see this not only with the novel's refutations of racial or cultural coherence but also in its revelation that, structurally, racial or cultural concepts of group identity are no different from the typologies and stereotypes that they might promise to replace. Geraldine-as-type is highly reminiscent of the sociological type produced at the beginning of the twentieth century. "We must limit ourselves," write Thomas and Znaniecki, "just as the natural scientist does, to a few *representative* cases whose thorough study will yield results as nearly applicable as possible to all other cases concerned."[43] In their reading of Władek Wiszniewski's untitled autobiography, Thomas and Znaniecki developed three "ideal types which social personalities tend to assume": the philistine, the bohemian, and the creative.[44] Park, eschewing class as a competent marker of group identity, recommended instead urban "vocational types" for sociological study:

> Among the types which it would be interesting to study are: the shopgirl, the policeman, the peddlar, the cabman, the night watchman, the clairvoyant, the vaudeville performer, the quack doctor, the bartender, the ward boss, the strike-breaker, the labor agitator, the school teacher, the reporter, the stockbroker, the pawnbroker; all of these are characteristic products of the conditions of city life; each with its special experience, insight, and point of view determines for each vocational group and for the city as a whole its individuality.[45]

Park's work was deterministic: "Individuals did not act against the forces of the city and create their own individuality; rather, the city created 'individual types'" (*OASS*, 363). And so Park, on accidentally meeting Wright after the publication of *Native Son,* is said to have asked him: "How in hell did you happen?"[46]

One has to laugh with Park, who, in this moment of self-irony, manages to see the way in which the real Wright escapes Park's sociological scheme. Although Park can't understand (or pretends not to understand) how Wright's environment might have produced someone who exceeds any type, this problem of how the real might not exactly fit into the boundaries of the type has in fact been central to the experience not just of Chicago sociology but of realism itself, as Peter Demetz has argued of Honoré de Balzac. Demetz shows how Balzac and his followers understood that the new realism's reaction to Sir Walter Scott's romanticism entailed—prefiguring Park—the use of types to capture the forces of modernity, urbanization, and industrialization: "[T]he modern novelist, Balzac implies, follows the methodological example of the natural scientist [in particular, French zoologist Etienne Geoffrey St.-Hilaire] by closely observing a multitude of individuals, isolating their common traits, separating them from the individual case, and concentrating them in a new model inclusive of all the individuals of the group, or class."[47]

In noting an alignment between the empirical observation of types promoted by the Chicago school of sociology in the 1920s and 1930s (articulated by Park) and by "l'école réaliste" of the 1840s and 1850s (articulated by Balzac),[48] my point is not to indict Chicago sociology for repeating an answer arrived at by Parisian realism eighty years before but to suggest that both Balzac and Park, in their similar ways, had stumbled upon the problematic limits of group identity—the conundrum of which is the theoretical insight of Morrison's *The Bluest Eye.* Balzac and Park believed that through intense observation of individual lives in the modern city, one might empirically discern the pattern that describes the identity of the group to which they belong. But this pattern, called a type, is fashioned by the shedding of excess alterity, such that mere similarity is left, a similarity that is considered essential (in both the practical and ontological senses of that word) in a way that the singularity is not. During this extended process, of course, we've lost the attention to detail and difference that realism and sociology promised; the sociological type and the literary type have become our set of expectations of what the real must be like. Hence Park's ostensible astonishment at the existence of Wright, who had exceeded the type.

But to back up one more time, my purpose is not just to reveal this affinity between the sociological type of the 1920s and the literary type of the 1840s—both of which, in any case, are now out of favor in current disciplinary practices. What I want to suggest is, first, that the sociological type and the literary type were no different structurally than the ignominious stereotype that has generated much discussion in racialized minority critical discourse. The stereotype has negative content, of course, but as a pattern in which some essential traits are retained as the condition of (mis)recognizing the new while other qualities are dropped as not essential to the pattern (such that a kind of common denominator is located), the stereotype is identical to social-science typology and the literary type (even if the latter two were conceived as having both positive and positivist content).[49] *The Bluest Eye* tests the limits of typology in Geraldine just as it does its literary cousin, the stereotype. As with Geraldine's literary-sociological typology, *The Bluest Eye* rehearses the literary stereotype with gusto. The prostitutes living above the Breedloves, for instance,

> did not belong to those generations of prostitutes created in novels, with great and generous hearts, dedicated, because of the horror of circumstance, to ameliorating the luckless, barren life of men, taking money incidentally and humbly for their "understanding." Nor were they from that sensitive breed of young girl, gone wrong at the hands of fate, forced to cultivate an outward brittleness in order to protect her springtime from further shock, but knowing full well that she was cut out for better things, and could make the right man happy. (55–56)

This is a "they" that appears in the novel before Geraldine's typology: "They were not young girls in whores' clothing, or whores regretting their loss of innocence. They were whores in whores' clothing. . ." (57). Rather than literary stereotypes, Morrison's characters here are excessive, extra-ordinary, atypical.

Pecola's strange question after she visits these women ("Were they real?" [58]) thus resonates with the history of realism and the stereotype. At some stages in its history, realism has been committed to establishing types as an appropriate method of paying proper empirical attention to urban modernity. At other stages, and this is especially true of minority literary politics, realism's attention to detail and to the real has been understood as a means of combating the ethnic or racial stereotypes that circulate in other literary texts and in the culture as a whole. But given realism's longstanding interest in typology, it is a strange choice as a form appropriate to combating stereotypes, since the type and the stereotype share the same structure.

I want to extend this argument by suggesting that not only do the type and stereotype share an essential structure but that this structure also characterizes most conceptions of both biological race and ethnic culture. This becomes especially apparent in Geraldine's typology, where the type and the description of culture are seen to overlap and to be, in fact, indistinguishable. This ethnographically sophisticated description of cultural practice covers the major areas of anthropological detail: living conditions, housing, employment, education, hygiene, sexuality, gesture, and values. The voice is that of the field anthropologist, making notes on the natives ("They") and seeing meaning in their practices. In other words, what Morrison's typology is talking about is culture. And yet what becomes apparent is that cultural description as a mode of discourse is not structurally different from the literary stereotype or the sociological type as a mode of discourse. Both are understood to be devoted to essentialist concepts of identity. Much of Morrison's passage describes situation-specific behaviors that should make Geraldine who she is, but somehow they don't. Although she can't pass for white because she's too black (or "colored," as she puts it), she is adopting the middle-class values of propriety associated with whiteness. The group identity described in the passage, however, is grounded not in a performative model of culture but (and it doesn't really try to disguise this fact) in race. I think this is the theoretical insight of *The Bluest Eye*. In the midst of two competing paradigms for minority citizenship in the United States—one founded on a concept of culture and one on a concept of race—these supposedly complex models of group identity are not merely interdependent but structurally identical to each other (indeed the former depends on the latter) *and* to the outmoded forms of the stereotype and the sociological and literary type.

The novel thus rehearses its own hermeneutic disappointments as it constantly tries to put people into one kind of group identity or another but finds that they don't exactly fit. The "whores" aren't real whores. Nor is Claudia a real African American, exactly, as her rage at the white dolls exceeds the racial typology discovered by the Clarks' study. Geraldine isn't really culturally white, though she practices whiteness, but is sort of racially black, though she tries not to be. Thus, the intertextual dialogue between *The Bluest Eye* and *Invisible Man* contains not only Cholly's rape of his daughter, as Michael Awkward has shown, but also the hermeneutic anxiety of Ellison's narrator, who fears, as Trueblood tells his tale, that a particular act by a single individual will be understood to be a trait of group identity.[50] What remains in *The Bluest Eye* once these paradigms of group identity—literary stereotype, social-science typology, culture, and race—have collapsed is a systemic idiosyncrasy for Morrison's fictional characters. ("I chose a unique situation, not a representative one," Morrison recalls in her afterword to *The Bluest Eye* [210]). That idiosyncrasy comes as a relief because we have developed, like the novel itself, scheme fatigue.

The Bluest Eye is an inaugural text of U.S. literary multiculturalism. Its logic—that we have to figure out what culture we should have, a question answered racially—is representative of a central concern in our present multiculturalism as well as in the cultural nationalism out of which it came. Morrison's writing has worked toward substantiating an African American cultural presence, though that presence is often, according to many critics, rendered through tropes of loss, nostalgia, dispossession, and grieving.[51] But the typology of Geraldine suggests that even descriptions of loss can generate a content for black culture that is both positive and positivist; it is, we might say, real. Thus, in this politics of recognition beginning with *The Bluest Eye,* Morrison has advanced the Black Aesthetic's project of making blackness, as Henry Louis Gates Jr. puts it, into "a trope of presence" rather than absence.[52] That successful move has become a cornerstone of our current multiculturalism.

But while *The Bluest Eye*'s cultural pluralism is representative of our current paradigm of literary multiculturalism, its suspicion of group identity is not. The novel shows us, at the dawn of multiculturalism, that there is no real difference between the type (or stereotype) and a notion of culture. Both are ideal forms that are created by the elimination of a certain amount of alterity. Real ethnic cultural identity and false stereotypes—understood by much ethnic minority criticism to be in opposition—are really two sides of the same coin. The stereotype is considered bad in literary-critical and academic discourse. Culture is considered good in both because it is supposed to be truer or more disposed to complexity. But the concept of culture (or race) itself is not naturally truer or more complex than the stereotype, and often our application of the concept isn't either. The early twentieth century witnessed a call to abandon biological race as a coherent concept, and it is still a worthy endeavor to try to see through biological essentialism (of race or gender). The problem is that what often replaces it is a kind of cultural essentialism that serves the same function—as the unexamined origin of or explanation for a practice or belief.

We can't escape the need to think in patterns, and thus we probably need a concept of culture—not a concept of cultural identity but of cultural practices and cultural values. We should understand, however, that culture is as structurally dubious a proposition as race was, and as the stereotype is. We shouldn't perpetuate the illusion that culture is a naturally more complicated notion than the stereotype. As I have argued elsewhere, many mid-twentieth-century minority authors, such as Richard Wright, Zora Neale Hurston, Jade Snow Wong, Pardee Lowe, and even Black Elk (through John Niehardt), strategically adopted the social-science paradigm shift from biological race to ethnic culture.[53] This moment was the prehistory of the current state of literary multiculturalism, in which minority writers—who often felt compelled to confront explicitly the idea of group identity in a way that white writers could avoid—became self-conscious consumers of social-science ideas regarding culture and race. It is therefore deeply problematic for the social sciences and ethnic studies to use the literary texts that they helped make conceptually possible to substantiate either an idea about culture or what the cultural values or practices might really be—or, even worse, mean.

Social science and ethnic studies may use literary texts as evidence for particular conceptions of culture or as the content of what might constitute a culture, but this data sample is thoroughly muddied. Literary writers, especially racialized or ethnic ones, have long been using social-science research as an intellectual resource for their works.

I want to strengthen and broaden Werner Sollors's warning about the circularity in social science's use of literary texts as evidence by suggesting that the idea of culture itself is a historical creation of which literary writers have made extensive use. That is, many minority literary texts may not reveal pristine descriptions of real cultures but, rather, constructions that have already been enabled in part by popular and academic renderings of the notion of culture in the twentieth century. We know, for instance, that Wright's Chinese American contemporaries Pardee Lowe and Jade Snow Wong relied considerably on sociology, as did Hurston on anthropology. But even Morrison's interrogation in *The Bluest Eye* of a famous social-science study is not a guarantee that her work will be recognized by future social scientists as having been influenced by their discipline. This is a classic feedback loop, in which the cultural meme of culture, itself of complicated origin, is taken up by literature and social science, each time amplified and recirculated between them. Multicultural U.S. literature no longer gives us pristine images of cultures, if it ever did, but, rather, images constitutively infected by social-science ideas about culture—and it is this circuit between literature and social science that indeed laid the basis for our current paradigm of multicultural literature.

NOTES

1. Toni Morrison, *The Bluest Eye* (1970; reprint, New York: Penguin, 1993), 89; further references are to this edition and will be cited parenthetically in the text.

2. Walter Benn Michaels, *Our America: Nativism, Modernism, and Pluralism* (Durham, N.C.: Duke University Press, 1995), p. 119. I am indebted to Michaels's argument in *Our America* that, as he has written elsewhere, "any notion of cultural identity that goes beyond the description of our actual beliefs and practices must rely on race (or something equivalent, say, sex) in order to determine which culture is actually ours" ("Response," *Modernism/modernity*, 3 [September 1996]: 121). For critiques of Michaels's argument, see Marjorie Perloff, "Modernism without the Modernists: A Response to Walter Benn Michaels," *Modernism/modernity* 3 (September 1996): 103; and Charles Altieri, ("Whose America Is *Our America?* On Walter Benn Michaels's Characterizations of Modernity in America," *Modernism/modernity*, 3 [September 1996]: p. 111).

3. Hoyt Fuller, "Towards a Black Aesthetic," *Critic*, 26, no. 5 (1968): pp. 70–73; reprint, *The Black Aesthetic*, ed. Addison Gayle Jr. (New York: Doubleday, 1971), p. 8.

4. Addison Gayle Jr., "Introduction," *The Black Aesthetic*, ed. Addison Gayle Jr. (New York: Doubleday, 1971), p. xxii.

5. Larry Neal, "The Black Arts Movement," *Drama Review*, 12 (summer 1968): pp. 29–39; reprinted in *The Black Aesthetic*, ed. Addison Gayle Jr. (New York: Doubleday, 1971), p. 272.

6. Ibid., p. 290.

7. According to Dorothy Ross, "[t]he founding document of Chicago sociology" is "a research protocol entitled 'Race Psychology: Standpoint and Questionnaire, with Particular Reference to the Immigrant and the Negro.'" Published by William I. Thomas in 1912, "[i]t addressed the central issue that would occupy the ethnic and urban sociology of Thomas and [Robert E.] Park: 'the backwardness and forwardness of different social groups.' The theoretical standpoint Thomas had constructed was crucial to the enterprise, for it placed his subjects in the middle of a changing liberal society, and it assumed racial equality" (*The Origins of American Social Science* [Cambridge: Cambridge University Press, 1991], p. 351); further references are to this edition and will be cited parenthetically as *OASS*).

8. See Michael Omi and Howard Winant, *Racial Formation in the United States from the 1960s to the 1980s* (New York: Routledge, 1986), p. 10. For Boas's influence on Thomas, see Martin Bulmer, *The Chicago School of Sociology: Institutionalization, Diversity, and the Rise of Sociological Research* (Chicago: University of Chicago Press, 1984), 59.

9. Robert E. Park, unpublished autobiography, printed in Fred J. Baker, "The Life Histories of W. I. Thomas and Robert E. Park," *American Journal of Sociology* (September 1973): p. 258; see also Ross, *Origins*, p. 307. Park—later of the Chicago school of sociology, which advocated the use of life-writing as empirical data collection—outlined and drafted some of Washington's life-writing, including *My Larger Education*, the sequel to *Up from Slavery* (see Louis R. Harlan, *Booker T. Washington: The Wizard of Tuskegee*, 1901–1915 [New York: Oxford University Press, 1983], p. 291).

10. See Lee D. Baker, *From Savage to Negro: Anthropology and the Construction of Race, 1896–1954* (Berkeley and Los Angeles: University of California Press, 1998), p. 168; further references will be cited parenthetically as *FSN*.

11. According to Baker, "Franz Boas and his students at Columbia University (on West 119th Street and Amsterdam Avenue, just up the steps of Morningside Park from Harlem) were reshaping the anthropological discourse on race literally in the middle of the Harlem Renaissance" (*FSN*, 166–167).

12. See Werner Sollors, "Of Mules and Mares in a Land of Difference; Or, Quadrupeds All?" *American Quarterly*, 42 (June 1990): pp. 167–90.

13. See Robert E. Hemenway, *Zora Neale Hurston: A Literary Biography* (Urbana: University of Illinois Press, 1977): pp. 329–337.

14. Juan Williams, *Thurgood Marshall: American Revolutionary* (New York: Random House, 1998), 199–200; further references will be cited parenthetically as *TM*.

15. This is the "conventional narrative" of the social sciences' influence on the Supreme Court in *Brown* that Sanjay Mody critiques; see "*Brown* Footnote Eleven in Historical Context: Social Science and the Supreme Court's Quest for Legitimacy," *Stanford Law Review*, 54 (April 2002): p. 793. Even if Mody is right—that the Court (like *Invisible Man* two years before it) was rejecting originalist intent as a framework for American legal practice—the Court was accepting the assimilation

model of that social science, even if it wasn't accepting the empirical arguments for psychological damage of the social science itself.

16. See Kenneth B. Clark and Mamie P. Clark, "Racial Identification and Preference in Negro Children," in *Readings in Social Psychology,* (New York: Holt, 1947): pp. 169–78; further references will be cited parenthetically in the text as "RI."

17. Questions 1 through 4 in the Clarks' test are as follows: "Give me the doll that you like to play with": " . . . is a nice doll"; " . . . looks bad"; " . . . is a nice color." Questions 5 through 8: "Give me the doll that looks like a white child"; " . . . a colored child"; " . . . a Negro child"; " . . . like you."

18. See Kenneth B. Clark and Mamie P. Clark, "Emotional Factors in Racial Identification and Preference in Negro Children," *Journal of Negro Education,* 19 (summer 1950): p. 348.

19. Ibid., p. 350.

20. See Jill Matus, *Toni Morrison* (Manchester, Eng.: Manchester University Press, 1998): p. 43.

21. The rejection of these mid-century social-science doctrines was at the heart of the 1960s demand for new black studies programs. As Ramon A. Gutierrez reports, students "demanded that the study of race and ethnicity be removed from the disciplinary homes they had long occupied in departments of sociology and anthropology, where race and ethnicity were pathologized, problematized, or exoticized" ("Ethnic Studies: Its Evolution in American Colleges and Universities," in *Multiculturalism: A Critical Reader,* ed. David Theo Goldberg [Oxford, England: Blackwell, 1994], p. 158). The programs formed to counter this school of social-science research were, of course, the forerunners of today's ethnic studies programs. As Gutierrez notes, the intellectual context was the crisis in the minority-citizenship model (158).

22. See William Walling, "'Art' and 'Protest': Ralph Ellison's *Invisible Man* Twenty Years After," *Phylon,* 34, no. 2 (1973): p. 128.

23. Fuller, "Towards a Black Aesthetic," p. 3.

24. "An Interview with Toni Morrison," by Rosemarie K. Lester, Hessian Radio Network (Frankfurt, West Germany, 1983); in *Critical Essays on Toni Morrison,* ed. Nellie McKay (Boston: G. K. Hall, 1998): p. 51.

25. Zora Neale Hurston, "Court Order Can't Make Races Mix," *Orlando Sentinel,* 11 August 1955; reprinted in Carla Kaplan, *Zora Neale Hurston: A Life in Letters* (New York: Doubleday, 2002): pp. 738–740.

26. See Walling, "'Art' and 'Protest,'" pp. 125–126, 127.

27. Neal, "Black Arts Movement," p. 273.

28. Arthur P. Davis, "Integration and Race Literature," *Phylon,* 17, no. 2 (1956): p. 142.

29. See Madhu Dubey, *Black Women Novelists and the Nationalist Aesthetic* (Bloomington: Indiana University Press, 1994): pp. 33–34.

30. Liz Gant, review of *The Bluest Eye, Black World,* May 1971, p. 52; and Sharyn J. Skeeter, review of *The Bluest Eye, Essence,* January 1971, p. 59.

31. Ruby Dee, review of *The Bluest Eye, Freedomways,* 11, no. 3 (1971): p. 319.

32. Nicholas S. Timasheff, *Sociological Theory: Its Nature and Growth,* rev. ed. (New York: Random House, 1957): p. 155.

33. See Carla Cappetti, *Writing Chicago: Modernism, Ethnography, and the Novel* (New York: Columbia University Press, 1993): pp. 20–23. For *The Polish Peasant*'s inaugural use of personal documents in sociology, see Bulmer, *Chicago School*, pp. 54–55.

34. Michael A. Elliott, introduction to *The Culture Concept: Writing and Difference in the Age of Realism* (Minneapolis: University of Minnesota Press, 2002): p. xviii.

35. *Personality in the Making: The Fact-Finding Report of the Mid-CenturyWhite House Conference on Children and Youth*, ed. Helen Leland Witmer and Ruth Kotinsky (New York: Harper, 1950): pp. 143–144.

36. On Richard Wright's relationship with University of Chicago sociology professor Louis Wirth, see Hazel Rowley, *Richard Wright: The Life and Times* (New York: Holt, 2001), p. 82. For further analysis of Wright's use of Chicago sociology, see Carla Cappetti, "Sociology of an Existence: Richard Wright and the Chicago School," *MELUS*, 12 (Summer 1985): pp. 25–43; Cappetti, *Writing Chicago*; and John M. Reilly, "Richard Wright Preaches the Nation: *12 Million Black Voices*," *Black American Literature Forum*, 16 (Autumn 1982): p. 116.

37. Werner Sollors, *Beyond Ethnicity: Consent and Descent in American Culture* (New York: Oxford University Press, 1986): p. 9.

38. Midge Wilson and Kathy Russell, *Divided Sisters: Bridging the Gap between Black Women and White Women*, (New York: Anchor, 1996), pp. 43, 40.

39. Paul L. Rosen, *The Supreme Court and Social Science* (Urbana: University of Illinois Press, 1972): p. 157.

40. LeRoi Jones, *Blues People: Negro Music in White America* (New York: Morrow, 1963): p. 219.

41. Reviewing the antiracist science in the years before *Brown*, Kluger notes: "Though physiologists had shown that Negroes have more sweat glands than whites, it was the social psychologists who finally reached the not very profound conclusion that white belief in powerful Negro bodily aroma was inspired—to the extent that the phenomenon may have existed at all—not by a natural-born funk that ran with the genes but by the lack of bathing facilities and laggard sanitary habits among poor people living in warm climates who also tended not to have very large wardrobes or much chance to wash the clothes they owned" (*Simple Justice*, 310).

42. See Toni Morrison, *Playing in the Dark: Whiteness and the Literary Imagination* (New York: Vintage, 1992).

43. William I. Thomas and Florian Znaniecki, introduction to Władek Wiszniewski, untitled autobiography, in Thomas and Znaniecki, *The Polish Peasant in Europe and America*, 2 vols. (New York: Knopf, 1927), 2:1855. Wiszniewski's three-hundred-page autobiography is appended to *The Polish Peasant*.

44. Thomas and Znaniecki, introduction to *The Polish Peasant*, 2:1837, 1856.

45. Robert E. Park and Ernest W. Burgess, *Introduction to the Science of Sociology*, 2nd ed. (Chicago: University of Chicago Press, 1924): p. 714.

46. See Rowley, *Richard Wright*, p. 250.

47. Peter Demetz, "Balzac and the Zoologists: A Concept of the Type," in *The Disciplines of Criticism: Essays in Literary Theory, Interpretation, and History*, ed. Peter Demetz, Thomas Greene, and Lowry Nelson Jr. (New Haven: Yale University Press, 1968): p. 407.

48. Ibid., p. 412.

49. See, for instance, Josephine Knopf, "Meyer Wolfsheim and Robert Cohn: A Study of a Jewish Type and Stereotype," *Tradition: A Journal of Orthodox Jewish Thought*, 10 (1969): pp. 93–104. Despite Knopf's proclaimed attempt to distinguish between the type (or archetype) and stereotype, their structural identity is betrayed in the fact that the ground for any distinction is revealed as only positive content (of the "shlemiel" type) against negative content (of the stereotype of the "villainous Jew").

50. On the intertext of *The Bluest Eye* and *Invisible Man*, see Michael Awkward, "Roadblocks and Relatives: Critical Revision in Toni Morrison's *The Bluest Eye*," in *Critical Essays on Toni Morrison*, ed. Nellie Y. McKay (Boston: G. K. Hall, 1988): pp. 57–68.

51. See, most recently, Caroline Rody, "Toni Morrison's *Beloved*: History, 'Rememory,' and 'Clamor for a Kiss,'" *American Literary History*, 7 (spring 1995): pp. 92–119; Michael Nowlin, "Toni Morrison's Jazz and the Racial Dreams of the American Writer," *American Literature*, 71 (March 1999): pp. 151–74; Madhu Dubey, "Narration and Migration: Jazz and Vernacular Theories of Black Women's Fiction," *American Literary History*, 10 (summer 1998): pp. 291–316; Ashraf H. A. Rushdy, "Daughters Signifyin(g) History: The Example of Toni Morrison's *Beloved*," *American Literature*, 64 (September 1992): pp. 567–97; Linden Peach, Toni Morrison, 2nd ed. (New York: St. Martin's, 2000); Dwight A. McBride, "Speaking the Unspeakable: On Toni Morrison, African American Intellectuals, and the Uses of Essentialist Rhetoric," *Modern Fiction Studies*, 39 (Fall–Winter 1993): pp. 755–776; and Dubey, *Black Women Novelists*.

52. Henry Louis Gates Jr., *The Signifying Monkey: A Theory of African-American Literary Criticism* (New York: Oxford University Press, 1988), p. 237.

53. See Christopher Douglas, "Reading Ethnography: The Cold War Social Science of Jade Snow Wong's *Fifth Chinese Daughter* and *Brown v. Board of Education*," in *Asian American Literature: Form, Confrontation, and Transformation*, ed. Samina Namji and Zhou Xiaojing (Seattle: University of Washington Press, 2005): pp. 101–124.

Chronology

1931   Born Chloe Anthony Wofford on February 18 in Lorain, Ohio, the second child of Ramah (Willis) and George Wofford.

1953   Graduates with B.A. in Englsh from Howard University. Changes her name to Toni during the years at Howard.

1955   Receives M.A. in English from Cornell University for thesis on the theme of suicide in William Faulkner and Virginia Woolf.

1955–57   Instructor in English at Texas Southern University.

1957–64   Instructor in English at Howard University.

1958   Marries Harold Morrison, a Jamaican architect.

1961   Morrison's first son, Harold Ford is born.

1964   Divorces Harold Morrison and returns with her two sons to Lorain.

1965   Becomes editor for a textbook subsidiary of Random House in Syracuse, New York.

1970   Published her first novel, *The Bluest Eye*. Takes editorial position at Random House in New York, eventually becoming a senior editor.

1971–72   Associate Professor of English at the State University of New York at Purchase.

1974   Publishes *Sula* and an editor of Middleton Harris's *The Black Book*.

1975   Sula nominated for the National Book Award.

1976–77   Visiting Lecturer at Yale University.

1977   Publishes *Song of Solomon*, which receives the National Book Critics Circle Award and the American Academy and Institute of Arts and Letters Award. Is appointed to the National Council on the Arts.

1981   Publishes *Tar Baby*.

1983   Morrison leaves her editorial job at Random House.

1984–89   Schweitzer Professor of the Humanities at the State University of New York at Albany.

1986   Receives the New York State Governor's Art Award. Dreaming Emmett, Morrison's play about the murder of Emmett Till, premiers in Albany.

1986–88   Visiting Lecturer at Bard College.

1987   Publishes *Beloved*, which is nominated for the National Book Award and the National Book Critics Award.

1988   Receives Pulitzer Prize in Fiction and the Robert F. Kennedy Award for *Beloved*.

1989   Becomes Robert F. Goheen Professor of the Humanities at Princeton University.

1992   Publishes *Jazz* and *Playing in the Dark: Whiteness and the Literary Imagination*.

1993   Receives the Nobel Prize in Literature.

1994   Morrison's mother, Ella Ramah Wofford, dies.

1996   Receives the National Book Foundation Medal for Distinguished Contribution to American Letters.

1997   Publishes *Paradise*.

2002   Toni and her son, Slade, start work on a book series called *Who's Got Game?*. They also write the picture book *The Book of Mean People*.

2003   Publishes *Love*. Publishes with Slade, *The Ant or the Grasshopper?* and *The Lion or the Mouse?*.

2004   Publishes with Slade *Poppy or the Snake?*

2007   *The Bluest Eye* is adapted for the stage by Lydia R. Diamond.

Contributors

HAROLD BLOOM is Sterling Professor of the Humanities at Yale University. He is the author of 30 books, including *Shelley's Mythmaking* (1959), *The Visionary Company* (1961), *Blake's Apocalypse* (1963), *Yeats* (1970), *A Map of Misreading* (1975), *Kabbalah and Criticism* (1975), *Agon: Toward a Theory of Revisionism* (1982), *The American Religion* (1992), *The Western Canon* (1994), and *Omens of Millennium: The Gnosis of Angels, Dreams, and Resurrection* (1996). *The Anxiety of Influence* (1973) sets forth Professor Bloom's provocative theory of the literary relationships between the great writers and their predecessors. His most recent books include *Shakespeare: The Invention of the Human* (1998), a 1998 National Book Award finalist, *How to Read and Why* (2000), *Genius: A Mosaic of One Hundred Exemplary Creative Minds* (2002), *Hamlet: Poem Unlimited* (2003), *Where Shall Wisdom Be Found?* (2004), and *Jesus and Yahweh: The Names Divine* (2005). In 1999, Professor Bloom received the prestigious American Academy of Arts and Letters Gold Medal for Criticism. He has also received the International Prize of Catalonia, the Alfonso Reyes Prize of Mexico, and the Hans Christian Andersen Bicentennial Prize of Denmark.

ROSALIE MURPHY BAUM is associate professor of English at Central Florida University.

THOMAS H. FICK is professor of English at Southeastern Louisiana University.

DONALD B. GIBSON is emeritus professor of English at the Rutgers University, New Brunswick.

SHELLEY WONG is associate professor of education at George Mason University.

LINDA DITTMAR is professor of English at the University of Massachusetts, Boston.

SHARON L. GRAVETT is professor of English and Assistant vice-president of academic affairs at Valdosta State University.

JANE KUENZ is associate professor of English at the University of Southern Maine.

ALLEN ALEXANDER is assistant professor at Nicholls State University in Thibodaux, Louisiana, where he teaches American, Southern, and Louisiana literature.

CAT MOSES is an independent scholar living and working in Santa Fe, New Mexico.

CARL D. MALMGREN is professor of English at New Orleans University.

JENNIFER GILLAN is associate professor of English at Bentley College.

JEFFREY M. BUCHANAN is an assistant professor of English and Teacher Education at Youngstown State University in Ohio.

DEBRA T. WERRLEIN teaches composition at George Mason University.

CHRISTOPHER DOUGLAS is assistant professor of English at the University of Victoria.

Bibliography

Atlas, Marilyn J. "The Issue of Literacy in America: Slave Narratives and Toni Morrison's *The Bluest Eye*." *Midamerica: The Yearbook of the Society for the Study of Midwestern Literature*, 27 (2000), pp. 106–118.

Blumenthal, Rachel. "Morrison's *The Bluest Eye*." *Explicator*, 65:2 (2007 Winter), pp. 117–119.

Daly, Brenda. "Taking Whiteness Personally: Learning to Teach Testimonial Reading and Writing in the College Literature Classroom." *Pedagogy: Critical Approaches to Teaching Literature, Language, Composition, and Culture*, 5:2 (2005 Spring), pp. 213–246.

De Lancey, Dayle B. "Sweetness, Madness, and Power: The Confection as Mental Contagion in Toni Morrison's *Tar Baby*, *Song of Solomon*, and *The Bluest Eye*." *In Process: A Journal of African American and African Diasporan Literature and Culture*, 2 (2000 Spring), pp. 25–47.

Fick, Thomas H. and Gold, Eva. "Authority, Literacy, and Modernism in *The Bluest Eye*." pp. 56–62. McKay, Nellie Y. and Earle, Kathryn, editors. *Approaches to Teaching the Novels of Toni Morrison*. New York, NY: Modern Language Association of America, 1997.

Hébert, Kimberly G. "Acting the Nigger: Topsy, Shirley Temple, and Toni Morrison's Pecola." pp. 184–198. Ammons, Elizabeth (ed. and introd.) and Belasco, Susan (ed. and introd.). *Approaches to Teaching Stowe's* Uncle Tom's Cabin. p. 66. New York, NY: Modern Language Association of America, 2000.

Lee, Soo-Hyun. "[*The Bluest Eye*: Tragic Aspects of Black Consciousness of the Self]." *Studies in Modern Fiction*, 9:1 (2002 Summer), pp. 195–217.

Luebke, Steven R. "The Portrayal of Sexuality in Toni Morrison's *The Bluest Eye*." pp. 87–94. Karolides, Nicholas J., editor. *Censored Books, II: Critical Viewpoints, 1985–2000*. Lanham, MD: Scarecrow, 2002.

Rice, Alan. "Erupting Funk: The Political Style of Toni Morrison's *Tar Baby* and *The Bluest Eye*." pp. 133–47. Madsen, Deborah L., editor. *Postcolonial Literatures: Expanding the Canon*. London, England: Pluto, 1999.

Towner, Theresa M. "Black Matters on the Dixie Limited: *As I Lay Dying* and *The Bluest Eye*." pp. 115–27. Kolmerten, Carol A., Ross, Stephen M., and Wittenberg, Judith Bryant, editors. *Unflinching Gaze: Morrison and Faulkner Re-Envisioned*. Jackson, MS: University Press of Mississippi, 1997.

Yancy, George. "The Black Self within a Semiotic Space of Whiteness: Reflections on the Racial Deformation of Pecola Breedlove in Toni Morrison's *The Bluest Eye*." *CLA Journal*, 43:3 (2000 Mar), pp. 299–319.

Acknowledgments

Rosalie Murphy Baum, "Alcoholism and Family Abuse in *Maggie* and *The Bluest Eye*"; *Mosaic: A Journal for the Interdisciplinary Study of Literature*, 1986 Summer; 19 (3): pp. 91–105. Reprinted by permission of the publisher.

Thomas H. Fick, "Toni Morrison's 'Allegory of the Cave': Movies, Consumption, and Platonic Realism in *The Bluest Eye*"; *Journal of the Midwest Modern Language Association*, 1989 Spring; 22 (1): pp. 10–22. Reprinted by permission of the publisher and author.

Donald B. Gibson, "Text and Countertext in Toni Morrison's *The Bluest Eye*"; *LIT: Literature Interpretation Theory*, 1989 Dec.; 1 (1–2): pp. 19–32. © 1989 Reproduced by permission of Taylor & Francis Group, LLC., http://www.taylorandfrancis.com.

Shelley Wong, "Transgression as Poesis in *The Bluest Eye*"; *Callaloo: A Journal of African American and African Arts and Letters*, 1990 Summer; 13 (3): pp. 471–481. © The Johns Hopkins University Press. Reprinted with permission of the Johns Hopkins University Press.

Linda Dittmar, "'Will the Circle Be Unbroken?' The Politics of Form in *The Bluest Eye*"; *Novel: A Forum on Fiction*, 1990 Winter; 23 (2): pp. 137–155. Copyright NOVEL Corp. © 1990. Reprinted with permission.

Sharon L. Gravett, "Toni Morrison's *The Bluest Eye*: An Inverted Walden?";
West Virginia University Philological Papers, 1992; 38: pp. 201–211. Reprinted by
permission of the publisher.

Jane Kuenz, "*The Bluest Eye*: Notes on History, Community, and Black Female
Subjectivity"; *African American Review*, 1993 Fall; 27 (3): pp. 421–431. Reprinted
by permission of the author.

Allen Alexander, "The Fourth Face: The Image of God in Toni Morrison's
The Bluest Eye"; *African American Review*, 1998 Summer; 32 (2): pp. 293–303.
Reprinted by permission of the author.

Cat Moses, The Blues Aesthetic in Toni Morrison's *The Bluest Eye*"; *African
American Review*, 1999 Winter; 33 (4): pp. 623–637.

Carl D. Malmgren, "Texts, Primers, and Voices in Toni Morrison's *The Bluest
Eye*"; *Critique: Studies in Contemporary Fiction*, 2000 Spring; 41 (3): pp. 251–262.
Reprinted with permission of the Helen Dwight Reid Educational Foundation.
Copyright © 2000. Published by Heldref Publications, 1319 Eighteenth St.,
NW, Washington, DC 20036-1802.

Jennifer Gillan, "Focusing on the Wrong Front: Historical Displacement, the
Maginot Line, and *The Bluest Eye*"; *African American Review*, 2002 Summer; 36
(2): pp. 283–298. Reprinted by permission of the author.

Jeffrey M. Buchanan, "'A Productive and Fructifying Pain': Storytelling as
Teaching in *The Bluest Eye*"; *Reader: Essays in Reader-Oriented Theory, Criticism,
and Pedagogy*, 2004 Spring; 50: pp. 59-75. Reprinted by permission of the
publisher.

Debra T. Werrlein, "Not So Fast, Dick and Jane: Reimagining Childhood and
Nation in *The Bluest Eye*"; *MELUS: The Journal of the Society for the Study of
the Multi-Ethnic Literature of the United States*, 2005 Winter; 30 (4): pp. 53–72.
Reprinted courtesy of *MELUS: The Journal of the Society for the Study of the
Multi-Ethnic Literature of the United States*.

Christopher Douglas, "What *The Bluest Eye* Knows About Them: Culture,
Race, Identity"; *American Literature*, Volume 78, no. 1, pp. 141–168. Copyright,
2006, Duke University Press. All rights reserved. Used by permission of the
publisher.

Index